How American Companies *Really*
Compete in the Global Economy

GLOBAL
ENGAGEMENT

Joseph P. Quinlan

CB
CONTEMPORARY BOOKS

Library of Congress Cataloging-in-Publication Data

Quinlan, Joseph P.
    Global engagement : how American companies really compete in the
global economy / Joseph P. Quinlan.
       p.   cm.
    Includes bibliographical references and index.
    ISBN 0-8092-2670-7
    1. Investments, American.   2. Competition, International.   I. Title.

   HG4538 .Q563   2000
   338.8′8973—dc21   00-31532

Interior design by Rattray Design

Published by Contemporary Books
A division of NTC/Contemporary Publishing Group, Inc.
4255 West Touhy Avenue, Lincolnwood (Chicago), Illinois 60712-1975 U.S.A.
Copyright © 2001 by Joseph P. Quinlan
Printed in the United States of America
International Standard Book Number: 0-8092-2670-7
01 02 03 04 05 06 MV 17 16 15 14 13 12 11 10 9 8 7 6 5 4 3 2 1

To Rudy and Grace Schneider, two great teachers in my life

Contents

Acknowledgments

I AM ESPECIALLY grateful to Robert Brown of Morgan Stanley Dean Witter for getting this project launched. Mimi Rodman of the Tribune Company and Gol Ophir of Morgan Stanley Dean Witter were also instrumental in jump-starting this undertaking.

Matthew Carnicelli, senior editor at NTC/Contemporary Publishing, has been a key part of this project from start to finish, providing invaluable ideas, suggestions, and editorial advice throughout the process. It was Matthew's support and vision that turned a book proposal into a reality, for which I am indebted. Kristy Grant of NTC/Contemporary Publishing also deserves mention for help in preparing the manuscript. I am particularly indebted to Susan Moore-Kruse of NTC/Contemporary Publishing for her last-minute heroics and assistance in pulling the book together.

I cannot emphasize enough the appreciation and gratitude I have for Raymond Mataloni Jr. of the Bureau of Economic Analysis in Washington, D.C. A leading authority on U.S. foreign direct investment, Ray's insights, comments, and ideas on the manuscript were invaluable. To a friend and colleague, I say thanks for putting up with all the phone calls and the incessant E-mails regarding "one final question." I would also like to acknowledge the assistance of William J. Zeile, Slyvia E. Bargas, and Mark New, all outstanding research professionals at the Bureau of Economic Analysis.

For his efficiency and due diligence in gathering research material, I am particularly indebted to Charlie Colombo, research librarian at Delaware Valley College in Doylestown, Pennsylvania. Charlie not only successfully found every arcane book or article I requested over the better course of a year but also showed infinite patience when I failed to return the books on time, which was quite often. Thanks, Charlie. Also, I wish to extend a special thanks to Harriet Roth, whom I seemed to visit every Sunday afternoon at the college.

I received extraordinary moral support from my friend and colleague Andrea Prochniak at Morgan Stanley Dean Witter, to which I'm thankful. Andrea's gentle prodding and, above all else, sense of humor were two key ingredients that kept me going when I wanted to stop.

Writing is a lonely endeavor, not only for the author but also for the author's family. This being the third time around for everyone, I am more indebted than ever to a family that has learned when to ask and not to ask about "the book." To PJ, thanks for crunching some numbers over break and checking in every Sunday from South Bend; to Brian, thanks for always humoring me in your own special way; and to Sarah Grace, thanks for bringing up the refreshments. To my wife and best friend, Karen, you're simply the best. Finally, I would be remiss and in trouble if I didn't mention Chloe.

INTRODUCTION

Beyond Trade

THIS IS A book about how American firms compete and sell products in the world marketplace. While that description immediately conjures thoughts about U.S. exports and imports, this is not a book about international trade. In fact, it seeks to dispel the myth that trade is the one and only gauge of global engagement. While trade is the common metric by which America's global sales are tallied, and the standard benchmark of global competitiveness, the cross-border exchange of goods and services renders an incomplete picture of U.S. global engagement.

One simple truth is neglected in the ongoing debate over U.S. trade policy, ignored by the U.S. media and overlooked by investors: American firms compete more through foreign direct investment—by establishing a local presence in various foreign markets, by being on the ground—than through arm's-length trade. In other words, U.S. global engagement is less about exports and more about General Motors manufacturing and selling automobiles in Germany, Intel integrating Ireland and Israel into its global production network, Eastman Kodak going head-to-head against its Japanese rival, Fuji, in China, and Home Depot bringing its do-it-yourself philosophy to customers in the suburbs of Santiago, Chile, to capture sales in one of Latin America's most dynamic markets.

Global engagement is also about Toyota of Japan relying less on Japanese imports to satisfy U.S. demand and more on hiring and training U.S. workers to build Camrys in Kentucky. It's about Deutsche Bank acquiring Bankers Trust, expanding the U.S. beachhead of one of Germany's largest banks. It's about Alcatel, the French telecom equipment manufacturer, making strategic acquisitions in Silicon Valley to buttress its technological capabilities.

U.S. global engagement is far more complex and intricate than the simple cross-border exchange of goods. It's beyond trade. American firms not only sell their goods and compete in overseas markets primarily through foreign direct investment, but they also do it better than anyone else in the world. The extraterritorial span of corporate America is unsurpassed on a worldwide basis. This global reach represents one of the most formidable strengths of the United States and is the primary focus of the following pages.

Global Engagement addresses the untold story of how U.S. firms *really* compete in the world markets. The sooner this story is told, the better, since policymakers and investors alike in America still view U.S. global engagement through the lens of trade and through the theoretical framework established more than two hundred years ago by David Ricardo and Adam Smith. This standard approach is particularly worrisome because America's trade deficit is a misleading indicator of how U.S. firms really stack up in the global marketplace and is therefore a dangerous variable shaping bilateral and multilateral relationships with other nations. When was the last time you heard a member of Congress speak about the difference between foreign affiliate sales and U.S. exports? Moreover, when the subject of U.S. foreign direct investment does arise in the United States, the common yet misguided assumption is that U.S. firms prefer to invest in low-wage countries, a strategy that robs American workers of jobs and adds to the U.S. import bill. Reality, as will be illustrated, is quite different.

To most Americans, the ultimate yardstick of U.S. participation in the global economy is the trade balance, and, by this measurement, who would not be concerned about the global competitiveness of U.S. industry? America has continually posted an annual trade deficit with the world for the past quarter century, with the U.S. trade gap in goods and services soaring to a record $265 billion in 1999. The widening gulf is worrisome, but there is much more to this story.

Benchmarks of Global Engagement: Foreign Affiliate Sales Versus Trade

One of the best-kept secrets in the United States is that American firms deliver their products to foreign customers via not one but two principal means: either through exports (trade) or through their overseas affiliates (investment). Often, firms deploy both modes of delivery. The former, though, is considered the ultimate scorecard of what and where U.S. companies sell goods abroad.

But how can trade alone be the sole benchmark of U.S. global engagement when over 23,000 U.S. foreign affiliates dot the global landscape? When sizing up the global competitive position of the United States, how can policymakers and investors discount the fact that the combined total output of U.S. foreign affiliates is greater than the output of most nations; that U.S. foreign affiliates in manufacturing employ over 4.6 million workers abroad, equivalent to nearly 25 percent of the total manufacturing workforce of the United States; and that collectively, U.S. foreign affiliates are among the largest exporters in the world? Above all else, how can trade be the yardstick of U.S. global engagement when foreign affiliate sales of goods and services are more than two and a half times the level of total U.S. exports in any given year?

Foreign affiliate sales totaled $2.4 trillion in 1998, the last year of available data, versus $933 billion in total exports in the same year. That is another way of saying that a great deal of global commerce was missing and not counted in U.S. exports. By the same token, a great deal of business is absent from U.S. import figures. U.S.-based foreign affiliate sales amounted to $1.7 trillion in 1998, versus total imports (goods and services) of $1.1 trillion. In other words, a significant proportion of what the U.S. actually buys from foreign-owned companies is missing from official U.S. trade statistics.

At best, the trade figures are incomplete and inaccurate indicators of global commerce. At worst, the traditional measurements of U.S. global engagement are tremendously dangerous in the hands of U.S. policymakers.

Bad data about trade beget bad policies shaping trade. So, it is not the out-sized U.S. trade deficit that represents the gravest threat to the global commercial interests of U.S. business. Rather, the greatest danger of all lies with America's failure to truly grasp how U.S. firms actually compete in the world economy and the policy errors that could emanate from this ominous misunderstanding.

The Plan of the Book

This book is organized into three main sections. Part I (Chapters 1–3) examines the central forces at work in the world economy, as well as the chief trends influencing global foreign direct investment flows. In particular, this section presents the long view of the world economy and highlights the reemergence of globalization in the 1990s. Key to globalization's renaissance is foreign direct investment—not trade—as the primary vehicle of global integration. Discussions of motives and determinants of foreign investment flows, as well as such specific dynamics as the boom in global mergers and acquisitions in the 1990s, the proliferation of strategic alliances, and the ever-growing influence of transnationals, set the stage for the rest of the book. The term *transnational*, incidentally, is the description used by the United Nations to describe the world's largest companies. It is used interchangeably with *multinationals* throughout this book.

Part II (Chapters 4–6) puts the spotlight squarely on U.S. foreign direct investment flows and the strategic role of foreign affiliates. Early in the postwar era, U.S. investment flows traveled basically one way: outbound. This reflected the global preeminence of the United States and the overriding competitiveness of American industry. As the overseas investment position of the United States increased over the past decades, so too did the importance of U.S. foreign affiliates, the global foot soldiers of corporate America. The 1980s and 1990s, however, saw the tide shift, with investment inflows outpacing U.S. outflows. This section investigates the forces behind this shift and analyzes global engagement from the perspective of foreign affiliate sales on the one hand versus trade (U.S. exports and imports) on the other. Trade tells one story of U.S. global engagement; investment and affiliate sales tell another.

Part III (Chapters 7–9) explores three distinct elements of U.S. global engagement. The first is the intense U.S.-Japanese commercial rivalry and the stunning asymmetrical nature of foreign direct investment flows between the two parties. The second is the globalization of service activities and the corresponding surge in U.S. foreign direct investment in services over the 1990s. And the third is U.S. investment ties with the developing nations, which are best described as a work in process.

Throughout most chapters, I have given as much historical data and information as possible, giving the reader a better understanding of how U.S. global commercial relationships have evolved and developed over time.

About the Data

Economic statistics always present some problems to users, although data on foreign direct investment are even more problematic. One caveat is that there is no universally applied international system or method for the collection of data on foreign direct investment flows. Accordingly, data collected and tallied by the United States is often not strictly comparable to figures collected by other nations. Most countries publish their own figures on foreign direct investment, creating large discrepancies regarding definitions, geographic coverage, industry classifications, and other variables. As such, when comparing and contrasting data among countries and regions, these limitations and data nuances should be borne in mind.

The Organization for Economic Cooperation and Development (OECD) and the International Monetary Fund (IMF) are two primary sources of investment flows. The United Nations publishes one of the most comprehensive annual guides on global investment trends (The World Investment Report), using data from both the IMF and OECD, as well as figures and estimates from its own database. United Nations data on cross-border mergers and acquisitions is sourced from the consulting firm KPMG. In Chapters 2 and 3, data analyzed are primarily from the United Nations.

Data presented on U.S. investment outflows and inflows (Chapters 4–9) were obtained from the U.S. government, in particular the Bureau of Economic Analysis (BEA), which provides the most comprehensive data on investment flows than any other government in the world. Another caveat: while U.S. foreign direct investment flows are relatively timely (reported on a quarterly basis), data on U.S. foreign affiliate activities (sales, employment, trade, etc.) is seriously dated given the difficulty in collecting and collating such information. Gathering data on the foreign operations of U.S. firms, as well as the operations of foreign-owned affiliates in the United States, is a difficult undertaking. The more positive aspect is that the U.S. government is one of the few countries in the world that collects this data, providing invaluable information, albeit with a lag, on the cross-border activities of U.S. firms and their foreign competition. The bulk of the statistics presented on U.S. foreign affiliates in Chapters 4–9 is on majority-owned affiliates versus minority-owned. Anyone interested in learning more about data regarding U.S. firms is advised to start with Raymond Mataloni's, "A Guide to BEA Statistics on U.S. Multinationals," published in the March 1995 edition of the *Survey of Current Business*. In addition, before delving into the text, it would help readers to become familiar with the following vocabulary of foreign direct investment.

Key Terms and Definitions

Developed nations Although the universe of developed nations has expanded over the past decade, throughout the book the developing nations are defined in the traditional sense and comprise the United States and Canada in North America; Japan, Australia, and New Zealand in Asia; and the following European nations: the United Kingdom, Germany, France, Italy, Greece, Spain, the Netherlands, Belgium, Austria, Denmark, Finland, Greece, Ireland, Luxembourg, Norway, Portugal, Sweden, and Switzerland.

Developing nations Those nations not cited above.

Direct investment income U.S. parents' return on capital that they have provided to their foreign affiliates. It includes claims on the earnings or profits of foreign affiliates and U.S. parents' interest receipts on loans to the affiliates.

Foreign affiliate A foreign business in which a single U.S. investor owns at least 10 percent of the voting securities, or the equivalent. Similarly, a *U.S. affiliate* is a U.S. business enterprise in which a single foreign investor owns at least 10 percent of the voting securities, or the equivalent.

Foreign direct investment (FDI) Acquisition by an investor based in the home country of an asset in another country (the host country), with the intent to manage the asset. The management dynamic is what separates foreign direct investment from *portfolio investment*. In addition, FDI involves a long-term commitment and entails a prolonged interest in the host nation. Portfolio flows, of course, are more "footloose" and volatile. For the United States, direct investment abroad is the ownership of at least 10 percent of a foreign business enterprise. There are three main categories of foreign direct investment:

equity capital Capital contributions of U.S. parent to existing affiliates or funds used to acquire and establish new affiliates.

intracompany loans There are two types of intracompany loans, according to the government: *U.S. parent receivables*, loans that a U.S. parent extends to its foreign affiliate; and *U.S. parent payables*, loans that a foreign affiliate extends to its U.S. parent. An outflow occurs when the parent extends a new loan to its affiliate; an influx occurs when an affiliate repays part of a loan from its parent.

reinvested earnings One of the largest components of U.S. foreign direct investment, reinvested earnings are derived from the earnings base of the affiliate; they represent the earnings that are not distributed as dividends by affiliates or remitted to the parent. Such retained profits by affiliates are reinvested.

U.S. foreign direct investment position The U.S. government provides three alternative valuation positions: (1) foreign direct investment on a *historical-cost basis*, reflects prices at the time of investment; (2) *current-cost basis* figures, which revalue that portion of the position that represents U.S. parents' claim on the tangible assets of affiliates, using appropriate price indexes; and (3) *market-value basis*, which revalues both the tangible and intangible assets on which U.S. parents have claim. The latter are revalued based on aggregate stock price indexes and are therefore more volatile. The current-cost and market-value estimates are produced only at the global level, not by country or industry. In general, historical cost figures tend to understate the current value of the positions because of inflation. For instance, U.S. foreign direct investment abroad on a historical-cost basis in 1997 was $861 billion, versus $1 trillion on a current-cost basis and $1.7 trillion on a market-value basis. Figures throughout the book consist of direct investment on a historic-cost basis since this series provides country and industry detail. The current-cost and market-value estimates are produced only at the global level and not at country or industry level.

Greenfield investment The act of constructing or establishing a new plant or facility, versus acquiring or merging with an existing foreign company.

Majority-owned affiliate An affiliate in which the combined ownership of all U.S. parents exceeds 50 percent. The bulk of the text in Chapters 4–9 refers to majority-owned affiliates.

PART I

SETTING THE GLOBAL STAGE

Today, American executives confront a global competitive landscape radically different from that of their predecessors. Multiple market opportunities, incessant technological advances, blurred industrial configurations, and unrelenting global competition create a daunting but dynamic global economic backdrop as the new century begins. In the global marketplace of the 21st century, speed and efficiency matter. So does being first to market. Use of enabling technology separates winners from losers. Such is the topsy-turvy world of global competition that firms increasingly compete through collaboration; a company's competitor of today may be its partner of tomorrow. Industry leaders must be global yet local, large but nimble, and simultaneously centralized and decentralized. These challenging paradoxes of the new decade frame the central thesis of this book—that successful global engagement requires U.S. firms to compete not through arm's-length trade but through foreign direct investment.

Understanding how American firms operate in the world economy requires an understanding of the dynamic global forces at work. The objective of Part I, then, is to prepare the stage, to expose the forces of the global market and the competitive environment in which U.S. firms and their foreign counterparts compete.

Chapter 1 provides a historical snapshot of the world economy and an introduction to key global agents of change. Chief among these is the fast-forward pace of technological advances, which has helped reduce the distance between markets and increase the cross-border mobility of materials, goods, capital, and information. The near universal embrace of free-market reforms is another component of change, resulting in open markets previously off-limits to U.S. firms. Both phenomena—advances in technology and market liberalization—helped relaunch globalization in the 1990s and created the framework by which the international production of transnationals has exceeded international trade as the primary means of global competition. Trade, using the terminology of the United Nations, is a "shallow" form of global integration. By contrast, international production via foreign investment is a "deeper" form of engagement.

Chapter 2 hones in on the theoretical underpinnings of foreign direct investment. It analyzes what factors determine whether a firm should invest abroad or simply export. This is difficult terrain to cover in that numerous and overlapping variables determine the overseas strategies of companies and therefore foreign direct investment flows, which precludes any neat and all-encompassing theories. Against this hazy backdrop, the scholarly research of John Dunning (see the Bibliography) is strongly recommended to readers as a starting point in understanding the dynamics of foreign direct investment. Chapter 2 also discusses the urge to merge among firms, with mergers and acquisitions the most popular mode of foreign direct investment in the last decade. The proliferation of strategic alliances, one of the global macrotrends of the 1990s, is also presented.

Chapter 3 delves into the rise of transnationals and their expanding global reach and influence. While global money managers are often considered the most powerful players on the world economic stage, they share the platform with many of the world's largest companies, some of which boast annual sales and/or market capitalization greater than the total output of many nations. The chapter also includes a macrosummary of global foreign direct investment flows, analyzing the largest providers and recipients of such capital flows over the past decade. A central character in this story, of course, is the United States, one of the world's top sources and recipients of foreign direct investment over the past quarter century. This unique role is detailed in Part II.

1

The Global Economy at the Dawn of a New Century

It was shaping up to be a bad day for Brian Cleveland, executive vice president for global operations of IKF Industries. Actually, it was turning out to be a rather lousy week, and it was only Wednesday morning. In the last 48 hours, the company's manufacturing facility in Germany had come to a virtual halt because the firm's French affiliate, a supplier of parts to the Munich plant, had experienced an unexpected bout of labor unrest. This had the operations manager in Barcelona fuming, since intermediate goods sourced out of Germany were essential to the Spanish facilities. The firm's European manufacturing base was anchored in Spain, where various parts of production from across the region were brought together for final assembly and then readied for export to other markets in Europe, the United States, and Asia.

As the effects of the production snafu rippled through the firm's European value chain, the distribution guys in Rotterdam were becoming nervous about meeting their shipping schedules. The firm's marketing team in London, which had just launched a $10 million global advertising campaign, was even more uptight and incensed with the French. As the strike dragged into the third day, each locale was looking to Brian to fix the problem and to fix it fast.

To make up for the production shortfall in France, Brian had considered sourcing some of the parts from the company's new plant in

5

Poland. But, judging by the correspondence from the country manager in Gdansk lamenting the quality of Polish craftsmanship and the high tariff barriers of the European Union, that was not an option. His message was simple: despite the firm's $500 million investment in upgrading and renovating the one-time state company, the Polish operation was not quite ready to be integrated with the company's broader European network. What was assembled and manufactured in Poland was good only to be sold in Poland and its surrounding eastern neighbors.

Another option was to airlift the essential components either from a facility near Pittsburgh or from a plant in Argentina. The second source was the more compelling alternative, since the Argentine facility, courtesy of a recession in neighboring Brazil, was operating at just 42 percent of capacity, which was embarrassing to Brian and others who had lobbied hard for the $1 billion state-of-the-art manufacturing and research facility a few miles outside of Buenos Aires. No sooner was the facility up and running than Brazil experienced a run on its currency and a host of ensuing problems, including a spike in interest rates, a halt in private investment, and a dive in industrial activity. Brazil, the Latin giant, was on its back—again. This meant that Argentina, given its ever-increasing trade and investment ties with Brazil under the auspices of the large regional trading bloc Mercosur, was in trouble. And so too was the firm's shiny new facility.

Buenos Aires or Pittsburgh? Brian would have to talk with the guys in logistics to determine the cost and time, pros and cons of each location. As it stood now, some production from the plant in Argentina was destined for Asia.

Following the financial crisis of 1997–98, Asia was back and with a vengeance. Twelve months ago, Brian could easily have offset any production problems in Europe by shipping product from the firm's plant in Singapore. He had done just that at the onset of Asia's recession. Now, however, sourcing anything from Asia was out of the question. The region's vigorous recovery had caught everyone off guard. Soaring regional growth had the company's plants in Australia, Taiwan, and Singapore working flat-out. Demand was so strong that all three Asian facilities were expecting shipments from South America and sister affiliates in Texas and Mexico in the next few days.

Satisfying the production needs of Asia with output from outside the region was particularly galling to Brian. At the height of the Asian crisis, he had strongly suggested to the IKF board that the company pursue and purchase distressed Asian assets. Then, many Asian competitors were on the financial ropes and looking to broker deals—joint ventures or sales of entire divisions—to remain solvent. Brian had blessed a number of acquisitions proposed by the people in Hong Kong, but the board, horrified at the losses coming from Asia, was reluctant to ante up any new funds until the division was showing a profit again. That myopic decision was now coming back to haunt both Brian and the company.

What little capital the company had sunk into Asia in the past three years had gone to two joint ventures: one in Japan, the other in China. The operation in Osaka showed great promise, but given Japan's stronger-than-expected economic rebound, production in Japan was consumed in Japan. The launch of the Chinese operation had been more problematic, largely because of the partners involved: a former state enterprise that was more or less foisted upon IKF by the local government. The implicit agreement was that if the company helped resurrect the plant outside of Shanghai, thereby avoiding another round of massive layoffs, the firm would be handsomely rewarded later on. Taking the long view, which meant giving in to the Chinese now in the hope of sweeteners later, Brian and the board went ahead with the joint venture. The deal had thus far been costly, and any rewards at this point seemed elusive at best. That was one reason why Brian was heading over to China next week. As the phone rang again, however, Brian thought to himself that the route to the Middle Kingdom would take him first to Europe.

The Beat Goes On

Brian Cleveland is a fictional character, but the complexities he confronts in orchestrating and executing a global business strategy are quite real for many executives throughout the ranks of corporate America. As the new century begins, their jobs have never been more complex.

The competitive dynamics of today dictate that U.S. companies and their managers be adept at maintaining a flexible and malleable global workforce. Being an "insider" is increasingly critical in markets around the world where customer demands are unique and competitive forces shift constantly. Being first to new markets is equally important. In many cases, collaborating with a competitor is just as important as competing against him. Operational nimbleness is a must in a world of unfettered capital flows that can inflate an economy one year and deflate it the next.

A global vision is another prerequisite of managers, since the "backyard" of many U.S. firms, be they Ford Motor or Wal-Mart, is no longer a different state in the United States, but a different region of the global economy. The competitor down the road is no longer a familiar American counterpart, but a German, Japanese, or Spanish affiliate ready to do battle on corporate America's home turf. And a firm's production chain no longer extends from Illinois to New Jersey, but from Peoria to Pudang to Prague. The global manager is faced with a remarkable set of circumstances, in which geography means both everything and nothing at all.

If all this sounds a bit overwhelming, that's because it is. Few American firms are truly global players. But out of both desire and necessity, the strategic thrust of many U.S. firms is to expand and deepen their level of engagement in the global marketplace. The rewards of engagement far exceed those of a stay-at-home strategy, not only because the risks of doing nothing at all have grown so high, but also because there are few places for an isolationist manager or company to hide. Competition is everywhere. The increasing pervasiveness of global competition has eroded the "home court advantage" of many companies, both in the United States and abroad.

As stated in the Introduction, this is not a book about U.S. trade, but about U.S. foreign direct investment. Both represent modes by which American firms deliver goods and services to foreign customers. They are not equal, however. The scenario just outlined is typical of how many American firms operate in the global economy. IKF Industries does not compete through trade, but rather through foreign direct investment—by being local in various regions of the world and having the wherewithal to leverage the global parts of the firm for the benefit of the whole. Trade is almost a residual activity or second-best solution for IKF. That is true of many U.S. firms. In fact, how Brian Cleveland decides to fill the production gap in France, sourcing from either Argentina or Pittsburgh, has a direct bearing on global trade flows, which highlights the influence of foreign investment and the strategies of global firms on cross-border trade.

There will be more on those subjects in the following pages. But first, to help understand where the global economy stands today, it is important to put into context the evolution and development of the world economy over the past century. Just how has the world economy evolved to the point where geography apparently means little to U.S. firms and their industrial counterparts? What global forces are at work that allow a firm like IKF Industries to have a dispersed yet integrated global production network stretched across the world? A summary of these issues follows. The chapter ends by making the case that the United States is far more integrated with the global economy than most Americans realize.

The Global Economy: The Long View

It is difficult to create a time line of global economic activity over the past 100 years, since there has been nothing linear about the evolution of the world economy during that time. To the contrary, the past century was punctuated by phases of economic advancement and stagnation, of integration and disintegration, neatly summarized below with the assistance of research by economic historian Angus Maddison.[1]

Phase I (1870–1913): The "Golden Age"

This was a period of buoyant world trade, robust capital flows, and fluid international migration. It was a period of accelerating global interdependence, starting really in the late 19th century (1870) and continuing up until the eve of the First World War. Over this time frame, exports grew by 3.5 percent a year, versus annual real growth of 2.7 percent in output; by 1913, the share of exports in world output had increased to 11.9 percent, a level not reached again until 1970.[2]

The cross-border flow of people and capital was just as robust. According to the United Nations, "The international integration of labor markets reached unprecedented levels. Intercontinental migration from the European periphery to the expanding North and South American economies— above all else the United States—predominated. Between 1870 and 1915, 36 million people left Europe, two-thirds to the United States. But the process was more widespread. Intracontinental flows were significant in Asia. . . . Intra-European flows also reached significant levels."[3]

With the absence of capital controls, money moved relatively freely, with the gold standard providing an anchor for the world financial markets. Among the larger financial markets of Europe, foreign ownership of securities was not uncommon. In fact, foreign securities accounted for nearly 60 percent of all traded securities in London in 1913; in France, the share was even higher.[4] Meanwhile, the global stock of worldwide foreign direct investment had reached an estimated one-third of world foreign direct investment, with the United Kingdom the world's largest investor.[5] The United States, among the most attractive emerging markets of the time, was one of the largest host countries.

Phase II (1914–1950): Global Disintegration

The second phase of global economic development was among the darkest of the century. This stage was marred by two world wars, a world depression, and a general collapse of the world trading system. The outbreak of World War I and its aftermath destroyed the productive capacity of Europe and ultimately led to a series of quantitative restrictions on trade and capital. Inflation was rampant. A gold standard was reinstated in 1925, although the attempt to restore financial stability failed. Many nations removed trade restrictions after the war, but in the face of plummeting commodity prices, some nations raised tariffs in 1929. In June 1930, the United States passed Smoot-Hawley legislation, raising duties on imports by 23 percent. Other nations retaliated with their own tariffs and quantitative controls, causing global trade and growth to wither.

The world depression resulted in an 18 percent decline in aggregate output of the industrialized nations, with America taking an even bigger hit: U.S. output declined 28 percent during the 1929–32 depression.[6] Capital outflows of all types slowed or slid back. The trade and investment linkages created during the so-called golden era were severed.

Phase III (1950–1973): The Golden Era Part II

This was a period of revival and rebuilding following the ravages of war. Robust growth was bolstered by the establishment of strong multilateral institutions (e.g., the World Bank, International Monetary Fund) and framework agreements such as the General Agreement on Tariffs and Trade and the Bretton Woods agreement that helped promote and underwrite global economic growth. The rebuilding of Europe and Asia following the devastation of war was another powerful stimulus to growth.

So too was technology, with improvements and advances in transportation, satellite, and information technologies all instrumental in expanding the boundaries of commerce, lowering the cost of doing business, and promoting greater cross-border linkages.

The rapid growth of international trade was among the most defining features of this period. World trade increased at an average annual rate of 6.7 percent between 1948 and 1953 and accelerated to an annual rate of 7.4 percent between 1958 and 1963. Helped by the introduction of containerized shipping in the early 1960s, the rate of world trade growth accelerated to 8.6 percent between 1963 and 1968.[7] As noted by British scholar Peter Dickens, "A particularly important feature of the postwar period was that *trade increased more rapidly than production*, a clear indicator of *increased internationalization* of economic activities and of the greater *interconnectedness* which have come to characterize the world economy."[8] Trade in manufactured goods was notably strong during this period, expanding eightfold between the early 1950s and the early 1970s.

Phase IV (1974–1988): The Scourge of Inflation

The golden era came to an abrupt end in the early '70s, with the sudden and dramatic rise in world oil prices. The fourth phase saw a marked deceleration in growth and acceleration in inflation in the industrialized nations. Adding to the sense of crisis, the Bretton Woods system, which had provided a stable, international fixed exchange-rate system over most of the golden era, collapsed in August 1971. Currency volatility subsequently increased. Rising oil prices led to higher levels of external debt among the world's oil importers. In turn, balance-of-payment difficulties surfaced in various parts of the world, including Latin America and Asia. For Latin America, buried under a mountain of foreign debt, the 1980s ultimately turned out to be the "Lost Decade."

Early in the 1980s, Europe and the United States, in addition to high-profile emerging economies in Latin America and Asia, slipped into recession. It was not until the second half of the decade, assisted by lower global interest rates and the rebound of the world economy, that global trade flows recovered. Even more powerful were the surge in global foreign direct investment and the attendant rise in the international production of transnationals. This dynamic reintroduced an old concept to the new post–cold war global economy: globalization, or the process of global integration through rising cross-border flows of money, goods, information, and, to a lesser extent, people.

Phase V: Back to the Future

When the economic history of the 1990s is written, globalization will undoubtedly be christened the defining precept of global economic activity in the final decade of the 20th century. But this period, actually beginning in the late 1980s and continuing through the 1990s and beyond, cannot be characterized as new or different so much as a continuation of trends established more than 100 years earlier. The world economy has come full circle over the last decade. Many of the defining characteristics of global economy in the 1990s and today—robust and unfettered global capital flows, market-liberalization measures, buoyant trade growth—are quite similar to the primary features of the world economy more than a century ago.

Consistent with the first period of globalization, growth in world trade has expanded at a faster pace than world output. The latter rose by an annual average rate of roughly 3.1 percent between 1991 and 2000, versus growth in world trade volume of 6.1 percent over the same period. In some years, notably 1994 and 1995, the growth rate of world trade was over two and a half times faster than that of world output. As a result, the share of world trade to world output rose from approximately 19.3 percent in 1990 to 23 percent in the latter stages of the decade.[9]

Similarly, robust foreign direct investment flows played a key role in both phases of globalization. Over the balance of the 1990s, foreign direct investment (FDI) inflows expanded at a faster rate than both world gross domestic product and international trade. By the late 1990s, there were nearly 60,000 transnationals with more than 500,000 affiliates spread around the world. From this global production base, sales of foreign affiliates topped $11 trillion in 1998, versus global exports of goods and services of $6.6 billion, evidence that in the last few decades of the 20th century, international production by transnational corporations had surpassed international trade as the most important mechanism for international integration.[10] In addition to local sales, global exports by foreign affiliates were valued at $2.3 trillion in 1998. Their global assets topped $14.6 trillion in the same year, while the global value added of affiliates was equal to $2.7 trillion. Foreign affiliate exports were nearly 36 percent of world exports, while GDP attributed to foreign affiliates accounted for around 7 percent of global GDP.[11] Throughout the 1990s, then, the expansion of international production had intensified the interdependence of the world economy beyond that achieved by international trade alone.

Put another way, the global investment strategies of transnationals have emerged as among the most powerful forces of the world economy. Where, why, and how companies such as General Electric, Honda, and Siemens decide to invest around the globe lies at the core of the current round of globalization. The preferred mode of global engagement—trade versus investment—has unequivocally tipped toward the latter, a topic explored in greater detail in later chapters. But first, let's look at some of the global forces influencing corporate decisions and the competitive playing field of today.

Globalization Part II: Forces of Change

Change of any significance is rarely the outcome of one event, but rather of different forces emanating and converging from different sources. So it is with the reemergence of globalization in the 1990s. Using a framework devised by the Organization for Economic Cooperation and Development (OECD),[12] the forces of global change are grouped into four main categories, as presented in the accompanying table (Figure 1.1).

Technology-Related Forces

Technology has been at the forefront of enabling and fostering greater mobility of people, materials, money, and information. It is the engine of globalization, allowing firms to unbundle production and service activities, and to perform the activities in virtually any part of the world. In the process, the internationalization of economic activity has spread, as has the global reach of transnational companies.

Figure 1.1

Forces Shaping Globalization

Technology

- Declining computing and communication costs
- Shortened product lives and cycles
- Rapid growth of knowledge-intensive industries
- Increased importance of R&D

Macroeconomic Factors

- Productivity differentials
- Exchange rates
- Growth and industrial development
- "Catching up" by lagging nations
- Availability of production inputs

Government Policies

- Privatization
- Trade and investment reform
- Promotion of regional integration
- Competition policies
- Liberalization of capital flows

Firm Behavior

- Strategic: preemptive and imitative behavior
- Exploitation of competitive advantage
- Access to trained and skilled labor, technology, raw materials, and lower-cost labor
- Organizational changes

Source: OECD, Globalization of Industry, *pp. 20–21.*

Technology has been central to both periods of globalization. Just as the first round was driven and supported in large part by technological advances, namely falling transportation and communications costs (e.g., the introduction of steamships, railroads, telegraph, and cables), so the second round has been paced by falling costs for microchips, computers, satellites, fiber optics, and of course, the proliferation of the Internet.

The *enabling* factors of new technologies have altered and expanded the global reach of firms. Technology enables firms to effectively and confidently manage far-flung operations that used to be more isolated than integrated. Technology enables companies to process, interpret, and disseminate information faster and more cheaply to various parts of the world than in any time in the past. Technology enables firms to segment and transfer various functions (or services) that were not transportable or tradable, creating an international division of labor to the advantage of the firm. At the core, the technological advances of the past decade, by enabling transnationals like IKF Industries to round up what used to be geographically dispersed and fragmented affiliates into regional or global integrated production networks, have deepened the level of global economic integration beyond any point the world economy has ever experienced.

Macroeconomic Forces

Numerous economic variables have helped promote the process of globalization. One is the increased availability of productive inputs—land, capital, labor, and raw materials—on a global basis. Transnationals are always keen on leveraging resources from all over the globe, a task that became much easier over the balance of the 1990s, when the supply of global labor was great, access to capital was easy, and the availability of raw materials was abundant.

Other macroeconomic factors of importance include productivity levels and fluctuations in exchange rates. Differences in economic growth has been another element, with more and more firms wishing to spread their operations and sources of revenue around the world in order not to have "their eggs all in one basket." Global growth is rarely synchronized, and companies that enjoy sustained profitability are those with the wherewithal to offset weak growth in one region of the world with strong demand in another. Countries "catching up," like the nations of central Europe, freed from the longtime shackles of the Soviet Union, have also facilitated the process of globalization.

Government Policies

A more liberal attitude and policy framework toward trade, investment, and capital flows have played a lead role in the rebirth of globalization as well. Except for a few reluctant holdouts, the general bias of most governments has been toward trade reform, the promotion of inward foreign direct investment, and reduced capital controls. In addition, "less is more" has become the guiding mantra of many governments, including those across Europe and Latin America that have hived off hundreds of state enterprises over the past decade. As the standard-bearers of the Anglo-Saxon model of capitalism, the United States and the United Kingdom have been at the forefront of downsizing the role of the state.

This is not to suggest that governments have abdicated their responsibilities and left the "commanding heights," or the most important elements of the economy, to the markets. But governments have been in retreat over the past decade for having failed to promote sustainable growth on the one hand, while having grown too expansive and bloated on the other. The economic decay of the Soviet Union ultimately led to market liberalization not only in what later emerged as Russia, but also across central Europe. Communism lives on in China, although the Chinese leadership continues to move toward market-opening measures in both trade and investment. Brazil has adopted the same philosophy. Even in India, where the role of the government remains critical, the tide has shifted away from the state and more toward the markets, with one of Asia's largest markets becoming more amenable to external forces. The same is true across Europe, where over the past decade governments have sold everything from telephone companies to post offices.

As Daniel Yergin and Joseph Stanislaw wrote in *The Commanding Heights*, "The world over, governments have come to plan less, to own less, and to regulate less, allowing instead the frontiers of the market to expand. The decamping of the state from the commanding heights marks a great divide between the 20th and 21st centuries. It is opening the doors of many formerly closed countries to trade and investment, vastly increasing, in the process, the effective size of the global market."[13]

Firm Behavior

Globalization has also been fostered in part by the actions and strategies of firms as they adapt to the shifting market dynamics around them. In many cases, the urge of a firm to go overseas lies with its competitive advantage and the opportunity to exploit this advantage outside the home market.

Sustaining long-term profitability is a strategic prerequisite of any company, which increasingly entails the global utilization of resources. Firms must go where the skilled labor is located or to markets that have the appropriate technology for their needs. Many must move labor-intensive production to low-wage areas in order to remain competitive. Rising costs of research and development, coupled with shrinking product cycles, mandate that firms search for more markets and pool their competencies with other firms around the world.

Finally, often a move by one competitor or a group of competitors in an industry prompts a preemptive move by another, activating and accelerating the pace of industry consolidation on a global scale. Change or be changed. Acquire or be acquired. Standing still is not an option, often forcing companies into moves that they might not otherwise have made.

All of the catalysts of global change represent risks and rewards for U.S. firms. As the 1990s came to a close, U.S. firms never before had such a global menu from which to choose where and how to do business. The number of markets "open" for business had never been greater, which stands in contrast to the first period of globalization, in which significant parts of the world did not participate. U.S. firms such as General Electric, Citigroup, and Avon—transnationals at the forefront of globalization, which have embraced greater global openness and interdependence with gusto—have exploited these circumstances. At the other end of the spectrum are firms such as Bankers Trust, Wang Laboratories, and Packard Bell, which have more or less been subsumed by the forces of globalization and no longer exist today as separate entities.

Risks abound for players blinded to the global forces outlined here. Perhaps the biggest risk of all is for U.S. firms and U.S. policymakers to simply ignore the tectonic change extending over the world, on the assumption that America is some island of stability amid a sea of turbulent change. That belief is rampant in America, but nothing could be further from the truth.

The United States and the Illusion of Being an Island

Even as the pace of globalization quickens and the level of cross-border interdependence rises, many people in the United States like to think of America as a distant island sheltered from the gale forces of globalization. In other words, globalization has changed everything but the way many Americans think. This sense of security is wrong-minded but, at the same time, not hard to understand.

As the new century begins, the United States sits astride the global economy as the world's sole military and economic superpower. The last

15 years of the 20th century proved to be America's "Industrial Renaissance," with corporate cost-cutting on the one hand and heavy investment in technology on the other transforming the American economy from a global laggard in the 1980s to a global leader in the 1990s. Utilizing critical inputs such as advanced technology, world-class management skills, and flexible labor-market practices, the U.S. economy expanded by roughly 2.7 percent on an annual average basis during the 1990–99 period, ahead of the 2.4 percent average annual rate of growth for the developed nations as a whole during the same period. For Japan, the global pacesetter of the 1980s, the last decade of the 20th century was the "Lost Decade." The world's second largest economy grew by around 1.3 percent in the 1990s, versus 4 percent annual average growth in the 1980s.

Not even the great Asian financial crisis could slow the American economic juggernaut. While other regions or countries of the world—Latin America, Europe, and Russia—felt Asia's pain, the U.S. economy motored on, relatively immune, it seemed, to the Asian contagion and attendant downturn in global economic growth. In 1998, when the full brunt of Asia's unexpected collapse weighed on the rest of the world, the U.S. economy grew by a surprisingly robust rate of 4.3 percent, versus global growth of just 2.5 percent.

To many economists, the stellar performance of the U.S. economy in the face of what President Clinton called "the biggest financial challenge facing the world in half a century" was proof that the U.S. economy was an island of stability and prosperity. After all, so went the argument, corporate America's exposure to world markets was minimal, with U.S. exports accounting for one of the smallest shares of gross domestic product among the industrialized nations. Why worry, then, about events in Asia, developments in Russia, or unfolding trends in Latin America when such a large percentage of the U.S. economy is nontradable or detached from the global economy?

Unfortunately, perception does not match reality in this case. The United States is hardly segregated from the rest of the world. The U.S. economy is more attached than detached, more linked than delinked, to the global economy than most people in the United States even remotely realize. This general lack of awareness—which permeates Wall Street, Washington, and the general media—stems from the fact that the common measurement of U.S. global engagement is trade, or the "shallow"

Figure 1.2

Modes of U.S. Global Engagement, 1998

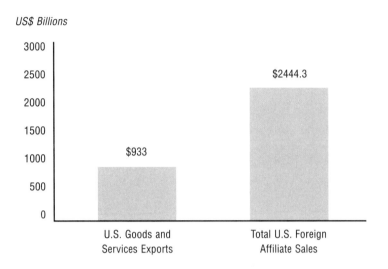

US$ Billions

Source: U.S. Department of Commerce.

form of global integration. By this benchmark, the United States does enjoy a relative degree of immunity from the rest of the world, with U.S. exports accounting for less than 12 percent of total U.S. output in 1998. Yet, in the "real world," or in the world of global manager Brian Cleveland, where the degree of U.S. global engagement is determined and measured by foreign direct investment and affiliate sales, the linkages between corporate America and the rest of the world are much greater and deeper. Therein lies the general thrust of this book—that exports and imports are poor measures of the scope and depth of U.S. global exposure, since U.S. global commerce entails far more than just shipping and receiving goods from overseas.

While trade paints a picture of global immunity, with U.S. exports totaling $933 billion in 1998, foreign investment, represented by the overseas sales of over 23,000 global U.S. foreign affiliates, reveals a radically different picture of U.S. exposure to the world economy. Sales of U.S.

overseas affiliates amounted to more than $2.4 trillion in 1998, two and a half times U.S. exports of goods and services in the same year (Figure 1.2). While the latter accounted for a relatively small share of total U.S. output in 1998, foreign affiliate sales in contrast were equivalent to roughly one-third of the U.S. gross domestic product in the same year.

This leads us back to an earlier point, that "in the last decades of the 20th century, international production by transnational corporations has superseded international trade as the most important mechanism for international integration." This is particularly true of the United States, the global leader in foreign direct investment and home and host to more transnationals than any other nation in the world.

2

WHY FIRMS INVEST ABROAD

Understanding the Dynamics of Foreign Direct Investment

"Too many people think you can succeed in the long run just by exporting from America or Europe. But you need to establish yourself locally and become, for example, a Chinese, Indonesian, or Indian citizen."

PERCY BARNEVIK, FORMER CHAIRMAN OF ABB,
AND CURRENT CHAIRMAN OF INVESTOR, THE
SWEDISH INVESTMENT GROUP. "TIMES UP FOR
THE MAN FROM HEAD OFFICE,"
FINANCIAL TIMES, OCT. 8, 1997.

HAVING SUCCESSFULLY BUILT and steered one of the world's premier engineering companies, Asea Brown Boveri (ABB), Barnevik knows a thing or two about the rules of global engagement. Under his guidance, the Swiss-Swedish electrical engineering firm emerged as a model global enterprise in the 1990s, with foreign affiliates rooted in virtually all regions of the world. Year after year, ABB has consistently ranked among the most global firms in the world, based on the United Nations' index of transnationality, which measures a firm's foreign assets, foreign sales, and foreign employment relative to each total. The cross-border reach of ABB, as Barnevik strongly suggests, is not based upon trade. Rather, the company's globality revolves around foreign direct investment and the establishment, in some shape or form, of a local presence in various markets around the world. Even though the company has its roots in not one but two countries that have long played a significant role in international trade, arm's-length transactions, a.k.a. trade, are a secondary strategy. ABB is not unique in this respect.

U.S. corporate leaders approach the world markets in a similar fashion, knowing that a successful and sustainable global advantage relies more on foreign direct investment than trade. As a result, roughly half of IBM's total assets and workforce were based outside the United States in 1997. In the same year, General Electric's foreign workforce represented 40 percent of the company's total, while roughly one-third of the firm's total assets lay beyond U.S. shores. Ford Motor employed nearly 175,000 foreign workers in 1997, or roughly half of its aggregate workforce. Approximately a quarter of the firm's assets were outside the United States. The list goes on: hundreds of U.S. firms have followed in the footsteps of Ford, "Big Blue," and other American corporate leaders in establishing overseas operations.

What motivates a company to expand beyond its own boundaries, and what determines whether a firm should invest abroad or simply serve the market via exports, are dissected in the following pages. The intent is to place the dynamics of foreign direct investment within a broad analytical framework. The material is presented in the context of U.S. firms. Examining all of the many theories of foreign investment falls beyond the scope of this text, although a few prominent theorists are mentioned. Particular attention is paid to global mergers and acquisitions, the primary mode of foreign direct investment in the 1990s. The proliferation of global strategic alliances—an increasingly important form of global engagement—is also examined. The chapter concludes by probing the linkages between foreign direct investment and trade.

What Motivates Firms to Invest Overseas?

Given that the U.S. economy represents the largest and wealthiest market in the world, and enjoyed near-unprecedented prosperity throughout the 1990s, what motivated U.S. firms to invest just over $800 billion abroad during the decade? For example, what possessed Ford to buy the auto division of Volvo of Sweden, and its financing arm, Ford Credit, to buy a local financial service company in Thailand? What compels Otis

Elevator, a subsidiary of United Technologies, to stick it out in Russia? Why has America Online set up back-office operations in the Philippines? What prompted Charles Schwab to take its discount brokerage model to Japan? Why have hundreds of other U.S. firms made it a strategic imperative to venture from home and seek opportunities beyond the 50 states?

There is, of course, no single answer to these questions. The global motivations of firms are as diverse and complex as both their business lines and the global markets themselves. They are in constant flux, changing and adjusting to prevailing market circumstances. Notwithstanding, theorists and academics have identified and broadly grouped four types of foreign direct investment (see Figure 2.1).

Resource Seeking

As the label implies, resource seekers prowl the world for resources, be they raw materials, semiskilled laborers, or highly trained workers. The motivation of resource-seeking investment is to acquire a specific resource that is either unavailable or in short supply in the home market. The world's top energy and mining firms are one such group of resource seekers. Consumer electronics manufacturers, textile firms, and other companies seeking cheap, semiskilled labor represent a second group of resource seekers. A third group consists of entities such as IBM and Microsoft that are in need of skilled, technologically trained labor.

Market Seeking

The strategic objective of market seekers is either to exploit new market opportunities in a particular country or to protect an existing market presence or position established via exports or through other means. Therefore, market size and prospects for growth along with per-capita income in the host nation, are all critical factors in the market-seeking investment decisions of transnationals. Import barriers and discriminatory government policies that mandate a local presence are also important. Market-seeking investment includes the foray of General Motors into China; Schwab's entry into Japan; the decision of McDonald's to buy Aroma, a chain of coffee and sandwich shops in the United Kingdom; and Wal-Mart's overseas investments in Mexico and Canada, and more recently, in Germany

Figure 2.1

Selected Variables Influencing the Motives of Transnational Corporations

Type of FDI	Economic Determinants of Host Country
Resource Seeking	• Availability of raw materials • Physical infrastructure (ports, roads, power, telecommunications) • Labor—skilled and unskilled • Availability of local partners to jointly promote knowledge and/or capital-intensive resource exploitations • Government restrictions and investment incentives
Market Seeking	• Market size and per-capita income • Adjacent regional markets (NAFTA, EU, etc.) • Market growth • Government policies • Quality of material and local infrastructure • Customer preferences; demographics
Efficiency Seeking	• Cost of resources and related production-cost variables (labor, materials) • Presence and competitiveness of related firms: e.g., leading industrial suppliers • Availability of local service support facilities; quality of infrastructure; degree of educated workforce; and other specialized factors: e.g., science and industrial parks • Membership in regional integration schemes conducive to the establishment of regional corporate networks
Strategic Asset Seeking	• Availability of knowledge-based assets • Availability of a pool of skilled labor • Business culture, entrepreneurial class, managerial competencies • Risk capital

Source: UNCTAD, World Investment Report: Trends and Determinants, *1998, p. 91.*

and the United Kingdom. In each instance, foreign investment is motivated by the desire to attract, gain, or maintain customers.

The advantage of market-seeking investment is that local production brings closer customer proximity, allowing firms to quickly and accurately adjust products to local tastes and trends. In addition, market seekers become closer not only to their customers but also to their competitors, both indigenous and global. As for the latter, some market-seeking investment is "follow-the-leader" type, or a response to a global competitor's major investment in a host country. The renewed rush to Brazil by the world's major automobile manufacturers in the mid-1990s is an example. Cost is another advantage of having local production, with the establishment of an in-country presence expected to reduce transport costs and other production expenses.

Efficiency Seeking

Efficiency seekers aim to rationalize existing structures in such a way as to gain economies of scale and scope. According to John Dunning, a leading theorist on transnationals and foreign direct investment flows, efficiency-seeking foreign direct investment takes two principal forms: "The first is that designed to take advantage of differences in the availability and cost of traditional factor endowments in different countries. . . . The second kind of efficiency-seeking investment is that which takes place in countries with broadly similar economic structures and income levels and is designed to take advantage of the economies of scale and scope, and of differences in consumer tastes and supply capabilities."[1] An example of the first type is the investment linkages between U.S. manufacturers and Mexican *maquiladores*, with many U.S. firms shifting production across the border into lower-cost Mexico and then assembling and exporting finished goods back to the United States. An example of the second is U.S. investment in Europe. The region's steady march toward economic integration over the past half century has given U.S. firms far greater opportunities and scope for increased efficiencies and rationalization. As Dunning explains, "In order for efficiency-seeking (or rationalized) foreign production to take place, cross-border markets must be well developed and open. This is why it flourishes in regionally integrated markets."[2]

Strategic Asset Seeking

Of all the motives underlying foreign direct investment over the 1990s, strategic asset seeking was among the most prominent. The intent of the strategic asset seeker is to add to the firm's existing portfolio of assets in a manner that bolsters and buttresses the firm's existing competitive advantage. Gaining access to marketing networks or distribution chains is one priority in this respect. Gathering intangible assets is of even more importance. Semiskilled labor and natural resources are secondary to the strategic asset seeker. What counts is the availability and accessibility of intangible assets such as intellectual capital and technological capabilities, as well as other "created assets." The common denominator, according to the United Nations, is "knowledge."[3]

Transnationals are venturing from home in search of knowledge and related attributes, since the basis of global competition has shifted from tangible inputs such as energy and cheap labor to intangible assets such as financial and intellectual capital. As stated by the United Nations regarding transnational corporations, or TNCs:

> The importance of created intangible assets in production and other economic activities has increased considerably. A large proportion of the costs of many final goods and services, ranging from simple products such as cereals through books and computers to automobiles, consists of the costs of such created assets as R&D, design, advertising, distribution, and legal work. Less than 10 percent of the production cost of automobiles now consists of labor costs; the rest relates to the contributions of various created assets. Moreover, international competition increasingly takes place through new products and processes, and these are often knowledge-based. R&D activities leading to new products and processes are costly and risky. At the same time, markets for knowledge-based resources and assets are becoming more open, and enterprises embodying these assets can be bought and sold. The result is that TNCs have taken advantage of these opportunities and used FDI as a major means of acquiring created assets and enhancing corporate competitiveness.[4]

Examples of strategic asset–seeking investment include Ford's purchases of Volvo (the auto division) of Sweden and Jaguar of the United Kingdom, and Land Rover from BMW in early 2000, three acquisitions that helped boost the firm's product niche in the luxury automobile market and meet the challenge of other luxury car manufacturers. A second example is Caterpillar's purchases of Perkins of the United Kingdom, a deal that allows Caterpillar access to Perkins's cutting-edge low-pollution engine technology. Similarly, in Japan, having a viable distribution network is requisite to long-term success, which helps explain in part the asset-seeking investment of companies such as GE Capital and Merrill Lynch.

Strategic asset investment has been at the core of booming foreign direct investment inflows into the United States over the past decade. A bundle of factors—a large and skilled labor pool, a wealthy consumer market, a first-class infrastructure, attractive government incentives—have motivated market-, resource-, and efficiency-seeking investment in the United States at various points. They remain key determinants to be sure. Yet, in the 1990s, it was the "created assets" of the United States, most of all America's technological capabilities, that unleashed a tidal wave of foreign investment in the U.S. technology sector. Over the second half of the decade, European firms led the way, snapping up U.S. technology companies such as Fore Systems (bought by GEC of the United Kingdom), VLSI Technology (Philips Electronics of the Netherlands), Xylan (Alcatel Alsthom of France), and Argon Networks (Siemens of Germany), to name just four deals. Many European telecommunication firms (British Telecom, Ericsson of Sweden, Nokia of Finland) have also made strategic asset investments in the United States over the past few years. In a similar vein, the Anglo-Dutch conglomerate Unilever bought SlimFast Foods, Ben & Jerry's, and Best Foods in rapid succession in early 2000. The logic: to acquire global and local brands, or intangible, "created" assets.

The premium now placed on "created assets" goes a long way in explaining the concentration of global foreign direct investment flows in the developed nations in general, and of the United States in particular. U.S. firms have been at the forefront of shedding the mass-production, mass-consumption economy of the past while embracing the knowledge economy of the future. And other transnationals from around the world are following in their footsteps. According to the United Nations, "It is precisely the rise in the importance of created assets that is the single most important shift among the economic determinants of FDI location in a liberalizing and globalizing world economy."[5] As the new millennium begins, access to knowledge—brains as opposed to brawn—has emerged as a predominant underlying motive of transnationals.

Some Theories on Foreign Investment

Two questions are pertinent to the determinants of foreign direct investment: Why do firms opt to enter foreign markets directly rather than export? and How do foreign firms new to a market successfully compete locally against indigenous firms that presumably have the home court advantage? Again, there is no one answer to these questions. While the literature on international trade is rich and generally well known, the theoretical underpinnings of foreign direct investment are more thinly developed. Up until the 1960s, the body of scholarly research on foreign direct investment was rather slight. Since then, however, the literature on cross-border investment flows has grown along with the rising magnitude and importance of foreign direct investment.

One pioneer in this endeavor was Stephen Hymer, who, in the early 1960s, was among the first to separate the theory of portfolio investment from the theory of foreign direct investment. Hymer's thesis was that the two forms of international capital flows—portfolio and foreign direct investment—behaved differently from each other. The former was related to interest rates, while the latter was composed of more than just the transfer of capital but also of other resources. Hymer postulated that capital movements of the firm were different from portfolio flows, motivated by the desire of control, whereby firms were interested in the control of a foreign enterprise in order to remove competition between the foreign company and firms in the host nations.[6]

In 1966, American scholar and leading theorist on multinationals Raymond Vernon developed the product life cycle, which became one of the first theories to link the relationship between international trade and international production (investment).[7] Vernon argued that a firm's ability to innovate and organize yielded a superior product that was initially produced in and for the home market. Given the advantages of the product and acceptance of the home market, the good, over time, was exported to other nations as foreign demand rose. That demand was initially satisfied through exports. However, as the product matured and became more standardized, as cost efficiencies and competition intensified, and as the size of the foreign market expanded, the feasibility of locating production in the host country grew. At this stage, one option was to broker a licensing agreement with a local firm. Another, assuming the right market conditions in the host country, was to establish a subsidiary or affiliate, whose production eventually substituted for exports.

Although the theory was powerful when first conceived, the explanatory powers of the product life cycle have diminished over the past few decades as the strategies of transnationals have grown more complex and product cycle times have been compressed. Still the model can serve as a framework in tracing the means by which many U.S. firms began to engage in overseas commerce. Many of America's most powerful manufacturing companies were global traders first and global investors second, a sequence outlined in Figure 2.2.

Since the publication of Vernon's thesis, many theories have been put forth to explain why firms invest overseas, with considerations ranging from market imperfections to proprietary knowledge of the firm to the culture of the home market. Some scholars have contended that firms venture abroad to take advantage of a favorable host government or to "jump" existing tariff barriers. Other theorists say that leveraging organizational

---

Figure 2.2

From Traders to Foreign Investors: The Linear Sequence

- Domestic production and sales are traditionally the principal objectives. Foreign markets enter the purview of most entrepreneurs later.

- When foreign markets become interesting, exports begin usually with arm's-length sales, initially through domestic or foreign agents. In the past, FDI did not enter into the reckoning.

- Intermediaries are replaced by export departments at headquarters, leading, perhaps, to some FDI: e.g., in storage facilities or foreign trading affiliates.

- Exports are often followed by licensing of foreign producers to manufacture a product with proprietary technology.

- Once experience with these and other, mostly nonequity, forms of production abroad has been gained, firms gradually begin to build up production capacities, beginning with assembly operations or other partial production (sometimes in joint ventures with local partners), before turning toward production in majority or wholly owned foreign affiliates, often as stand-alone clones of their parent companies.

- While a firm may simultaneously export to many countries, investment in production facilities usually begins in one country, typically not too distant from the home country in "psychological distance—that is, the distance measured in "factors preventing or disturbing the flows of information between firms and market" (Johanson and Wiedersheim, 1993), such as differences in language, culture, political systems, level of education, and level of development.

- If successful, the experience with the first foreign producing affiliate can lead to affiliates in other countries, on the basis of separate, local market-oriented, multidomestic strategies, relying on stand-alone affiliates.

- Eventually, foreign affiliates may begin to export.

Source: World Investment Report: Investment, Trade and International Policy Arrangements, *1996, p. 76.*

efficiencies or marketing skills has been the catalyst to the overseas expansion of some companies. International diversification and the avoidance of exchange-rate risks are two more explanations offered, while still another is that firms invest abroad neither to maximize profits nor to leverage a particular advantage, but rather follow competitors abroad to avoid giving them unrivaled access to an attractive market.

To capture the multiple strands motivating the behavior of transnationals, and to help explain the fact that the motives of foreign direct investment vary across industries and countries, John Dunning crafted the "eclectic theory" of foreign direct investment in the early 1980s.[8] According to Dunning, three interrelated factors are necessary for firms to undertake foreign investment: (1) The firm must possess or control specific advantages that existing competitors do not have (ownership-specific advantages); (2) To exploit these advantages, it is more profitable for the firm to internalize those advantages as opposed to selling or leasing them to other firms (local production under foreign ownership); and (3) It must be more profitable to leverage the firm's assets and advantages overseas rather than domestically (location-specific advantages). A summary of each determinant follows.

Ownership Advantages

Ownership advantages refer to the assets possessed by the firm and can include product innovations, brand recognition, marketing capabilities, management structure, distribution capabilities, patents, technology capabilities, finances, and a host of other factors. These factors give the foreign firm an edge over local firms in the host country; theoretically, without this benefit, firms would lack the ability to overcome the better understanding of local conditions by local firms and therefore remain at a competitive disadvantage.

Extending theory to reality, one ownership advantage of Microsoft is its technological prowess and dominant position in developing software. Cisco Systems' advantage lies in hardware. Capital, technology, and brand recognition are firm-specific advantages of Citigroup, while IBM and Coca-Cola have ownership advantages in such areas as marketing, brands, and patents. Many of America's most globally successful firms have developed multiple and complementary ownership advantages, making them among the most formidable competitors in the world. Ford Motor's advantage in manufacturing production, for example, has been augmented by overseas investment of Ford Credit, giving Ford a leg up not only in vehicle production but also in financing and after-sales service. General Electric's firm-specific advantages run the gamut, from high technology to process engineering to commercial loans. In short, ownership advantages are unique capabilities of the firm that enable it to successfully compete overseas.

Internalization

Internalization goes to the decision of the firm to internalize its particular ownership-specific advantage. The pivotal question is whether firms should invest directly overseas, establish a licensing agreement with an indigenous firm, or simply export. Numerous advantages are associated with internalization: The strategy eliminates uncertainty and avoids such problems as negotiating costs and selecting partners. It gives the firm more control and ensures a steady supply of product. It reduces the threat of creating competitors through borrowed or licensed technology, and avoids unacceptable performance of foreign agents. It also allows firms to bypass domestic intermediaries in host countries, in many cases bestowing greater marketing flexibility and customer proximity. Internalization is prevalent among companies (IBM, Oracle, Rambus, and Eastman Kodak, for example) whose ownership-specific advantage relates to technology, and who often prefer to establish their own subsidiaries overseas rather than sell or license their technology to other firms.

Locational Variables

Locational factors relate to the "where" of production and differing conditions (political and economic) among potential production sites. For Exxon, Royal Dutch/Shell, and other energy firms, overseas investments are dictated by location-specific factors and the corresponding availability of natural resources. The investment decisions of consumer product companies such as Unilever, Sony, and Procter & Gamble are influenced in part by such locational variables as the size of a particular foreign market, the level of income, and country demographics. For a computer manufacturer such as Compaq or a consumer electronics firm such as Philips, operative locational factors include the availability of skilled labor, wage costs, and other general operating variables.

Government policies, whether composed of incentives or disincentives, are also considered primary locational factors. Tax exemptions, low corporate taxes, the creation of export processing zones, and related policies favor greater investment inflows. So do government initiatives that promote regional economic integration. In the early 1950s, the bulk of U.S. overseas investment was directed to Canada and the developing nations, notably in Latin America. The following decade, however, the general overseas thrust of corporate America shifted toward Europe, due in large part to the formation of the European Community in 1957. Thereafter, the expansion of the European Economic Community, followed by the creation of the European Single Market, and the introduction of the European Monetary Union were all propitious locational-specific variables that sustained the long-term rise in U.S. investment. By the same token, the creation of the North American Free Trade Agreement and South America's formation of Mercosur in the 1990s have had similar stimulating effects on U.S. foreign investment outflows to Mexico and Brazil since the mid-1990s.

Looked at from a country basis, the location advantages of Ireland include the nation's favorable corporate taxes, a relatively inexpensive, English-speaking workforce, and membership in the European Union. Heading south, proximity and accessibility to the U S. market is one reason why more firms from around the world are investing in Mexico. In China, cheap labor costs and the prospects of a relatively large market are considered major locational factors. Brazil's more hospitable policies toward foreign direct investment, in addition to its large market and Mercosur membership, have embellished the locational attractiveness of that country. The favorable location specifics of the United States are manifold, ranging from a first-class infrastructure to highly developed capital markets to a wealthy and large consumer market and, above all, to America's possession of "created assets."

At the other end of the spectrum are government policies that impede investment. These include policies that exclude foreign firms from certain sectors, limit foreign ownership, require a minimum level of technology transfer, and restrict the remittances of profits. Local-content rules, union practices, and environmental regulations can also serve as a locational deterrent to investment.

In summary, foreign direct investment takes place when a firm combines its ownership-specific advantage with a host nation's location-specific advantage through internalization. Internalization can be accomplished primarily either through a "greenfield" investment, in which a transnational builds a plant or facility to internalize its ownership advantage abroad, or through an acquisition or merger with an existing firm in the host country. Build or buy? In the 1990s, buying was far and away the preferred method of transnationals.

The Urge to Merge

Cross-border mergers and acquisitions, versus greenfield investment, were the most popular mode of foreign direct investment in the 1990s. Typically, greenfield projects require more time than a merger or acquisition, and in many cases, they require more up-front capital. While a merger can have a relatively quick impact on the bottom line of a company, the contribution from a greenfield investment comes after a considerable lag. Before any revenue materializes, a company usually has to commit and tie up massive amounts of capital, construct the facility, and then begin operations. The payoff comes later, while the dividends from M&A typically materialize faster.

The greenfield process is seen as particularly glacial in a competitive environment marked by the accelerating pace of technology, intensifying global competition, and rapidly shifting industry configurations. Being first to market and penetrating it quickly are competitive advantages for transnationals that can be satisfied more effectively through a cross-border merger or acquisition. For the acquiring company, the deal can be a swift and efficient way to gain market presence, reach new customers, augment core competencies, access technology, and/or take control of existing supplier networks or distribution systems.

Mergers can also be less taxing on a company's capital base. Many of the recent global megadeals do not involve cash payment, but rather have been funded by stock swaps between the acquiring and acquired firm. The stock-exchange method of payment has allowed many big deals to go through with few funds involved, which has helped fuel the ever-rising number of deals.

After falling steeply in 1991 due to the onset of recession in the United States and Europe, global mergers and acquisitions soared, climbing from a level of $80.7 billion in 1991 to over $500 billion in 1998.[9] According to preliminary estimates from the United Nations, cross-border mergers and acquisitions grew by 35 percent in 1999 to $720 billion. While cross-border M&A deals are not strictly defined as foreign direct investments, due to different valuation methods, global M&As and global foreign investment flows mirror each other to a large degree (Figure 2.3).

Not only were there more foreign M&A deals in the 1990s, but there were also larger deals, helping to inflate the total value of global mergers. While $1 billion agreements were rare and notable early in the decade (the first $1 billion deal, in fact, did not occur until 1991), they became commonplace over the course of the years. Indeed, megadeals became the rage. Over 1995–97, for instance, the average size of large-scale cross-border arrangements rose from $1.7 billion to $2.8 billion. The number of corporate marriages worth more than $1 billion totaled 58 in 1997, up from 35 in 1995. The largest foreign M&A deal in 1997 was between Zurich Versicherungs and BAT Industries, a deal valued at $18.4 billion that shocked the international investment community with its price tag.

Thereafter, the megadeals grew in number and size. For instance, there were 89 deals of $1 billion or more in 1998, with the largest merger, between British Petroleum and Amoco, valued at $55 billion. In the same year, Daimler-Benz and Chrysler stunned the automobile industry and others with their $40.5 billion merger of equals. The global pharmaceutical industry was shaken by the $31.8 billion deal between ZENECA Group of the United Kingdom and Astra of Sweden and by the $21.2 billion merger between Germany's Hoechst and Rhone-Poulenc of France. In 1999, the deals only grew in size, with the Vodafone AirTouch ($66 billion) acquisition one of the largest of the year. The richest of all was the purchase of Mannesmann of Germany by Vodafone AirTouch of the United Kingdom for nearly $185 billion. The deal was announced in 1999, to be realized in 2000.

One salient characteristic of global M&A activity is that the bulk has been concentrated among the developed nations. In particular, in both sales and purchases, the United States and the United Kingdom stand out, with the duo involved as either sellers or purchasers in 63 out of the 89 megadeals of 1998. On the sales side of global M&A activity, U.S. sales registered more than $200 billion in 1998, up from $65 billion in 1997 and a previous peak of $71 billion in 1996. Of the 89 megadeals (defined as $1 bil-

Figure 2.3

FDI Inflows and Cross-Border M&As[a]

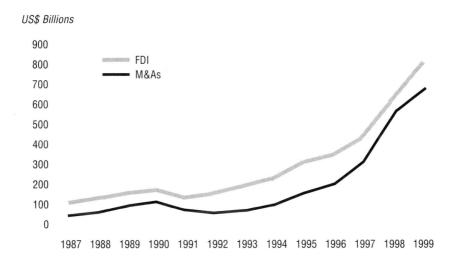

[a]Cross-border M&As that result in the acquisition of more than 10 percent equity share.

Source: UNOTAD, FDI/TNC database.

lion or higher), the United States was involved in 30 as sellers, with such American firms as PacificCorp (purchased by Scottish Power of the United Kingdom), Bankers Trust (Deutsche Bank—Germany), Bay Networks (Northern Telecom—Canada), Simon & Schuster (Pearson—the United Kingdom), Illinois Central Corporation (Canadian National Railroad-Canada), and others all falling under foreign ownership. Again in 1999, the United States was the single country with the largest value of sales.

On the purchase side of the equation, the United States ranked as the world's largest purchaser in every year of the 1990s but two—1998 and 1999, when the United Kingdom ascended to the number one slot. It was in fact aggressive buying among United Kingdom firms in the United States that vaulted the nation to the top spot: 12 out of 17 megadeals made by U.K. firms in 1998 were for U.S. firms, which helps explain the promi-nent position of the United Kingdom in U.S. foreign direct investment inflows. According to the United Nations, only 10 percent of cross-border deals by U.K. firms were with other European firms in 1998.[10] Continen-tal European firms, in contrast, exhibited a tendency to conclude more cross-border deals among themselves than with either the United Kingdom or the United States for most of the decade.

Meanwhile, Japan's participation in global mergers and acquisitions, at least up until the late 1990s, has been nominal at best. Japan was involved in only 2 of the 89 megadeals in 1998 and was a bit player over most of the decade. That is not surprising in the face of Japan's predisposition toward greenfield investment and bias against foreign mergers and acquisi-tions. Fueling this bias is the popular belief in Japan that M&As are preda-tory actions that should be shunned, in addition to cultural difficulties and cross-shareholdings among Japanese firms. And it doesn't help that the Eng-lish word *takeover* is translated into Japanese as *hijacking*. However, "hijack-ings" (a.k.a. mergers and acquisitions) are becoming more popular and acceptable in Japan, a secular trend brought on by Japan's lingering reces-sion and long-term profits squeeze. More on that subject in Chapter 7.

In the developing nations, the number and value of mergers and acquisitions are small but are expected to grow as M&A activities become more acceptable forms of business, as they have in Japan. The develop-ing nations accounted for only 3 percent of total M&A purchases in 1998, down from a 10 percent share the prior year. On the sales side, the devel-oping nations accounted for just 12 percent of total global M&A activ-ity in 1998, although in prior years, the share was as high as 30 percent (in 1993, 1994, and 1996), owing to the process of privatization, or the selling off of state-owned enterprises to foreigners in such locations as Latin America and central Europe. Brazil alone, due to the privatization of Telebras and other deals within the telecommunications sector, emerged as the fifth largest seller country in 1998, with sales of nearly $25 bil-lion, twice the value of total M&A transactions in 1997.

In the future, the level and scope of mergers and acquisitions in the developing nations will depend less on privatization—the primary force behind M&A activity in the 1990s—and more on the willingness of both corporations and governments in such emerging countries as Poland, Brazil, South Korea, and China to accept cross-border mergers and acqui-sitions as a form of private sector corporate restructuring. At best, it has been a lukewarm embrace to date, since most developing nations prefer greenfield foreign direct investment to mergers and acquisitions, and for relatively good reasons. The latter involve merely a change in ownership of existing assets and hence little in the way, at least initially, of new capital in the productive stock of the host country. In contrast, greenfield investments typically entail an injection of funds and greater capital formation. They often lead to the transfer of technology, the creation of new jobs, and, in many countries, a rise in export capabilities. For all of these reasons and more, the bias is toward new and additional foreign investment as opposed to merely the swapping of ownership between a local party and a foreigner. In times of duress, however, or the Asian financial crisis for instance, mergers and acquisitions have become more acceptable.

A final characteristic of global mergers and acquisitions is greater industry concentration. At the tail end of the 1990s, global mergers and acquisitions were particularly prevalent in industries newly liberalized and deregulated (electricity, banking, finance, insurance, and telecommunications); in industries suffering from overcapacity (defense, chemicals, automobiles, pulp and paper, basic materials, oil); and in sectors facing high research and development expenditures (pharmaceuticals and technology). In many cases, global mergers and acquisitions represented a form of industry consolidation and corporate restructuring, creating ever larger firms in their wake. As the size of the deals grew, so did the companies. Today, the sales of many merged firms are greater than the total output of many countries.

Global mergers and acquisitions emerged as a basic global strategy for companies such as Cisco, Lucent, Ford, IBM, and Merrill Lynch in the 1990s. And when these companies were not buying or building, they were busy crafting strategic partnerships, another principal form of global engagement that requires special mention.

My Enemy's Enemy Is My Friend: The Rise of Alliance Capitalism

"Corporate leaders are beginning to learn what the leaders of nations have always known: In a complex, uncertain world filled with dangerous opponents, it is best not to go it alone." [11]

KENICHI OHMAE

Foreign direct investment and trade are the primary, although not the only, means of global engagement. Firms also interact, compete, and serve customers through a host of nonequity forms of investment. These include subcontracting agreements, management contracts, turnkey deals, franchising, licensing, and product sharing. Of particular importance, and the focus here, has been the rise of strategic alliances or partnerships, which have become nearly as prominent—if not more so in some industries—over the past decade as global mergers and acquisitions.

Where foreign direct investment is the acquisition and therefore control (minority or majority) of one firm in one country over another firm in another country, cross-border strategic alliances represent nonequity linkages between two firms or among a group of firms. The popularity of such deals has swelled in the past decade, with the number of technology-related pacts alone totaling more than 8,200 over the 1980–96 period, according to data from the United Nations.[12]

The global forces driving the proliferation of strategic alliances are similar to the ones behind the surge in cross-border mergers and acquisitions: market liberalization, intensifying global competition, and above all else, soaring costs of research and development juxtaposed against shortened product life cycles and rapid technological obsolescence in a number of advanced industries (telecommunications, biotechnology, and semiconductors). As the degree of innovation in competition has increased over the past decade, so has the number of competitive collaboration agreements. Greater market access and lower transaction costs are two other forces driving the growth of alliances, although over the 1990s, an increasing number of partnerships were crafted to protect or embellish the created assets of participating firms.

Many companies have concluded that going solo is just too expensive and time-consuming. It is more advantageous, according to prevailing wisdom, to find a partner or partners to spread the costs and risks of developing new products, to entering new markets, to gain access to critical technologies and to leverage existing distribution channels. In practice, however, a large percentage of these corporate partnerships do not work as envisioned and ultimately fail.

When they are successful, strategic alliances not only diffuse risks but also allow for speedier access to new technology, enhanced market flexibility, and greater economics of scale and scope.[13] Through alliances, companies can preempt or neutralize a strategy of a competitor, quickly shed noncore businesses and turn their focus to core competencies, and develop closer relations with their customers. Alliances can also be deployed to overcome barriers to entry imposed by governments, a tactic used by the world's major airlines, which, facing government limitations on foreign ownership, have coalesced into a handful of mega-alliances. The Star Alliance is one such group, whose members include United Airlines (United States), Lufthansa (Germany), SAS (Scandinavia), Thai Airways (Thailand), Air Canada, (Canada), Singapore Airlines (Singapore), Varig (Brazil), Ansett (Australia), and ANA (Japan).

From the perspective of United Airlines, the Star Alliance gives the company far greater global breadth than it could have accomplished otherwise. No one airline can afford the expense of maintaining both a global fleet and a global infrastructure. United and its counterparts have achieved greater economies of scale by alliance building—pooling assets, whether they are planes, code-sharing capabilities, frequent-flyer programs, catering services, training, maintenance, or even aircraft buying programs. Expanded market reach without the large up-front capital cost typically associated with an acquisition is one of the primary benefits of strategic alliances. In early 2000, however, the potential for global mergers within the industry was raised again with the planned merger of British Airways with Royal Dutch Airlines.

Another benefit of alliances is knowing your competitor better. As Gary Hamel and C. K. Prahalad observed:

> Collaboration can also be used to calibrate competitors' strengths and weaknesses. Toyota's joint venture with GM, and Mazda's with Ford, give these automakers an invaluable vantage point for assessing the progress their U.S. rivals have made in cost reduction, quality, and technology. They can also learn how GM and Ford compete—when they will fight and when they won't. Of course, the reverse is also true: Ford and GM have an equal opportunity to learn from their partner-competitors.[14]

The automobile sector has experienced a number of strategic alliances over the past few years, in addition to a few mergers and acquisitions. In many cases, competitors are also collaborators. General Motors has agreed to buy transmissions and engines from Honda, a deal that will save millions of dollars in research and development costs. Ford Motor's web of strategic alliances among major suppliers, equipment manufacturers, technology leaders, and auto manufacturers themselves is shown in Figure 2.4. As environmental and performance standards have risen, so has the number of

Figure 2.4

The Portfolio of Technology Agreements of Ford, 1983–1996

Suppliers of Inputs for Components	
1983	Garrett Corp. (United States)
1986	Phoenix Steel Corp. (United States)
1986	Ceradyne Inc. (United States)
1988	Occidental Petroleum (United States)
1989, '92	General Electric (United States)
1994	Engelhard Kali-Chemie (Germany)

Manufacturing Technology Providers	
1984	American Robot Corp. (United States)
1985	Bendix Industry Group (United States)
1985	Boeing Computer Services (United States)
1985	Measurex (United States)
1985	Teknowledge (United States)
1986	Iscar Ceramics (Israel)
1988	Inference Corp. (United States)
1989	Guest Keen & Nettlefolds (United Kingdom)
1989	Grob Werke Gmbh (Germany)
1989	ABB Robotics (Sweden)
1989	Advanced Assembly Automation (United States)
1990	AT&T (United States)

Ford

Equipment Suppliers	
1984	Yamaha Motor Co. (Japan)
1985	JBL Inc. (United States)
1987	Matsushita Elec. Industrial (Japan)
1990	Ge. Silicones (United States)
1991	Hewlett-Packard (United States)
1994	Siemens (Germany)
1994	Directed Technologies (United States)
1995	Cambridge Industries (United States)
1996	Lear Sitting Holding (Italy)

Auto Manufacturers	
1988, '91[a], '93[a], '96[a]	General Motors (United States)
1993, '94 (2), '95	Chrysler (United States)
1986	Iveco (Italy)
1987, '89	Nissan (Japan)
1989	Motor Iberica (Spain)
1994	Daimler-Benz (Germany)
1995	Audi NSU (Germany)
1995	BMW (Germany)
1996	Mazda Motor Co. (Japan)

[a]Signed two technology agreements that year.
Source: MERIT/UNCTAD database; World Investment Report, *1998, p. 27.*

collaborative alliances between automakers to develop fuel alternatives, greater engine efficiencies, and improved pollution-control capabilities.

The proliferation of the Internet has been another key driver of strategic alliances, with the beginning of the new millennium witnessing the formation of a host of business-to-business (B2B) alliances among manufacturing firms in the same industries. As the next step in collaborative commerce, numerous online Internet exchanges have sprung up in the past year across the spectrum, ranging from trucking to mining to aerospace. The goal of these e-alliances is manifold: to reduce procurements costs, streamline intercompany transactions, eliminate redundancies, increase efficiencies, promote greater industry transparency, and a host of other objectives.

On balance, global cooperative alliances have become an increasingly important form of global engagement. Behind this trend have been the spread of globalization, the rising cost of research and development, and the widening gap between a firm's strategy on the one hand and its resources and capabilities on the other. Even Microsoft, arguably one of the most powerful companies in the world, has had to enter into multiple strategic alliances (with Ericsson, British Telecommunications, Telmex, and others) over the past few years. Like many other companies, Microsoft hopes to position itself in the center of a global constellation, thereby leveraging global resources. In the process, the rules of global engagement promise to become even more intricate.

Foreign Direct Investment and Trade: The Interlinkages

> *"The issue of whether foreign direct investment and exports are substitutes or complements has been rather extensively investigated empirically, and the bulk of the evidence points toward a complementary relationship rather than a substitutive one."* [15]

Given the linear sequence of how companies typically become involved in global markets—exporting first, and then investing locally on a step-by-step basis later—foreign direct investment is often viewed as a substitute for trade. The underlying assumption is that a rise in outward foreign direct investment invariably leads to a corresponding decline in exports of the home country, precipitating a fall in employment and balance-of-payment pressures. The result: a "hollowed-out" economy and the potential for worker unrest as jobs are lost to overseas locations.

The reality, however, is somewhat different and much more complex. Foreign direct investment and trade are alternative means of delivering goods (and to a lesser extent, services) to foreign markets. But whether one form of delivery is a substitute for another is unclear. Numerous studies have shown that depending on the industry and the host and home countries involved, foreign direct investment can be either trade-replacing or trade-creating, or both.[16]

To the extent that a firm invests in a host country to avoid trade barriers, or out of the threat of market restrictions, then foreign investment can substitute for trade. The surge in foreign direct investment in the United States by Japanese electronics and automobile manufacturers in the 1970s and 1980s is one such example. Another is the global rush among the world's top automakers to invest in China in the 1990s. High-import barriers meant that foreign direct investment was the only feasible option available to General Motors, Volkswagen, and others who wanted to sell cars in China. However, the mainland's pending entry into the World Trade Organization could result in a future rise in automobile trade. In these examples, where local production of foreign affiliates substitutes for imports (or exports, from the viewpoint of the home country), "the line of causality did not run from higher FDI to lower trade; it ran from import restrictions to smaller imports by the host country (or exports from the home country), to higher FDI."[17]

Foreign direct investment can also complement trade or, in many cases, create cross-border movements in goods and services. U.S. parent companies, for instance, can be major suppliers to their foreign affiliates, which means that while the establishment of an American foreign affiliate can replace or reduce the level of U.S. exports, the corresponding needs of the affiliate (capital goods, parts, components, intermediate goods, services) create demand for exports from the home country.

Over time, of course, foreign affiliates can be expected to increase local sourcing, reducing their dependence on the parent for supplies. Rarely are the parent-affiliate ties completely severed, however, a point underscored by the fact that a significant share of U.S. trade is intrafirm, or between parents and their foreign affiliates. In 1997, the most recent year of data, intrafirm shipments between U.S. parent companies and their foreign affiliates accounted for 26.3 percent of all U.S. merchandise exports and nearly 17 percent of total merchandise imports. In addition, exports between foreign-owned U.S. affiliates and their foreign parents accounted for roughly 10 percent of total U.S. exports in 1997, while imports between the related parties accounted for nearly one-quarter of total U.S. imports. Due largely to the significance of intrafirm trade, U.S. foreign investment and trade are more closely linked than most people realize.

As an example, much of the auto-related trade between the United States and Canada, and the United States and Mexico, is intrafirm related, with U.S. parents (Ford, General Motors) exporting parts and components to their affiliates in Canada and Mexico. In return, U.S. affiliates export components as well as finished products (cars, minivans, and trucks) to the United States and other parts of the world. In this case, the foreign direct investment of Detroit is both trade-replacing and trade-supporting.

Over the decades, the conceptual models of foreign investment and trade have been developed separately of each other. However, the global spread and influence of transnationals, epitomized by the accelerating dissemination of integrated international production networks, has fundamentally altered the relationship between foreign direct investment and trade. The two variables are more fused than isolated. For investors and policymakers alike, a greater understanding of this interlocking dynamic is essential.

3

BEYOND TRADE

Transnationals and Global Foreign Direct Investment Trends

"The aim in a global business is to get the best ideas from everywhere."

JACK WELCH, CEO, GENERAL ELECTRIC.
"THE GLOBAL ECONOMY: PART ONE,"
FINANCIAL TIMES, OCT. 1, 1997.

GLOBAL MONEY MANAGERS are considered among the most powerful players on the world economic stage, and with good reason. With their penchant for shifting billions of dollars into and out of various countries each day, these moneymen can bring an economy either to new heights or to its knees. This group is held to be so influential, in fact, that some observers have claimed that certain nations have "surrendered" to the markets and are no longer in control of their own destiny.[1]

That's an exaggeration. Global traders, to be sure, are powerful. But they share the global stage with an equally, if not more, influential group of players called transnational corporations. It is transnationals, with their extended yet integrated global production networks, that have been at the forefront of globalization. As the chief distributors of foreign direct investment capital, transnationals are not only a major source of global financing but also a major driver of global economic activity, accounting for large shares of world output and trade. Where money managers' investment can often be footloose and fickle, transnational investment is more strategic and long term, with a lasting impact on the host country. Money managers' "hot money" is primarily a source of capital, while foreign direct investment provides not only funds but also technology, managerial skills, employment opportunities, and other critical inputs to growth.

Transnationals, then, not global money managers, have radically reshaped the world economy over the past half century. Here we'll learn first how they have emerged and evolved. The rest of the chapter examines the key sources and recipients of global foreign direct investment flows over the 1990s.

The Making of a Transnational

Operating abroad is hardly a new endeavor for some American firms. Mira Wilkens traces the origins of U.S. overseas participation to the colonial period, when "merchants—preferring not to depend on agents abroad—dispatched members of their families to England to act for their concerns. This is the first approximation of a foreign branch house, for in most cases the overseas representative was installed at the expense of the American enterprise."[2] U.S. foreign direct investment began to rise in earnest during the mid-1800s and gathered pace later in the century with the introduction of the steamship, the telegraph, railroads, and trans-Atlantic cables. New technology helped shrink the world and expand the cross-border capabilities of firms such as Singer, J. P. Morgan, and oil giant Standard Oil as well as American entrepreneurs such as Thomas Edison and George Westinghouse.

By the first decade of the 20th century, such familiar names as Eastman Kodak, Quaker Oats, and Coca-Cola had already established overseas beachheads. Ford Motor opened its first foreign plant in 1904, in Canada. Following World War I, Ford established a presence in Europe, where it was soon joined by its American rival General Motors. In 1929, General Motors bought Opel, one of the oldest names among European automakers and one that remains one of the flagships of German industry.

For most of the 20th century, U.S. firms with production facilities outside the United States were known as multinationals. Typically, foreign affiliates or subsidiaries of multinationals were scattered around the world and acted relatively independently from the parent company. There was little or no coordination among foreign subsidiaries. According to the United Nations, "in most cases (with the natural-resources sectors being an obvious exception), foreign affiliates would follow a *stand-alone strategy*, replicating more or less in total the entire value chain of the parent firm . . . thus performing all tasks necessary for servicing the host country and/or neighboring markets."[3] This relationship symbolized the parent-affiliate partnership in the initial period following the Second World War. From there, the stand-alone strategy of affiliates grew and evolved as a result of technological advances and the global trend toward greater trade liberalization. As their capabilities increased, affiliates adopted more *simple integration strategies*, "where affiliates undertake—typically with technology obtained from the parent firm—a limited range of activities in order to supply their parent firm with specific inputs that they are in a more competitive position to produce. Such strategies have given rise to new forms of cross-border linkages (such as subcontracting relations) and allow for greater two-way flows of information, technology, and value-added activities between parent firms and affiliates."[4]

In the last quarter century, notably in the 1990s, the strategies of multinationals became even more sophisticated.[5] Falling trade barriers, investment reforms, industry liberalization, further advances in communications technology, the proliferation of regional trading blocks—the intersection of these variables has *enabled* firms to pursue more sophisticated international production strategies, which, in turn, has enhanced their overall competitive position and their global clout.

In the words of the United Nations, "simple integration strategies" have evolved into "complex integration strategies." These entail greater intrafirm linkages, interdependence, and coordination not only between affiliates and their parents but also among various affiliates themselves. The affiliate, rather than being a stand-alone entity, functions for the firm as a whole. It's part of the firm's value chain. Specific functions (production, distribution, marketing, research and development) are segmented and are carried out by operating units in countries best suited for that particular activity. Under this process, affiliates maintain multidimensional linkages not only with the parent but also with other affiliates in other nations and with unrelated firms. An international intrafirm division of labor is developed. The company looks more like a network than a hierarchy. The current-day transnational has emerged from this global configuration, about which scholars Christopher A. Bartlett and Sumantra Ghoshal have stated: "Transnationals integrate assets, resources, and diverse people in operating units around the world. Through flexible management processes . . . transnational companies can build three strategic capabilities: global-scale efficiency and competitiveness; national-level responsiveness and flexibility; and cross-market capacity to leverage learning on a worldwide basis."[6]

The Transnational Profile

Figure 3.1 succinctly summarizes the global might of transnationals and their affiliates. One caveat: Consider these figures the best estimates available, since even the United Nations, the primary source of the data, concedes that the numbers understate the true universe of firms that operate as transnationals. Quantifying the actual positions is difficult because different valuation measurements of foreign direct investment exist, and many firms have cross-border relations and control of foreign assets through other, nonequity arrangements, which are not included in the official investment calculations.

The transnational universe included some 60,000 parent firms and more than 500,000 foreign affiliates in 1998; the comparable figures were 37,000 and 170,000, respectively, in 1990. Foreign direct investment stock exceeded $4 trillion in 1998, up from $1.7 trillion in 1990 and just $480 billion in 1980. In other words, in the last two decades of the 20th century, the stock of global foreign direct investment rose more than eightfold, marking one of the most explosive periods of global integration in history.

Transnationals remain clustered in the industrialized nations; of the world's top 100 transnationals in 1997, nearly half were headquartered in the European Union (45), followed by the United States (27), Japan (17), and Canada (3). As for industry concentration, four sectors—automotive, electronics and electrical equipment, petroleum, and chemicals/pharmaceuticals—account for roughly two-thirds of the total. Based on the value of foreign assets, General Electric, Ford Motor, Royal

Figure 3.1

FDI Indicators and International Production

	Value at Current Prices (US$ Billions)			Annual Growth Rate (%)				
	1996	**1997**	**1998**	**1986–90**	**1991–95**	**1996**	**1997**	**1998**
FDI inflows	359	464	644	24.3	19.6	9.1	29.4	38.7
FDI outflows	380	475	649	27.3	15.9	5.9	25.1	36.6
FDI inward stock	3,086	3,437	4,088	17.9	9.6	10.6	11.4	19.0
FDI outward stock	3,145	3,423	4,117	21.3	10.5	10.7	8.9	20.3
Sales of foreign affiliates	9,372	9,728	11,427	16.6	10.7	11.7	3.8	17.5
Gross product of foreign affiliates	2,026	2,286	2,677	16.8	7.3	6.7	12.8	17.1
Total assets of foreign affiliates	11,246	12,211	14,620	18.5	13.8	8.8	8.6	19.7
Exports of foreign affiliates	1,841	2,035	2,338	13.5	13.1	–5.8	10.5	14.9
Employment of foreign affiliates (thousands)	30,941	31,630	35,074	5.9	5.6	4.9	2.2	10.9
Global exports of goods and services	6,523	6,710	6,576	15.0	9.3	5.7	2.9	–2.0

Source: UNCTAD, World Investment Report, *1999, p. 9.*

Dutch/Shell, General Motors, and Exxon Corporation ranked as the top five transnationals in the world.

Because foreign assets, taken in isolation, do not fully capture a firm's involvement in the world economy, the United Nations has developed an index of transnationality. The index is a composite measure of a firm's share of foreign assets, foreign sales, and foreign employment, and serves as a better tool for gauging just how globalized the operations of major transnationals are. By this measurement, the transnational universe remains concentrated in the industrialized nations, although the company rankings dramatically shift toward firms based in relatively small economies. Given the limited size of their home markets, transnationals such as Asea Brown Boveri (Switzerland/Sweden), Thomson (Canada),

Nestlé (Switzerland), Unilever (United Kingdom/Netherlands), and Solvay (Belgium) have always had a powerful incentive to expand overseas and in the process have accumulated large foreign asset, sales, and employment bases relative to their respective home operations. Accordingly, they ranked among the top transnationals based on the index of transnationality in 1997.[7]

Besides giving effect to the global reach of transnationals, the table in Figure 3.1 reinforces the influential role of foreign affiliates, which have emerged in their own right as among the most dominant players in the global economy in the past few decades. Total foreign affiliate assets rose from $1.9 trillion in 1982 to $5.6 trillion in 1990, and nearly tripled between 1990 and 1998, to $14.6 trillion. From this production base, the U.N. estimates that the gross product or value added of affiliates reached $2.7 trillion in 1998, a figure that exceeds the annual GDP of all but the largest economies in the world. In the same year, the ratio of sales of foreign affiliates ($11.4 trillion) to world exports ($6.6 trillion) was 1.7:1. That compares with a ratio of 1.1:1 in the early 1980s and 1.2:1 in 1990, and underscores the commonly overlooked but essential fact that firms use overseas affiliates more than exports to service foreign markets.

The U.N. figures actually understate the extent to which U.S. firms use foreign investment to penetrate foreign markets. The ratio of U.S. affiliate sales to exports is discernibly higher than the world average, a topic developed later in this chapter. The U.N. calculations, however, support the central theme of this book: global engagement is less about trade and more about foreign direct investment and the deliverance of goods and services to customers via foreign affiliates. The role of affiliates has grown along with the flourish in global foreign direct investment.

The Global Boom in Foreign Direct Investment

Global foreign direct investment flows were nothing short of explosive in the last 15 years of the 20th century.[8] From an annual average of just $42.4 billion over the 1980–84 period, global FDI outflows rose to a yearly average of $156 billion in the second half of the 1980s. That marked an impressive increase at the time, but it was only the beginning. Annual outflows topped $200 billion for the first time in 1989. They rose again in 1990, although the following year, due to the global slowdown in growth, FDI outflows fell for the first time since 1982. At the time, some experts warned that the powerful cycle of global investment had come to an end, but in reality 1991 was just a blip on the radar screen. Global flows rebounded in 1992, and over the 1990–94 period, annual outflows averaged $234 billion. In 1995, outflows reached nearly $360 billion, and they continued to increase thereafter.

Not even the great Asian crisis of 1997–98 slowed the momentum of global foreign direct investment. Outflows soared by 25 percent in 1997, to $475 billion, roughly double the annual total at the beginning of the decade. More impressive still was the fact that in the face of a global economic slowdown in 1998, FDI outflows climbed 35.6 percent year-over-year, to a record $644 billion. They jumped by more than 25 percent in 1999, to an estimated $827 billion, capping an astounding decade of growth.

Sources of Global FDI Outflows

Transnationals from the industrialized nations have dominated investment outflows for the past 100 years, with the United Kingdom and the United States at the vanguard.

Britain was the major source of foreign investment in the early 20th century, reflecting, in large part, the country's premier global economic status and colonial reach. According to the United Nations, the world stock of foreign direct investment totaled $44 billion in 1914. The United Kingdom accounted for roughly 40 percent of the total, or $18 billion, well ahead of France ($9 billion), Germany ($6 billion), and Belgium ($5.5 billion).

In the intervening decades, Britain's global influence waned, and the United States assumed the role as the world's top investor. Spared most of the ravages of World War II, and reigning as the undisputed global economic leader at the time, the United States accounted for at least half of total global FDI outflows in the 1950s. In 1960, according to figures from the United Nations, the U.S. share of world outward stock of foreign direct investment was around 50 percent, with the United Kingdom a distant second. Combined, the two parties represented two-thirds of total world investment stock in 1960 (see Figure 3.2).

Figure 3.2

Global Foreign Direct Investment

(Percent Share in World Outward Stock of FDI)

Country of Origin	1960	1980	1985	1990	1995	1996	1997	1998
United States	49.2	42.9	36.6	25.4	24.5	25.4	25.1	24.1
United Kingdom	16.2	15.7	14.6	13.6	11.0	11.4	10.9	12.1
Japan	0.7	3.8	6.4	11.8	8.4	8.3	7.9	7.2
Germany	1.2	8.4	8.7	8.8	9.5	9.4	8.9	9.5
France	6.1	3.5	4.6	6.4	6.5	6.5	5.5	5.9
Netherlands	NA	8.2	6.5	6.4	6.3	6.2	6.1	6.4
Switzerland	NA	4.2	3.1	3.8	5.0	4.6	4.7	4.3
Italy	NA	1.4	2.1	3.3	3.4	3.4	3.7	4.1
Developing Nations	NA	2.6	4.1	4.3	8.3	9.0	10.0	9.5

NA = Not available.
Source: UNCTAD.

The duo remained the dominant providers of foreign investment well into the second half of the 20th century. In 1980, in fact, the two nations accounted for nearly 60 percent of the global total of outward stock; five years later they still maintained an impressive global share of just over 50 percent, although their dominance waned in the second half of the 1980s as other global transnationals began to emerge. In particular, Japan proved a new arrival with which to be reckoned.

Japan Goes Global

Counted among the largest and wealthiest countries in the world, and home to a number of well-known companies with strong global brands, Japan has a distinguished history in foreign direct investment. Yet, following World War II, the nation's efforts were directed toward the development of exports and industrial self-sufficiency. In other words, global engagement meant primarily trade, not foreign investment. The latter was actually discouraged and restricted by the government up until the late 1960s, given Japan's own capital needs.

By the mid-1970s, the pace of overseas investment had begun to accelerate. The appreciation of the yen and rising domestic wage costs compelled Japanese manufacturers to shift labor-intensive production to the low-wage newly industrialized nations of Taiwan, South Korea, Hong

Kong, and Singapore. In the mid-1970s and in the following decade, Japan's overseas investment thrust shifted to the United States in response to growing U.S. threats of protectionism and market restrictions which were incited by the lopsided Japan-U.S. trade relationship. This, coupled with the dramatic strengthening of the yen in the wake of the 1985 Plaza Accord Agreement, set off a near tidal wave of Japanese foreign direct investment over the second half of the 1980s. At the time, Japan seemed to emerge from virtually out of nowhere to become the top global provider of FDI outflows in the second half of the 1980s. Outflows from Japan averaged $27.8 billion a year during 1985–90, exceeding the annual average of $21.6 billion from the United States and $25.2 billion from the United Kingdom. As a share of world outward stock of foreign investment, Japan's portion rose to 11.8 percent by 1990, up from 6.4 percent in 1985 and just 3.8 percent in 1980.

In the United States, Japan's buying binge wrought concern and consternation in the halls of Congress and in the executive suites of many American companies. The overriding fear in the United States was that corporate Japan, having upped the competitive ante first via trade and now through foreign investment, was on the verge of assuming unrivaled control and influence over the American economy.

These fears were unfounded. Japan's influence in global FDI outflows coincided with the rise and decline of its "bubble economy." While Japan was flush with liquidity, FDI outflows peaked in 1990, accounting for one-fifth of world outflows. When the infamous "bubble" burst in the early 1990s, Japanese companies were forced into a global retreat. Profit losses, tight lending practices, mounting debt, plummeting asset prices—all of these variables and more stanched Japanese outward investment in the early 1990s. Foreign direct investment reached a trough in 1993, when FDI outflows slumped to $13.8 billion, down 71 percent from 1990's total. Thereafter, outflows recovered but remained just a sliver of the global total. In fact, still struggling to break out of an economic slump that lasted nearly a decade, Japan accounted for less than 4 percent of world FDI outflows in 1998, a far cry from its 20 percent share at the beginning of the 1990s.

Europe Steps Up

With Japan sidelined by its own economic ills, the global boom in foreign direct investment in the 1990s was largely a trans-Atlantic affair, led by

American, British, and continental European firms. While the United States was the largest individual source of global FDI over the 1990–98 period, the European Union was the largest regional provider of outflows, accounting for nearly 60 percent of the global total in 1998, versus 55 percent in 1990. In 1999, the United Kingdom became the largest investor in the world, topping the United States for the first time since 1988.

A variety of determinants—intense global competition, the creation of the single market, nascent market opportunities in central Europe, strategic positioning in the United States, and finally, the adoption of a single currency—precipitated a massive surge in cross-border investment from Europe in the 1990s. The introduction of the euro reconfigured the competitive landscape of Europe, as did market-deregulation initiatives agreed upon earlier in the decade. Government privatization allowed one-time state enterprises to either acquire other companies or be acquired.

Accompanying these structural trends were the gale forces of globalization, which, among many other variables, stirred a strategic rethinking among corporate Europe. Gone were the days when firms could comfortably compete within the confines of the home market. For many European companies, sustained growth, let alone corporate survival, depended on greater regional and global expansion. Stay-at-home or close-to-home strategies were not feasible against a backdrop of intense U.S. competition in Europe's own home markets, coupled with deeper import penetration among Japanese and other Asian manufacturers. Meanwhile, next door, the fall of the Berlin Wall led to the rebirth of new markets and new competitors to the east.

Shareholder pressure for industry consolidation was another driver of Europe's cross-border investment boom in the 1990s, with more and more Anglo-American institutional investors, despite regional resistance, influencing the pace and extent of corporate restructuring in Europe in the second half of the decade. Just as shareholder activism in the United States goaded management into change, the same dynamic became more evident in Europe, introducing an element of urgency in boardrooms across the region.

All of these pressures were catalysts for change, and for greater European investment outflows. French companies invested more than $256 billion outside their home market over 1990–98. German firms invested even more. Companies such as Siemens, Volkswagen, and Bayer were compelled to engage in more cross-border investment not only because of the regional and global forces mentioned but also on account of domestic considerations. Germany's outward investment of $320.5 billion over 1990–98 was motivated in part by the nation's high wage structure, rigid labor practices, and punishing corporate tax policies. All three disincentives put the global competitiveness of German industry at risk in the 1990s, prompting resource- and efficiency-seeking foreign investment in such locations as eastern Europe, Latin America, and Asia. Market and strategic-asset access was another motive of corporate Germany, supporting a rise in German FDI outflows to one market in particular: the United States. Of total German foreign direct investment outflows for 1990–98, more than 28 percent went to the United States.

On balance, global FDI outflows historically have been concentrated among the industrialized nations. At the vanguard have been the United States and the United Kingdom, which combined accounted for 36 percent of the total world outward stock of foreign investment in 1998. British transnationals remained the top overseas investors among their European counterparts in the 1990s, though the United Kingdom's share of total European Union outflows fell from nearly one-third in 1985–90 to an annual average share of roughly one-quarter in the 1990s. Japan emerged as a major source of global FDI outflows in the last two decades of the 20th century but ranked only fifth in terms of total FDI outflows over the 1990–98 period. Cumulative outflows from Japan totaled $225 billion during the period, trailing the United States ($657 billion), the United Kingdom ($373 billion), Germany ($320.5 billion), and France ($256.5 billion).

As early as 1991, the United Nations remarked: "The global pattern of foreign direct investment can now be characterized as tripolar, with the EC, the United States, and Japan being the members of the Triad."[9] This pattern of global outflows became even more pronounced over the 1990s, with the Triad accounting for nearly 80 percent of global FDI outflows in 1990–98 (see Figure 3.3).

New and Emerging Transnationals

For the most part, the leading companies of the developing nations still utilize trade as the primary means of global engagement rather than foreign

Figure 3.3

Global FDI Outflows

(US$ Billions)

	Annual Average 1985–90	Cumulative Total 1990–98	Annual Average 1990–98
World	155.6	3,034.2	337.1
Developed Nations	145.0	2,669.0	296.5
United States	21.6	657.4	73.0
European Union	80.3	1,517.2	168.6
Japan	27.8	225.6	25.1
Developing Nations	10.6	357.6	39.7
Latin America and Caribbean	1.3	65.1	7.2
Brazil	0.3	8.9	1.0
Mexico	0.2	4.3	0.5
Asia (except Japan)	8.1	285.5	31.7
Hong Kong	2.1	147.3	16.4
China	0.7	20.4	2.3
South Korea	0.8	25.1	2.8
Malaysia	0.3	18.0	2.0
Taiwan	2.9	30.0	3.3
Singapore	0.6	31.0	3.4

Source: UNCTAD.

investment and overseas affiliates. However, the trade-led strategies of many firms are changing, and changing fast. The reasons are simple: firms such as Acer of Taiwan, Cemex of Mexico, Sappi of South Africa, Ranbaxy of India, and others confront the same competitive challenges as their U.S., Japanese, and European counterparts. These include shifting exchange rates, rising domestic costs, fierce foreign competition at home, and ongoing protectionist pressures in overseas markets. Acquiring new technology and having access to new markets are underlying motives as well, as is customer proximity, given the shifting dynamics of final demand. According to Antony Lo, chief executive of Taiwan-based Giant, one of the world's largest bike companies, "The main reason for transferring some production from the Far East to the Netherlands is to increase flexibility. Fashions are changing quickly, and market trends must be followed closely. Having a production base next to the market means we should be able to satisfy our customers better."[10] In short, many companies in the developing nations are venturing farther and farther abroad for the same reasons that compelled their industrial competitors to leave home before them. As evidence of this outward migration, transnationals from the developing nations accounted for nearly 13.7 percent of world investment outflows in 1997, up from 7.4 percent in 1990 and just 3 percent in 1980. In 1998, however, the Asian financial crisis and attendant squeeze on capital precipitated a near 20 percent plunge in investment from the developing nations. Outflows fell to $52.3 billion, representing just 8 percent of the global total. In Asia, which accounts for the bulk of outward investment from the developing nations, the combination of rising debt burdens, declining profits, plunging asset valuations, and, in some countries (e.g., Malaysia), capital controls greatly reduced regional investment outflows in 1998. Hence the steep decline in total flows from the developing nations at large.

Developing Asia provided 80 percent of total outflows of the developing nations over 1990–98. At the forefront was Hong Kong, whose level of outward investment exceeded even Japan's for the 1993–98 period—$133.8 billion versus $128.5 billion. The majority of this investment was directed at China and motivated chiefly by the mainland's relatively strong economic growth rates, and cheap land and labor costs. Politics—namely China's resumption of control over Hong Kong as of mid-1998—was another contributor to Hong Kong's expanding investment position in the mainland.

Hong Kong's counterparts, Taiwan, South Korea, and Singapore, also emerged as significant overseas investors in the 1990s. As with Hong Kong, Taiwanese manufacturers established a sizable investment stake in mainland China in an effort to offset rising wages at home and the underlying structural strength of the New Taiwan dollar. In fact, Taiwan firms pumped so much money into China over the 1990s that the Taiwanese government openly expressed its concern late in the decade that the nation's manufacturing capabilities and industrial base were becoming too closely tied with China's. The mainland was also a favorite target of many firms from Singapore, which, along with Hong Kong and Taiwan, exploited their Chinese connections in penetrating the large Chinese market.

To ensure market access in the industrialized nations, emerging transnationals from Taiwan, South Korea, and Singapore have undertaken sizable investments outside Asia, namely in the United States and the European Union, and alongside each country's/region's peripheral. "You have to be close to the customer," Cliff Chu, an executive with Singapore-based NatSteel Electronics, told the *Far Eastern Economic Review* in an interview in late 1999.[11] That explains the firm's rising investment commitment to Mexico and Hungary, outposts with strategic proximity to the United States and the European Union, respectively. NatSteel's competitors have followed suit, notably in Mexico, where more and more Asian contract manufacturers now have facilities to better serve their main customers, which include technology leaders such as Apple, Cisco, Ericsson, and Hewlett-Packard. In the global electronics industry, speed and proximity matter, forcing many companies in developing Asia to shift production to North America and Europe.

Finally, mainland China, the largest host nation among the developing nations, emerged as another source of foreign direct investment in the 1990s, with annual outflows totaling $20 billion on a cumulative basis over 1990–98. That's not a terribly large amount, but the figure is greater than the combined total FDI outflows of Latin America's two largest overseas investors, Brazil ($8.9 billion) and Mexico ($4.3 billion), for the same period.

Why would Chinese firms, with a huge and growing domestic market, in addition to a massive and relatively cheap labor pool, want to venture abroad? One motive is a desire to secure a stable supply of natural resources. This priority compelled the China National Petroleum Corporation to take a 60 percent stake in Kazakhstan's state-owned oil company in the mid-1990s. Chinese firms have also made large investments in forest-development projects in New Zealand.

A second motivation is trade. A significant amount of China's overseas investment is done by trading companies, whose mission is to uncover global trade opportunities and assist in the overseas expansion of Chinese construction companies, banks, transportation firms, and other companies. In this respect, China is following in the footsteps of Japan and South Korea, where large trading companies have been among the most aggressive overseas investors and traders for decades.

Finally, another strategic motive of China's foreign investment has been maintaining access to vital overseas markets, prompting Haier, China's leading producer of household appliances, to build a $30 million refrigerator plant in Camden, South Carolina, in 1999. The Konka Group, a Chinese manufacturing outfit, now makes televisions in Tijuana, Mexico, and has a research and development facility in San Jose, California. As a potential hedge against U.S. trade protectionism, the company, in addition to other Chinese firms, increasingly feels obligated to operate "inside" the North American market as opposed to conducting business on an arm's-length basis, a sentiment shared by many emerging transnationals from other countries.[12]

In total, investment outflows from the developing nations remain secondary to outflows from the developed nations, a situation that became even more pronounced in 1998 following the plunge in investment from Asia. However, it would be better to view the events of 1998 as a temporary, cyclical downturn rather than a structural shift away from the general trend of rising outflows over most of the 1990s. The long-term trend favors a resumption of outward investment in the future, not only from developing Asia but also from Latin America and central Europe. Just as the risks and rewards of global competition have motivated firms from the developed nations to move beyond their respective home markets, the same dynamics are at work in developing nations, spawning an ever expanding universe of transnationals beyond the "Triad." U.S. transnationals, then, can expect in the future to cross paths with such emerging corporate leaders as First Pacific Company (Hong Kong), China National Chemicals (China), LG Electronics (South Korea), Petronas (Malaysia), Acer (Taiwan), Souza Cruz (Brazil), TVK (Hungary), and Latvian Shipping (Latvia).

Global FDI Inflows: A Larger Claim for the Developing Nations . . . Even in Times of Crisis

Global investment inflows are more diverse and less concentrated than outflows. The latter, as previously discussed, are dominated by the industrialized nations, notwithstanding the structural rise in foreign investment from the developing nations over the past decade. Investment inflows exhibit a somewhat better global balance: the developing nations claimed nearly one-third of global inflows during 1990–98, versus a share of roughly 12 percent of outflows. According to preliminary estimates from the United Nations, the developing nations captured roughly 26 percent of total global inflows in 1999, slightly off the average for the decade.

The resilence of investment inflows to the developing nations was borne out over the last two years of the 1990s. Notwithstanding the Asian financial crisis and the spillover effect into other parts of the world, investment flows to the developing nations were basically flat in 1998, and then galloped ahead the following year. Inflows totaled $193 billion in 1998, up 1 percent from 1997, and then climbed to $218 billion in 1999, a near 13 percent difference.

In Asia, the decline in inflows in 1998 was steepest in Taiwan, Hong Kong, and Indonesia, which together experienced a fall of $11.5 billion in investment inflows that year. Indonesia was at the extreme end, experiencing net divestment in 1998. Total investment inflows approached $90 billion for Asia in 1998, accounting for more than half of the total of the developing nations. While down from the prior year, inflows were still higher than the precrisis level of 1996 and well above the annual average ($58.2 billion) of 1990–98 (see Figure 3.4). The following year, in 1999, inflows rose by an estimated 1 percent, to $91 billion.

In stark contrast to resilient foreign investment inflows was the poor showing in net portfolio flows and bank lending to Asia. Net portfolio flows plunged from $17.2 billion in 1996 to just $5 billion in 1998, while commercial bank lending swung from $80.1 billion in 1996 to minus $60 billion two years later. The dramatic swings speak volumes about the behavior of transnationals on the one hand and global money managers on the other. Asia, no doubt, experienced a sharp decline in private external capital in the wake of the regional financial crisis, with total flows sheared to just $4.2 billion in 1998, down from $66.8 billion in 1997 and $176 billion in 1996, according to the Institute of International Finance.[13] Yet, the decline reflected more the panic and rush to the exits of global investors and bankers than any serious loss of confidence among transnationals. Money managers and lenders pulled the plug on Asia in terms of external financing, resulting in negative lending and portfolio flows in the five so-called crisis economies (South Korea, Indonesia, Thailand, the Philippines, and Malaysia) in 1998. By contrast, foreign

Figure 3.4

Global FDI Inflows

(US$ Billions)

	Annual Average 1985–90	Cumulative Total 1990–98	Annual Average 1990–98
World	141.9	2,807.5	312.0
Developed Nations	116.7	1,838.4	204.3
United States	48.6	616.1	68.5
European Union	52.7	994.9	110.5
Japan	0.4	13.5	1.5
Developing Nations	24.7	886.4	98.5
Africa	2.9	42.7	4.7
Latin America and Caribbean	8.1	312.5	34.7
South America	3.8	190.7	21.9
Brazil	1.3	71.4	7.9
Mexico	2.6	72.5	8.1
Asia	13.5	524.0	58.2
China	2.7	246.1	27.3
Central and Eastern Europe	0.5	82.4	9.2

Source: UNCTAD.

direct investment to the same economies fell only 2 percent the same year, juxtaposing the long-term horizon of transnationals against the extremely short time lines of fund managers. By country, South Korea, the Philippines, and Thailand showed sharp increases, while inflows to Malaysia declined and Indonesia suffered through a year of divestment. A similar scenario unfolded during the Mexican peso crisis. Then, portfolio equity investment plunged to just $500 million in 1995 from $4.5 billion the year before, while foreign direct investment inflows contracted by only 13 percent in 1995 after more than doubling in 1994.

Asia: Transnationals Make the Most of the Crisis

Not only did developing Asia weather the financial crisis rather well, but more important perhaps, the crisis actually encouraged new foreign direct investment inflows. Above all else, Asia's crisis was a catalyst for change, a "shock" that altered deeply entrenched government policies and corporate business practices throughout the region. Needing capital, and overwhelmed by an overleveraged corporate sector, governments and companies rapidly adopted a more accommodating attitude toward foreign direct investment. Various barriers to entry in certain industries, notably in such service sectors as telecommunications, banking, and insurance, were removed, while rules governing foreign ownership, modes of entry, and financing were loosened. Specifically, South Korea introduced an automatic approval system; ASEAN (the Association of Southeast Asian Nations) formed a regional investment area; and within ASEAN, Thailand, among other measures, liberalized rules governing expatriate workers. Of particular significance was the widening acceptance of cross-border mergers and acquisitions, which were slow to gather pace in the immediate aftermath of the crisis but eventually became a more familiar mode of investment in Asia. In the five crisis economies alone, merger activity shot upward, with the annual average value of M&A transactions reaching $12 billion in 1998 and 1999, versus just $1 billion annually in the 1994–96 period. Whether this trend becomes entrenched in Asia remains to be seen, however, given stiff local resistance.

At the firm level, many transnationals from the United States and Europe were quick to snap up assets that had suddenly become very inexpensive. Devalued currencies, coupled with lower property values and bargain prices for corporate assets, reduced the costs of buying physical assets throughout Asia. Many parts of the region were up for sale and at extremely attractive prices for transnationals, prompting Jean-Marie Bernard, president of the French company Wheelabrator Allevard, to remark, "We were already thinking about making an investment in Asia before the crisis began. Now that the price was right, we are ready to move ahead rapidly."[14]

Asia's cheap currencies also had the effect of lowering local production costs, namely wages, in terms of foreign currency values, triggering a rise in efficiency-seeking foreign direct investment. Not surprisingly, export-oriented manufacturing and assembly investment rose sharply in such locations as Thailand and Malaysia, where devalued currencies made it more competitive for firms, whether local or foreign, to export goods. However, foreign affiliates and transnationals producing goods for sale in the local market, or market-seeking investors, were not as fortunate, with depressed economic conditions leading to depressed final sales. Against this backdrop, Asia's sudden and unexpected bout with recession imparted different consequences on different transnationals.

Whatever the effect, a consensus emerged in 1999 that Asia's financial crisis was nothing more than a blip on the radar screen of transnationals and the region would remain among the preferred locations in the world for transnational activity. Jack Welch of General Electric echoed this sentiment in the firm's 1998 annual report, saying that the region was "in need of various structural remedies but rich in opportunity."[15] Putting Welch's money where his mouth is, General Electric has been among the most aggressive overseas investors in Asia since the financial crisis.

Latin America: A Refurbished Image Equals More Capital Inflows

It is clear that the horizon of the transnational is infinitely longer than that of the money managers. But even transnationals have their limits and have been known to periodically step back from a particular country or region when local conditions become so extreme and unfavorable that firms have to either leave or greatly scale back their investment position. A case in point is Latin America.

At the end of the 1970s, Latin America, including the Caribbean, was the preferred choice of transnationals, with Brazil and Mexico the most popular locations for foreign companies within the universe of the developing nations. Then came the "Lost Decade," a period characterized by high inflation, limited growth prospects, burdensome debt levels, and a general sense of uncertainty that greatly raised the political and credit risk associated with investing in the region over the first half of the 1980s. Transnationals retrenched; investment inflows declined early on in the 1980s. By 1986, developing Asia surpassed Latin America for the first time as the largest host region for foreign direct investment among the developing nations.

But just as Asia began to gain favor among transnationals, Latin America began work to improve its overall macroeconomic environment, setting the stage for an impressive rebound in inflows during the 1990s. Over the second half of the 1980s and into the 1990s, fiscal discipline became the norm across the region. Mountains of external debt were restructured, creating the underpinnings for greater macroeconomic and political stability. Specific policies such as debt-equity swaps followed by privatization measures acted as catalysts for greater foreign direct investment. These measures were implemented within a general framework advocating investment liberalization and included policies that eased sectoral restrictions, simplified registration procedures, and strengthened intellectual property protection.

Improved prospects for regional integration acted as another force pulling investment into the region. For instance, the North American Free Trade Agreement (NAFTA) cracked open many markets (e.g., tourism, telecommunications, and retail) in Mexico that had long been off-limits to or protected from foreign competition. Technical barriers to trade, government procurement practices, product standards, environmental policies—all of these interrelated areas, and more, were liberalized under NAFTA, helping to generate a wave of foreign direct investment in Mexico. Annual global inflows jumped from $2.5 billion in 1990 to nearly $7 billion in 1993, one year before NAFTA began. The following year, investment inflows to Mexico bolted to more than $12 billion. The peso crisis and ensuing recession in 1995 caused a temporary deceleration in inflows during 1995–96, although the annual amount of investment topped $9 billion each year, well above pre-NAFTA levels. Mexico attracted a record amount of investment in 1997 (nearly $13 billion) and ranked second only to China (albeit by a wide margin) as the top destination of global investment among the developing nations during the 1990–98 period.

More impressive than the surge in investment in Mexico during the 1990s was the transnational rush to Brazil. The Latin giant reemerged as the unequivocal preferred location in Latin America in the late 1990s. The opposite was true as the decade began: Brazil, despite having the largest economy and population in Latin America, attracted slightly less than $1 billion in foreign direct investment in 1990, below Argentina ($1.8 billion) and Mexico ($2.5 billion). At the time, because of its questionable and unpredictable macroeconomic and political climate, Brazil was bypassed for more amenable environments.

The 1990s, however, brought about a sea of change, in which Brazil became far more attractive to transnationals. The regional laggard became the regional leader as Brazil slowly but surely implemented the trade- and investment-reform measures that other nations in the region had embraced earlier. As part of this process, the country eliminated a variety of trade barriers, deregulated a number of domestic industries, and repealed various pieces of protectionist legislation, such as laws restricting imports of computer equipment. The prerequisite policies to attract external investment were complemented by two overarching initiatives. The first was the creation and subsequent implementation of Mercosur, the regional trading bloc of the southern cone of South America, encompassing Brazil, Argentina, Paraguay, and Uruguay. As with NAFTA, the prospect of further regional integration, which, in most cases, bestows such benefits as greater economies of scale and wider market access to transnationals, yielded rising investment inflows not only to Brazil but to other Mercosur members as well.

The second initiative was Brazil's large-scale privatization program, which induced a substantial rise in privatization-related foreign direct investment, beginning in the middle of the decade. Throughout Latin America, privatization programs were instrumental in boosting foreign direct investment during the 1990s. But Brazil, not atypically, lagged behind the likes of Argentina, Chile, and Mexico in selling off state firms. According to the United Nations, Brazil owned 28 of the 50 largest public companies in Latin America (ranked by sales) in 1994. Where Mexico had privatized more than $20 billion of assets by the end of 1994, and Argentina $16 billion, Brazil had privatized only $6 billion.[16]

When various state enterprises in Brazil did come up for sale, foreign investors responded. Investment inflows more than doubled in 1995 ($5.5 billion) from the prior year but were nevertheless roughly half of Mexico's ($9.5 billion). In 1996, however, Brazil's inflows nearly doubled again, to $10.5 billion, while inflows to Mexico declined 3.6 percent due to the lingering effects of the currency crisis and recession. Brazil had regained its position as the region's most attractive location for foreign transnationals, a switch brought about not only through privatization but also through rising greenfield investment from the world's top automakers, all of which seemed to beat a path to Brazil at mid-decade. Along with new entrants into the Brazilian market, existing foreign-owned operations did their part to bolster investment inflows by restructuring and expanding their operations.

Throughout 1997 and 1998, Brazil consolidated its investment lead over Mexico and the rest of the region. Despite the turbulence in the developing nations in 1998, inflows amounted to nearly $29 billion, up more than 50 percent from the prior year. Part of the credit goes to aggressive foreign participation in the massive sale of the telecommunications giant Telebras. The enthusiastic response of foreign investors helped boost Brazil's share of total regional inflows to nearly 40 percent in 1998. Mexico ranked a poor second, with a share of 14 percent, followed by Argentina, Chile, and Venezuela, which each held a regional market share of 5–8 percent in 1998. Taken together, the Big Five—Brazil, Mexico, Argentina, Chile, and Venezuela—accounted for roughly 70 percent of total regional inflows during 1990–98.

Beyond the region's major markets, foreign investment inflows also played an important role in the resource-rich Andean countries (Bolivia, Ecuador, and Peru) during the 1990s, and in the Central American economies of El Salvador, Guatemala, Costa Rica, Jamaica, the Dominican Republic, and others. The offshore financial centers of the Bahamas, Bermuda, and the Cayman Islands were also large recipients, although manufacturing investment has been confined mostly to South America and among Caribbean and Central American economies that have developed with the help of foreign investment in high-volume, low-value manufacturing activities.

In both regions, privatization measures generated more investment in service activities in the 1990s, complementing more traditional resource-related, manufacturing-assembly investment. As a potential harbinger of the future, Costa Rica landed a $500 million investment from Intel in 1997, a development likely to lead to more sophisticated forms of foreign investment. For now, however, many countries in the region, such as Guatemala, Bolivia, and Honduras, remain of secondary importance to transnationals. Yet, transnationals are extremely important to these small host nations, since rising investment flows over the years have helped ensure a relatively steady supply of external financing in an environment of volatile short-term capital flows and burdensome debt obligations. Moreover, in many smaller recipient nations, foreign investment is an essential component of fixed capital formation and a significant contributor to gross domestic product.

Latin America reemerged on the radar screens of transnationals in a big way in the 1990s. Preliminary estimates from the United Nations in early 2000 indicated that the region as a whole was the largest recipient among developing nations in 1999, with inflows estimated at $97 billion, surpassing developing Asia ($84 billion) for the first time since 1986.

Inflows to Brazil reached a record $31 billion. For the region as a whole, annual investment inflows averaged roughly $34.7 billion over the 1990–98 period, better than a fourfold increase from the $8.1 billion average of 1985–90.

Central Europe and Russia: In from the Cold

Rising and with great upside potential: that is probably the best way to describe foreign direct investment inflows into the countries of central Europe and Russia. Largely off-limits to transnationals until the Berlin Wall was breached in 1989, nations such as Poland, Hungary, Russia, and others in the region opened for business in the 1990s. But the world's top transnationals did not pile in all at once, notwithstanding all the media hype about new markets, liberated consumers, and the availability of cheap labor. Rather, legal and regulatory problems, economic recession in some countries, a prolonged privatization process, political instability, and local business practices inimical to western firms all acted, in various forms, to offset the attributes of the region.

The region remained a work in progress to many transnationals during the 1990s, which helps explain the fact that over the past decade, transnationals have exhibited an overriding preference for Latin America and Asia. While average annual inflows to central Europe rose to $9.2 billion in 1990–98 from just $500 million during 1985–90, a marked improvement, the comparable levels in Latin America and Asia in the same period, $34.7 billion and $58.2 billion, respectively, were much higher. In the words of the United Nations, however, central and eastern Europe are "catching up with the rest of the world as evidenced in the growth rates of FDI inflows in 1993–1997: over that period the inflow of central and eastern Europe increased faster (28.5 percent per year) than those of the developing countries (23 percent), the developed countries (16 percent), and the world as a whole (19 percent). And this catching up may be even faster than data suggest because inflows into the region are often underreported."[17]

Despite the "catching up," though, one particular point needs to be made: Not unlike other regions of the world, the pattern of foreign direct investment inflows into central Europe strongly favors just a few countries. China, of course, is the overwhelming destination of choice for transnationals in Asia. Brazil and Mexico hold sway in Latin America. In central and eastern Europe, the preferred locations are Poland, Hungary, the Czech Republic, and the Russian Federation, which accounted for just over 80 percent of total regional inflows during 1990–98.

Poland—an early advocate of economic reform and possessing one of the largest markets in central Europe—heads the list, attracting more foreign direct investment ($23 billion) in 1990–98 than established emerging market superstars such as South Korea ($16 billion) and Taiwan ($12.7 billion). Inflows to Hungary, another earlier reformer, reached nearly $17 billion during the 1990s, exceeding not only South Korea and Taiwan but also India ($12.4 billion), the Philippines ($9.9 billion), and Venezuela ($16 billion). Combined, Poland and Hungary accounted for nearly half of total inflows to central Europe during 1990–98.

Not unexpectedly, the ruble crisis in 1998 had a severe impact on foreign investment flows to Russia, which slipped from a record $6.2 billion in 1997 to just $2.2 billion the following year. Yet, despite the Russian meltdown and the Asian financial crisis, central Europe weathered the storm relatively well. Total inflows to the region were off by only 4 percent in 1998. The collapse in investment in Russia was nearly offset by a stunning 26 percent gain in inflows to other parts of the region, proof that central Europe had come in from the cold and become more than just another blip on the radar screens of transnationals.

Sustained investment inflows are conditioned on greater macroeconomic stability, continued growth and development, an improved physical and financial infrastructure, and perhaps above all else, the likelihood of regional integration with the European Union. All of these fundamental building blocks of development must be fortified over time in order to attract long-term investment capital from the world's largest companies.

Africa: Lots of Potential but Still on the Margin

The same conditions apply to Africa, where the outlook for rising investment levels remains inherently uncertain. One positive development: foreign direct investment to Africa rose during the 1990s, with inflows hitting a record $9.4 billion in 1997 before drawing back to $8.3 billion in 1998. Annual inflows averaged $4.7 billion during 1990–98, versus an annual average of $2.9 billion for 1985–90. Notwithstanding that rise,

Africa accounted for less than 5 percent of total inflows to the developing nations in the 1990s, down from a share of nearly 12 percent for 1985–90. What's more, total inflows were skewed toward just a few nations. Egypt, Nigeria, and South Africa accounted for 51 percent of total regional inflows in 1990–98, with oil-rich Nigeria notching more than 26 percent of the regional total.

The irony of Africa is that the region offers plenty of investment opportunities to transnationals, but the necessary institutional and macroeconomic framework is not yet in place in most countries to attract long-term capital from some of the world's largest companies. Missing in many cases are simply the basics: an efficient physical infrastructure, an educated workforce, a viable financial sector, and a clear and transparent rule of law governing contracts, real estate, and related issues. In many nations, political instability is a problem, as is state corruption.

On a positive note, Africa is rife with natural resources, which is why more than half of the region's foreign direct investment stock is in resource-based investments. Various countries are home to a number of "strategic commodities," or commodities important to the world economy: Namibia has uranium, Guinea has bauxite, and South Africa has gold and diamonds. In Nigeria and Angola, oil and gas reserves are plentiful.

Other advantages of the region are low-cost labor and preferential access of most African countries to the European Union, which bodes well for more export-oriented foreign investment. According to the United Nations, "Possibilities of even closer integration of the countries of northern Africa with the European Union would provide additional impetus to FDI in this subregion."[18] In addition, in the absence of strong domestic competition, market-seeking investment in many African states should be profitable. In fact, U.N. figures show that between 1991 and 1997 the average return on foreign investment in Africa was higher than in any other region. Competition in services is also seriously lacking, offering, according to the same United Nations report, "considerable opportunities for foreign investors, especially since many service industries were closed to them until recently." Tourism and infrastructure are two more areas identified by the United Nations as being of promise for foreign investors.

Privatization initiatives helped stimulate investment levels in such nations as South Africa, Angola, Kenya, Morocco, Mozambique, and Tunisia in the 1990s. Strong economic growth and the appropriate macroeconomic policy mix have also been instrumental in attracting investment in such economics as Mauritius and Botswana, two of Africa's most dynamic markets. Politics has also played a part, notably in South Africa, which became a far more welcoming investment destination for transnationals following the historic elections of 1994.

The bad news is that despite the region's overriding potential and promise, and the upswing in inflows over the past decade, Africa still has an image problem among transnationals. The lack of skilled labor, militant unions, a poor infrastructure, impoverished masses, and the dearth of capital all hamper a sustained structural rise in capital inflows, keeping transnationals at bay. So too has the AIDS epidemic, the largest killer of young adults in the late 1990s. As the *Financial Times* reported in December 1999, "On one sugar estate in Kenya, where a quarter of the workforce was infected, company spending on funerals rose fivefold between 1989 and 1997, while direct health spending was up tenfold, according to UNAIDS."[19]

Pervasive levels of corruption, including extortion and bribery among various governments, act as even bigger obstacles to investment. Within this context, and with so many other countries from which to choose, many transnationals have not given Africa serious consideration. That will change in the years ahead for some nations, particularly those that can achieve growth, adopt more liberal investment regimes, push ahead with privatization, and pursue regional integration agreements. The region as a whole, however, absent any wholesale restructuring at both the macro and firm levels, is expected to continue to lag other regions in attracting its share of foreign direct investment.

The Chosen Few: Investment Flows to the Developing Nations

One final note is in order before ending the discussion on investment inflows to the developing nations. It concerns the asymmetrical nature of flows to the developing nations, or the fact that the tide of foreign investment has failed to lift all boats.[20] Transnational investment in the developing nations has been notably selective and concentrated in a handful of nations. Just 10 countries accounted for nearly 71 percent of total aggregate inflows to the developing countries over the 1990–98 period, creating a "haves" and "have nots" divide in a universe of more than 150 developing nations tracked by the United Nations. This gap is critical, since foreign direct investment has emerged as the largest and fastest-growing component of external financing for the developing nations over the past decade. In other words, where and why transnationals decide to invest overseas increasingly influences the long-term development of many nations. The problem is that just a few nations are at the receiving end (see Figure 3.5).

At the top of the list of "haves," by a wide margin, is China, which attracted nearly $250 billion in foreign direct investment during the 1990–98 period. The mainland accounted for roughly 28 percent of total investment inflows to the developing nations in the 1990s and nearly 9 percent of total global inflows. Only the United States—accounting for 22 percent of the global take—attracted more investment than China. The Middle Kingdom, of course, has many attractive attributes, including favorable trade and investment policies geared toward export-oriented foreign investment; relatively cheap land and wage costs, encouraging efficiency-seeking investment; and a potential consumer market (in the realistic range of 250–350 million people) greater than the population of the United States. For many transnationals, these inducements outweighed the multiple risks of doing business in China, as indicated by the hefty increase in investment over the last decade, and discussed in further detail in Chapter 9.

Notwithstanding the lure of China, and the nation's stunning ability to attract investment inflows, it would be incorrect to assume that the world's top transnationals largely spent the 1990s beating a path to China while ignoring the rest of the world. That's not the case at all. In fact, the United States invested four times more in Mexico than in China between 1990 and 1998. As for other countries, the mainland accounted for roughly 2 percent of total German foreign direct investment outflows over the same time frame, and just 3.7 percent of Japan's total outflows.

In other words, despite all the hype in the western media about the nation's cheap labor and 1.2 billion consumers clamoring for western products, American, German, or Japanese firms did not lead the rush to China, at least up until the late 1990s. Rather, overseas Chinese entrepreneurs spread throughout the region, based in such places as Taiwan, Hong Kong, the Philippines, Indonesia, and Singapore have been instrumental to

Figure 3.5

Concentration of Global FDI Inflows to the Developing Nations, 1990–1998

Rank	Country	Cumulative Total (US$ Billions)	% of Developing Nation Total	% of Global Total
1	China	246.1	27.7	8.7
2	Mexico	72.5	8.2	2.6
3	Brazil	71.5	8.1	2.5
4	Singapore	58.0	6.5	2.1
5	Argentina	40.0	4.5	1.4
6	Malaysia	38.9	4.4	1.4
7	Hong Kong	28.4	3.2	1.0
8	Thailand	24.8	2.8	0.9
9	Chile	23.3	2.6	0.8
10	Indonesia	23.3	2.6	0.8

Source: UNCTAD.

surging investment inflows. This silent but powerful cohort has largely financed China's integration with the rest of the world, forming, according to authors Murray Weidenbaum and Samuel Hughes, a "bamboo network" that has transformed the mainland.[21] While American, European, and even Japanese transnationals have been more circumspect in taking the plunge in China, given the multiple risks involved (legal, financial, commercial, etc.), overseas Chinese businesses and entrepreneurs have not hesitated to utilize their cultural, ethnic, linguistic, and above all else, family ties with the mainland to their advantage.

Thus, nearly three-fourths of total foreign investment to China during the 1990s was sourced from within Asia itself, excluding Japan. More than half of China's foreign investment came from Hong Kong's Chinese entrepreneurs, although much care is required when citing these numbers, given that "some—perhaps as much as one-fourth—of that 'foreign' investment is actually mainland money that is recycled in order to qualify for special import incentives," according to Weidenbaum and Hughes.[22] Taiwan ranked a distant second with a share of around 8.5 percent.

The share of U.S. investment in China is small but growing. U.S. investment in China totaled just $330 million in 1991, then soared to $1.2 billion in 1994 and a record $1.7 billion in 1998. Over the last three years of the 1990s, U.S. investment flows to China averaged $1.4 billion annually, more than three and a half times the annual average in the first half of the 1990s. Continued robust growth in U.S. investment, especially in services, is likely, given China's entry into the World Trade Organization (WTO). China's participation in the WTO is expected to encourage greater investment not only from the United States but also from Japan and Europe, ensuring the mainland's status as one of the most attractive locations in the world for transnational investment. For U.S. companies and others, however, the overseas Chinese already encased in China represent formidable competitors in various sectors.

In the mainland's shadow, but nevertheless preferred destinations of transnationals in the 1990s, were such countries as Mexico and Brazil, ranked number two and three. Argentina (fifth) and Chile (ninth) were also favored locations in Latin America during the past decade. In Asia, the most favored site after China was tiny Singapore, ranked fourth, followed by Malaysia (sixth), Asia's other city-state, Hong Kong (seventh), Thailand (eighth), and Indonesia (tied with Chile). Just behind Indonesia, but short of cracking the top 10, was Poland, the top destination of transnationals in central Europe.

The Sectoral Shift in Global Foreign Direct Investment

One of the most significant aspects of global investment flows is that the surge in investment over the past few decades has been accompanied by a pronounced shift in its sectoral composition. Where investment was concentrated in raw materials or resource-based sectors during the 1950s, flows shifted more into manufacturing industries in the 1960s and 1970s. Since the mid-1980s, while investment in both raw materials and manufacturing has remained important, the largest share has been directed at service-based activities.

According to the United Nations, services represented around a quarter of the total world stock of foreign investment at the beginning of the 1970s. By the late 1980s, the share of services in world stock of foreign investment was close to 50 percent and rising. The share continued to climb in the 1990s, aided in part by the rapid technological advances and

Figure 3.6

Cross-Border M&As by Sector

(US$ Billions)

	1990	1991	1992	1993	1994	1995	1996	1997	1998
Total	160.0	85.3	121.9	162.3	196.4	237.2	274.6	341.7	544.3
Primary sector	9.6	3.0	3.2	24.3	9.6	22.2	23.4	23.8	77.8
Mining/petroleum	8.1	2.7	3.0	24.0	7.7	21.4	22.9	22.8	76.3
Secondary sector	84.8	47.0	64.0	63.6	109.2	105.7	96.1	117.8	189.3
Paper and paper products	9.0	6.2	4.2	3.5	10.9	8.6	11.3	7.9	40.9
Chemicals	15.5	7.9	7.9	21.2	23.6	26.4	21.2	22.8	24.3
Motor vehicles	13.0	2.8	4.9	2.6	7.0	7.8	13.1	9.5	52.9
Tertiary sector	65.6	35.3	54.5	74.3	77.6	109.3	155.1	200.1	277.2
Electricity/water	1.6	0.4	8.8	10.3	10.5	17.5	25.4	32.3	42.5
Postal services/ telecommunications	10.6	3.4	2.6	17.1	9.0	17.9	15.5	20.2	50.4
Banking/finance	9.1	6.1	13.4	10.1	7.0	16.8	21.3	33.7	50.7

Source: UNCTAD.

the attendant decline in communications costs, and in part by market-deregulation efforts in various regions of the world. The upshot was a flurry of cross-border mergers and acquisitions among utilities, financial services, business service firms, and telecommunication firms.

Note from the table in Figure 3.6 that the total value of cross-border mergers and acquisitions in services was almost one-quarter less than M&A activity in manufacturing in 1991 ($47 billion in manufacturing versus $35.3 billion in services). However, over the decade, as barriers to entry fell and technology proliferated, numerous service sectors, in both the developed and developing nations, underwent sweeping change, accelerating the pace of mergers and acquisitions. Since 1995, the annual value of cross-border mergers and acquisitions in services has exceeded the value of manufacturing deals in every year. In 1998, cross-border M&A activity in services reached $277 billion, more than four times the total for 1990, and accounted for just over half of the value of all global mergers and acquisitions. The globalization of services is one of the most important aspects of the world economy and a key component of U.S. global engagement. More on that subject in Chapter 8.

PART II

U.S. Global Engagement Through Foreign Direct Investment

T he next three chapters take a close look at U.S. global engagement through the lens of foreign direct investment. While Part I provided a macropicture of global foreign direct investment, this section provides a microview of America's investment stake.

Chapter 4 compares and contrasts America's role in international trade with its foreign direct investment position. The United States is a leader in both, but trade tells one tale of how and where U.S. firms do business around the globe, while investment tells quite another. From the perspective of trade, the Asian financial crisis was no doubt an ominous event for the corporate interests of the United States. With foreign direct investment as a benchmark, however, the Asian crisis, in and of itself, was less of a risk to corporate America than most people realized at the time, given the shallow and relatively underdeveloped investment linkages between the United States and most countries in Asia. Chapter 4 brings all of this into perspective by presenting a historical overview of U.S. foreign direct investment outflows. Central to this presentation is the fact that U.S. foreign outflows are overwhelmingly geared toward the developed nations (i.e., Europe, Canada, Japan, and Australia), not the developing nations.

Chapter 5 analyzes the global scope and operations of U.S. foreign affiliates. The premise is that U.S. affiliates, very much like Rodney Dangerfield, "don't get much respect." Yet, affiliates are the global foot soldiers of corporate America. They do a great deal of heavy lifting and are critical to the success of any U.S. transnational. Where they were once outposts or outcasts of corporate headquarters, affiliates today are becoming integral components of the global network of the parent company. They are formidable economic players in their own right. Many of the specific functions and strategic objectives of U.S. foreign affiliates are identified in Chapter 5. Contrary to popular belief, the primary objective of most U.S. affiliates is to deliver goods and services to the local market, not to export products back to the United States. The bulk of U.S. foreign direct investment is market-seeking, which helps explain the fact that roughly two-thirds of worldwide affiliate sales are made in the host nation. The chapter concludes by explaining how the U.S. parent-affiliate relationship bears on the U.S. economy. As much as U.S. firms have extended their global reach over the past few decades, the operations of U.S. parent companies remain overwhelmingly rooted in the United States, a fact often overlooked or ignored by critics of U.S. transnationals.

Chapter 6 is the flip side of Chapter 5 and analyzes foreign direct investment in the United States and the corresponding role of foreign-owned affiliates in the U.S. economy. Just as U.S. companies sell more goods abroad through investment than through trade, the same holds true for the world's leading foreign transnationals, which have built a sizable investment position here in the United States over the past quarter century. In other words, foreign competitors compete in the United States not only via imports but also through foreign direct investment and foreign affiliate sales. Chapter 6 gives a historical overview of U.S. investment inflows, highlighting chief foreign investors and the sectors where they are prominent. While Japan emerged as a high-stakes foreign direct investor in the United States in the 1980s, the record growth in investment in the 1990s was spawned by European transnationals, with mergers and acquisitions the most popular vehicle of entry. The presence of foreign-owned affiliates in the United States is most evident in U.S. trade flows, as the chapter establishes. Concluding remarks address the United States as a host country to foreign investment, a rather recent role for America from a historical perspective.

4

Global Linkages Through U.S. Foreign Direct Investment

"In the new world economy investment is growing faster than trade."

Peter Drucker, "The Changing World Economy,"
The Economist Special Report, 1992.

American companies deliver their products to overseas customers through two principal means: exports (trade) or U.S. overseas affiliates (investment). Yet, there is little doubt which mode is the most popular and widely used benchmark of U.S. global engagement. So, it is no surprise that over the past decade, whenever an economic crisis has struck a particular nation or region—Mexico in 1995, Asia in 1997, Russia in 1998, and Brazil in early 1999—investors and Wall Street analysts immediately leaped to determine the trade ties between the stricken country and the United States. Many assumed that the greater the linkages, the greater the damage. Regrettably, each crisis failed to stir any debate about America's foreign direct investment position relative to the rest of the world, which, as this chapter will illustrate, is the superior measurement of global engagement.

Global Linkages: Trade Tells Just One Part of the Story

Using exports as a benchmark, Russia's meltdown in the summer of 1998 was largely a nonevent for corporate America. After all, Russia accounted for less than 1 percent of total U.S. exports at the time. It was Russia's outsized financial linkages with the rest of the world, notably with Europe, that caused the global financial tremor in August 1998. When economic turmoil struck Brazil in late 1998 and early 1999, the economic consequences were deemed more serious because the Latin giant represented one of the largest markets in the western hemisphere for U.S. exports. Worse still was the Mexican peso crisis of late 1994. The currency crisis sparked a recession in an economy that consumed around 9 percent of America's total exports at mid-decade, making Mexico one of the largest markets for U.S. goods not only in the region but also in the world.

All of these events pale in comparison with Asia's stunning economic collapse in 1997. Following decades of nearly uninterrupted development, the world's leading region in terms of economic growth suddenly became the global laggard. A region that had grown by an average annual rate of more than 6.5 percent in the 1980s, and more than 9 percent annually throughout the early part of the 1990s, hit a wall in late 1997. Decelerating export growth, excess levels of capital investment, widening trade deficits, highly leveraged corporations, worsening debt levels, currency instability, volatile capital inflows—all of these negatives first converged in Thailand, then spread to South Korea, Indonesia, and other parts of the region to bring Asia's economic growth to a screeching halt by the end of that year.

In the months following the Asian crisis, private capital investment in new plant and equipment evaporated. Capital spending on infrastructure also slowed sharply, with investment projects involving new airports, seaports, energy plants, and telecommunications worth billions of dollars either postponed or canceled. As unemployment festered across the region, personal consumption deteriorated, robbing many multinationals of newly cultivated consumers. Fiscal austerity meant reduced levels of government spending. All totaled, Asia ended the decade on the mend in the wake of the crisis, although many nations remained battered and bruised, a stunning reversal of fortune for a region that had emerged as the unequivo-cal growth champion of the world over much of the post–cold war era.

During Asia's reign of growth, what was good for the region proved exceptionally good for corporate America and many other multination-als. Asia had become the new frontier for many companies, the most promising market in the world for goods ranging from potato chips to computer chips. The region offered something for nearly everyone: global consumer product companies were attracted to Asia's young and increas-ingly wealthy population base; capital goods manufacturers cashed in on Asia's massive infrastructure investment; technology companies found new customers among the region's highly skilled and educated workforce; and global service leaders in insurance, finance, and entertainment tapped new consumers eager for western amenities.

With these dynamics of demand, developing Asia's total imports sprinted from just $56 billion in 1975 to $176 billion in 1980. At that point, the region accounted for less than 10 percent of total world imports, although the share rose to 13.4 percent in 1990 and to nearly 20 percent by 1996. Asia's import bill, excluding Japan, exceeded $1 trillion for the first time in 1996—roughly three times greater than the total imports of Japan, an economy that accounts for more than 80 percent of Asia's total output. At the time, the seemingly insatiable appetite of consumers in Malaysia, Tai-wan, South Korea, Hong Kong, Shanghai, and Singapore sparked Asia's import binge and fueled talk of the next century's belonging to Asia.

For the United States, the "Asian Century" arrived rather early. It was 1981 to be exact, the year U.S. exports to Asia exceeded shipments to Europe for the first time ever. The occasion was trumpeted as a seminal event in America's global trade relations and another significant marker of Asia's economic ascendance. Global economic power was shifting from west to east, and the changing pattern of U.S. trade was irrefutable evi-dence of this tilt. By the early 1980s, Japan had established itself as one of the most competitive and dynamic economies among the developed nations. Following in Japan's footsteps were the "Tiger" economies—South Korea, Taiwan, Hong Kong, and Singapore—both admired and feared by global multinationals. In the second half of the 1980s, Thailand, Malaysia, and Indonesia emerged as the region's champions in terms of average annual growth. And China's "opening" to the west, and subsequent economic rise in the 1980s and 1990s, added even more credence to the argument that

Asia was the future and that American firms absent from the region were missing out on one of the greatest market opportunities of the century.

These opportunities were not lost on many U.S. companies. Throughout the 1980s and most of the 1990s, U.S. exports to Asia soared, a point underscored in the accompanying chart (Figure 4.1). In 1997, when the Asian crisis broke out, 4 of America's top 10 export markets for goods, and 9 of the top 20, were in Asia. Collectively, the region, including Japan, accounted for nearly one-third of U.S. exports in 1996, notably above the share for Europe (22.4 percent) and Latin America (17.8 percent). Given this level of trade exposure, when the region plunged into recession, the mandarins on Wall Street concluded that U.S. firms were doomed. Their logic was compelling but, in fact, wide of the mark.

Asian Aftershocks

Asia's financial crisis did prove challenging to many American companies, but it neither derailed the U.S. economy nor sank the U.S. financial mar-

Figure 4.1

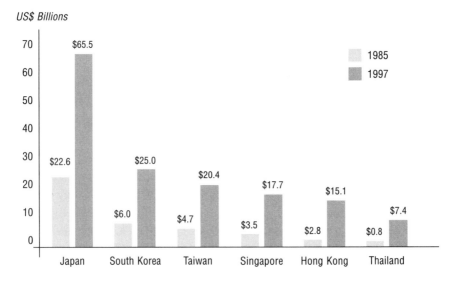

U.S. Merchandise Exports to Asia, 1985 Versus 1997

Source: U.S. Department of Commerce.

kets. Seemingly unfazed by Asia's economic debacle, the American economy expanded by over 4 percent in 1998 and 1999. In turn, this turbocharged performance helped lift all the major U.S. financial indexes, notably the Dow, the S&P 500, and the Nasdaq, to record highs in 1998 and again in 1999.

In other words, the robust performance of the U.S. financial markets largely defied the collective expectations and wisdom of Wall Street. Many doomsayers were left wondering what had gone right when so many things were expected to go wrong following Asia's collapse. How could corporate America remain immune to one of the greatest economic crashes of all times? Asia was in economic ruins. Millions of consumers were suddenly unable to purchase common staples, let alone luxury goods. Massive investment projects were either canceled or postponed, resulting in billions of dollars of lost revenue. A region drowning in excess capacity and competitively endowed with cheap currencies was poised to obliterate U.S. industry and wipe out international corporate profits. U.S. exports to the region sagged by over 12 percent in 1998, causing the U.S. trade deficit with Asia to balloon to a record $180 billion, up over a quarter from the prior year. How could the U.S. economy and financial markets seemingly shrug off the Asian debacle and forge ahead into the record books?

The reality is that corporate America was hardly immune to Asia's crisis. The region's stunning collapse produced plenty of pain across the U.S. industrial spectrum, though the adverse impact was more micro (i.e., felt within certain industries) than macro. U.S. farmers watched their overseas markets for agricultural products shrivel. American steel producers were inundated with cheap imports. Boeing, the giant aircraft manufacturer, recorded a series of canceled orders from Asia. The region's recession put a dent in the profits of consumer product companies across the board. The impact on the U.S. technology sector, however, was mixed: while wilting demand depressed final sales in the region, Asia's massive currency markdown translated to a discount on imported parts and components from the region.

Ironically, the initial aftershocks from Asia proved to be relatively benign—if not in fact beneficial—to the U.S. economy. With the world economy teetering on the edge, the United States Federal Reserve Board lowered interest rates three times in 1998. Easier credit conditions, in turn, buoyed U.S. personal spending and private capital investment.

Depressed industrial activity in Asia caused world commodity prices to fall, which in turn led to a decline in global inflation. Meanwhile, the strong dollar acted to lower U.S. import prices on a variety of goods from Asia, fueling even more consumption in the United States.

On the trade front, however, the wreckage from Asia's economic meltdown was all too apparent. As expected, U.S. overseas shipments took the brunt as one economy after another sank into recession, and demand for imports waned. U.S. merchandise exports to Thailand and South Korea, two of the so-called crisis economies, declined 29 percent and 34 percent, respectively, in 1998. Exports to Indonesia, another economy in "crisis," were halved, while those to both Taiwan and Japan slid by 11 percent.

Investors watched with rising anxiety as the casualties of U.S.-Asian trade piled up throughout 1998. Their worst fear—a collapse in trade with what had been the most dynamic region of the world—had become a reality. Yet, neither the American economy nor the U.S. financial markets crumbled under the weight of the Asian crisis, for two reasons. First, the residual effects of the crisis—lower U.S. interest rates supported by little inflationary pressures—helped prolong rather than abort the great U.S. economic expansion of the 1990s. Second, the economic linkages between the United States and Asia were never as great as many feared. Trade accounts for only one part of the global engagement story, while foreign direct investment accounts for another.

Global Linkages Part II: Foreign Investment and the Ties That Really Bind

Wall Street overestimated the impact of Asia's crash on corporate America because when the crisis struck, investors turned to trade—the most popular, yet outdated and "shallow," indicator of global engagement—to measure the damage. What they saw spooked them, and for good reason. Hopes of the "Pacific Century" were dashed. Near-Depression conditions engulfed the region, prompting Wall Street to send the Sell signal to investors, who were quick to comply. But in their rush to the redoubts, many investors remained oblivious to the primary gauge of U.S. global engagement: the foreign direct investment linkages of corporate America with the rest of the world. In their haste to sell U.S. stocks, money managers failed to realize the following:

• First, that the global competitive environment requires that successful and profitable U.S. companies build, maintain, and nurture an in-country presence. Being an "insider" abroad has long been a fundamental strategy of American firms, many of which have viewed an arm's-length relationship through exports with foreign customers as a beginning or interim strategy at best.

• Second, that sales of U.S. foreign affiliates have been greater than total exports for decades. In 1998, U.S. foreign affiliate sales of goods were roughly two and a half times larger than total U.S. exports of goods. The ratio of affiliate sales to exports is much higher in many nations, including the United Kingdom, Germany, and Brazil.

• Third, that Europe, and the developed nations in general, on the basis of investment rather than trade, have been the most important foreign market in the world for U.S. goods for the past quarter century, not withstanding the impressive rise of Asia and the attendant shift in U.S. exports since the early 1980s.

The bottom line? The dynamics and extent of U.S. global engagement are significantly different when viewed from the perspective of foreign direct investment and the overseas operations of U.S. foreign affiliates rather than trade. Using investment as a diagnostic, the Asian crisis was serious but not fatal to corporate America for the simple fact that America's investment exposure to the region was far less than investors realized or feared. That becomes clear after analyzing the historic pattern of U.S. foreign direct investment.

U.S. Foreign Direct Investment: A Historical Perspective

Competing through foreign direct investment has long been a hallmark of corporate America. As stated earlier, U.S. overseas investment became increasingly evident in the last decades of the 19th century. By the eve of World War I, the stock of U.S. foreign investment had grown to nearly $2.7 billion, and the United States ranked among the largest foreign investors in the world. Growth in investment declined during the war years but resumed shortly thereafter, with the familiar names of today—General Electric, Ford Motor, DuPont, and General Motors— leading the way. By 1929, overseas investment totaled $7.5 billion, but it slipped again with the Great Depression, which triggered a global wave of reduced earnings, forced liquidations, and nationalization measures by many governments.

Since the end of World War II, U.S. foreign direct investment has undergone two powerful cycles. The first extended from 1950 to 1979 and was followed by a half decade of slow growth in U.S. overseas investment in the 1980s. The second, the most potent investment cycle in U.S. history, was set in motion by a number of seminal events in the late 1980s, with the end of the cold war and the return of globalization the most prominent, and was still going strong as the new century commenced.

Before delving into each cycle, it helps to get a handle on the level and geographic distribution of U.S. foreign direct investment in 1950, or the beginning of the cold war era. U.S. foreign investment, on a historical-cost basis, stood at $11.8 billion in 1950. The sum was almost evenly divided between the developed nations, with a share of 48.3 percent of the total, and the developing nations, with 51.7 percent. Canada was far and away the most favored location of American firms. On a historical-cost basis, Canada accounted for nearly 63 percent of total investment to the developed nations in 1950 and 30.4 percent of the global total. Europe represented just over 15 percent of the total, while the American investment position in Japan and the rest of Asia was minuscule.

Latin America attracted the bulk of U.S. foreign direct investment in the developing nations in 1950, seeing much of this investment, as with Canada, going to mining and oil exploration and production. The region accounted for nearly 80 percent of total investment in the developing nations and almost 40 percent of the worldwide aggregate. Venezuela was the primary recipient of U.S. investment, accounting for 8.4 percent of the worldwide total, second only to Canada. The United Kingdom ranked third, with a 7.2 percent share.

The 1950–1979 Cycle: Europe Beckons

In the decades that followed, corporate America's penchant for overseas investment compounded even as U.S. firms, at least up until the early

1970s, enjoyed favorable economic conditions at home. America's investment outflows totaled $20.4 billion over the 1950–59 period; the amount more than doubled, to $42.2 billion, in the 1960s. The pace of outward investment accelerated in the 1970s, with aggregate outflows soaring to $122.7 billion in the 1970–79 period.

The swell in investment outflows was accompanied by a shift in geographic preference. Europe, trailing Canada and Latin America in 1950, emerged as the most favored destination of U.S. multinationals during this period. As the region rebuilt and recovered from the ravages of war and moved toward the creation of a common market, U.S. firms were quick to seize the opportunities across the Atlantic. U.S. foreign investment in Europe averaged just $400 million annually in the 1950s, but it more than quadrupled in the 1960s, to an annual average of $1.7 billion. Cumulative U.S. outflows to Europe totaled $16.6 billion during

---

Figure 4.2

U.S. Foreign Direct Investment Abroad

(Cumulative Totals, US$ Billions)

	1950 –59	% of Total	1960 –69	% of Total	1970 –79	% of Total	1980 –89	% of Total	1990 –99	% of Total
Canada	7.2	35.3	10.7	25.4	22.0	18.0	19.0	11.0	63.9	8.0
Europe	4.0	19.6	16.6	39.4	58.0	47.3	94.7	55.0	435.6	54.3
Latin America	5.4	26.5	5.6	13.2	24.0	19.5	32.8	19.1	156.8	19.6
Australia, New Zealand, and Japan	0.8	3.9	3.2	7.6	9.0	7.3	11.8	6.8	47.3	5.9
Developing Asia	0.6	2.9	1.4	3.3	6.1	5.0	14.0	8.1	74.2	9.3
Other	2.4	11.8	4.7	11.1	3.6	2.9	0.3	0.0	23.9	2.9
Total	20.4	100.0	42.2	100.0	122.7	100.0	172.6	100.0	801.7	100.0

Source: Bureau of Economic Statistics.

1960–69, or nearly 40 percent of the global share, up from slightly less than 20 percent in the 1950s. In the 1970s, Europe accounted for nearly half of total U.S. foreign direct investment (see Figure 4.2).

The United Kingdom was the early favorite of American multinationals, which felt more at home establishing an operation in a country with the same language and a similar legal system. In 1956, almost 60 percent of all U.S. manufacturing investment in Europe went to the United Kingdom, while over the 1950–59 period, the nation accounted for nearly half of total U.S. investment to Europe.[1]

In the following decades, U.S. firms branched out to embrace continental Europe as well. The tilt toward the continent was effected in large part by the formation of the European Economic Community (EEC) and the prospects of greater economic coordination among its initial members—Germany, France, Italy, the Netherlands, Belgium, and Luxembourg. Germany, of course, was at the core of this group, and having produced its own economic "miracle" in the 1960s, the country attracted one-fifth of total U.S. investment in Europe in the 1960s, second only to the United Kingdom, with a 29 percent share. Combined, the United Kingdom and Germany accounted for nearly half of total U.S. investment in Europe in the 1960s and roughly 45 percent in the 1970s. France ranked as the third most popular destination, followed by other members of the European Economic Community.

The surge in U.S. investment flows to Europe came largely at the expense of Canada and Latin America. Canada accounted for more than one-third of America's global investment and nearly half of total investment in the developed nations in the 1950s. However, as the horizons of U.S. manufacturers and American energy companies broadened in the succeeding decades, the share of investment earmarked for Canada declined. The nation's share of U.S. investment fell to 25.4 percent during the 1960–69 period and to just 18 percent the following decade.

U.S. firms cooled even more toward Latin America in the 1960s. Currency instability, financial risks, rising nationalism, political skirmishes, weak growth—all of these conditions and more conspired to crimp investment in Latin America in the 1960s and even created net capital outflows in some nations. American energy companies planted stakes elsewhere in the world, while U.S. manufacturers turned their attention toward the wealthy markets of Europe. As a result, U.S. foreign direct investment in Latin America stagnated in the 1960s, with cumulative investment outflows to the region ($5.6 billion in the 1960–69 period) rising just 3.3 percent from the prior decade.

On a country basis, the most significant development was the plunge in investment in Venezuela. U.S. outlays, the bulk in the petroleum sector, fell and actually reversed course in the 1960s, helping to reduce Latin America's share of total U.S. foreign investment to just 13 percent in the 1960s, half the share of the 1950s.

But thanks to the spike in world commodity prices in the mid-1970s and the recycling of petrodollars in the developing nations, economic growth in Latin America rebounded over the balance of the 1970s, as did U.S. foreign investment. Investment outlays to Brazil were particularly strong, helping to bump cumulative U.S. investment flows to Latin America to $24 billion in the 1970s, a global share of 19.5 percent.

As for Asia, the region gradually attracted more U.S. investment in the decades following World War II, but not nearly the amount sent elsewhere. Resource-rich Australia was the favorite destination of U.S. companies in both the 1950s and 1960s, with the "Lucky Country" accounting for roughly 40 percent of cumulative U.S. outflows to Asia during both decades. The bulk of this investment went to the mining and energy sectors. However, in the 1970s, as more and more U.S. manufacturers entered Asia, the predisposition toward Australia began to weaken, and U.S. investment spread to other countries in the region. U.S. investment to Japan rose sharply in the last two years of the 1970s and totaled $4.4 billion in the 1970–79 period, versus a total of $4.2 billion to Australia.

Meanwhile, U.S. firms discovered and began to utilize the strategic advantages of Hong Kong and Singapore in the 1970s. Not only did both entities offer sweeteners such as favorable tax incentives to global multinationals, but they also were endowed with low-cost labor, deep-water ports, and geographic proximity to larger regional markets. Hong Kong's free-wheeling economy, combined with the predictability of British rule, was particularly attractive to American goods and service companies. They sank more than $1.5 billion into Hong Kong over the 1970–79 period, the largest investment stake among the developing nations of Asia at the time. Energy-rich Indonesia ranked second in the 1970s, followed by Singapore.

On balance, Asia's share of U.S. foreign investment rose from 6.8 percent in 1950 to 12.3 percent in 1970. Yet, as the preferred location for U.S. firms, Asia still lagged Canada, Europe, and Latin America in the first postwar investment cycle of U.S. firms.

The Investment Boom Goes Bust in the Early 1980s

As the 1980s began, the investment position of the United States looked radically different from that of the 1950s. The geographic distribution of U.S. investment had shifted toward the developed nations, which accounted for nearly three-quarters of total U.S investment (historical-cost basis) in 1980, versus a share of less than 50 percent in 1950. Canada held the largest proportion of U.S. foreign investment, although the nation's 20.9 percent share of the U.S. total in 1980 was down considerably from previous periods. Europe was home to nearly 45 percent of the total foreign stock of American investment as the decade began. Even though Latin America still held the largest percentage of U.S. stock among the developing nations, the region's global share of U.S. investment declined precipitously between 1950 and 1980, from nearly 40 percent to 18.1 percent. In Asia, the largest U.S. investment stake was in Australia, at just 3.6 percent of the global total, followed by Japan.

The first half of the 1980s would prove to be an unpropitious time for U.S. foreign investment. Battered by the second "oil shock" in the late 1970s, the world economy stumbled into recession as the new decade began. Global growth slowed in the developed nations as policymakers, confronted with another round of inflationary pressures from rising global commodity prices, jacked up interest rates. Tight credit conditions, in turn, led to a deceleration in personal consumption, a slowdown in private investment, and ultimately, a marked downturn in economic growth among the developed nations. Problems in the latter were quickly transmitted to the developing nations, setting the stage for a global recession in the early part of the 1980s.

After reaching a postwar annual peak of $13 billion in 1980, U.S. foreign investment in Europe tumbled to just $3.5 billion in 1982. Europe's recession caused both total affiliate earnings and, more important, reinvested earnings—a significant component of U.S. overseas investment, discussed in greater detail in Chapter 5—to decline. Meanwhile, the strong U.S. dollar, by effectively reducing the dollar value of both earnings and the net worth of foreign affiliates, contributed to the precipitous outflow drop as well. Recovery was slow and arduous; it was not until 1987 that annual U.S. investment totals returned to similar levels as at the start of the decade.

U.S. investment outflows to Canada actually turned negative in 1981 and 1982 due to Canada's restrictive policies and programs. The government's Foreign Investment Review Agency, for instance, mandated such a rigorous review of the economic benefits of investment prior to approval that many U.S. firms did not bother and went elsewhere. The National Energy Program, meanwhile, encouraged the sales of U.S. existing investment in the politically charged sectors of petroleum and mining. Late in the decade, however, a bilateral trade agreement between Canada and the United States led to a revival in U.S. investment, although for the whole of the 1980s, cumulative U.S. foreign investment to Canada fell by more than 13 percent versus the prior decade. The total for the 1980–89 period came to $19 billion, a global share of just 11 percent.

Looking south, Latin America's debt crisis and the ensuing economic slowdown curbed U.S. investment outflows to the region in the first half of the 1980s. In fact, from 1980 to 1984, cumulative investment flows were actually negative. The second half of the decade brought a marked reversal in flows, spurred by the improved earnings performance of affiliates, new investment in Mexico's export-oriented *maquiladora* plants, and the general economic rebound of the region.

Across the Pacific, U.S. companies viewed Asia more favorably in the 1980s. Then, the world was coming around to the consensus that Asia, with its highly educated workforce and outward-looking economic policies, had found the magic recipe for rapid industrial development, a sentiment backed up by annual growth rates that easily exceeded the world average. Talk of an "Asian miracle," juxtaposed against debt-ridden Latin America, more-nationalistic Canada, and slumping Europe, inspired a friendlier view of the region among U.S. firms.

Accordingly, during 1980–89, cumulative U.S. foreign direct investment in Asia rose 71.5 percent from the previous decade, well ahead of the pace of Europe at 64 percent, Latin America at 37 percent, and Canada at minus 13.2 percent. More impressive still was the surge in U.S. investment in the developing nations of Asia, which extended to $14 billion in the 1980–89 period, from $6.1 billion for 1970–79. Because of this rising tide of U.S. foreign investment in such countries as Singapore, Hong Kong, Taiwan, Indonesia, and Thailand, U.S. investment outflows to Asia underwent a marked shift in the 1980s. While in the preceding decades, U.S. investment flows were concentrated in the developed markets of Australia, Japan, and, to a lesser degree, New Zealand, U.S. firms switched focus in the 1980s to the low-wage, nascent consumer markets of Asia. Despite this shift, however, developing Asia attracted only 8.1 percent of total U.S. outflows in the 1980s, less than half the amount invested in trouble-prone Latin America.

The Booming 1990s

While the early part of the 1980s brought a gloomy global investment climate for U.S. transnationals, that decade ended on a decidedly different note. In fact, the global investment backdrop for U.S. firms at the tail end of the '80s and early part of the '90s could be described as nearly perfect. Multiple forces—both cyclical and structural—were working in multinationals' favor: Falling telecommunication and transportation costs, in addition to other technological advances, gave U.S. firms the capabilities and confidence to venture further afield. Just as important, low interest rates and surging equity prices spawned excellent liquidity conditions and copious amounts of cash for global mergers and acquisitions.

The end of the cold war and the fall of the Berlin Wall proved another powerful catalyst. Markets long out of reach to multinationals were suddenly open for business. Free-market reforms became not only the economic mantra of Poland, Hungary, the Czech Republic, and even Russia, but also the core policy thrust of such priority countries as Brazil, Argentina, Mexico, India, and China. At the heart of these reforms were initiatives to promote trade and foreign direct investment and to privatize state enterprises.

The proliferation of regional trading blocs, such as the North American Free Trade Agreement and Mercosur, were additional enticements to U.S. firms. Enhanced regional cohesion meant easier access to more consumers and greater economies of scale, a win-win situation for many U.S. companies. Along these lines, Europe's bold strategy to create not only a single market but also a single currency was nearly made to order for many U.S. firms already entrenched in Europe. In both Europe and Latin America, billions of dollars in U.S. foreign investment were earmarked for the privatization of state companies.

All of these developments converged in the 1990s to breed the most powerful wave of U.S. foreign direct investment in history. During 1990–99, American firms invested more capital overseas—$801.7 billion—than they had in the prior four decades combined, a sum that represented nearly 70 percent of total U.S. foreign direct investment in the course of the past half century.

In its largesse, the United States did not miss a single region of the world, though the developed nations—particularly those of Europe—were the biggest beneficiaries. Despite the common assumption that the bulk of U.S. overseas investment is directed at low-wage, emerging nations, the developed nations accounted for two-thirds of total U.S. foreign investment during 1990–99, with Europe logging more than half (54 percent) of the global total.

Of the top 10 destinations of U.S. investment in the 1990s, 5 countries were in Europe, with 2 each from Latin America and Asia. Canada also was included (see Figure 4.3). The United Kingdom was the overwhelming country of choice, accounting for just over one-fifth of all U.S. foreign direct investment in the '90s. As one of the standard-bearers of the Anglo-Saxon model of capitalism, which swept the globe last decade and helped jump-start the drive toward globalization, the United Kingdom was a natural place for American firms to build or add to their investment stakes. After all, the country boasts a large, relatively affluent market, a shared language, and a similar business and legal architecture to that of the United States. Geographically, in addition to membership in the European Union, the country is ideally situated: perched at the rim of continental Europe, the United Kingdom offers easy access to the region at large.

France and Germany, two of Europe's largest and wealthiest markets, are particularly attractive to U.S. investors, as evidenced by the flurry of M&A activity throughout the '90s. More attractive still were the Netherlands and Switzerland, ranked numbers two and four, respectively, as the top locations for U.S. foreign investment last decade. Both countries act as strategic gateways to the greater European market and have attracted a great deal of U.S. investment from American holding companies. By sector, the Netherlands' petroleum sector drew a considerable amount of U.S. capital during the decade, as did Switzerland's pharmaceuticals industry.

Figure 4.3

Corporate America's Top 10 Favored Locations for Foreign Investment in the 1990s

(Cumulative Total 1990–99)

Rank	Country	US$ Billions	% of Total
1	United Kingdom	165.2	20.6
2	Netherlands	67.2	8.4
3	Canada	63.8	8.0
4	Switzerland	38.7	4.8
5	Brazil	34.0	4.2
6	Mexico	33.6	4.2
7	Germany	32.3	4.0
8	France	27.2	3.4
9	Australia	25.1	3.1
10	Singapore	20.8	2.6

Source: U.S. Department of Commerce, Bureau of Economic Analysis.

The NAFTA Surprise

Continuing a long-term trend, Canada's share of U.S. foreign direct investment fell throughout the '90s. The country nevertheless ranked third in terms of capital outflows from U.S. companies, attributable in large part to the creation of the North American Free Trade Agreement (NAFTA). In the first six years of NAFTA's existence, old, mature, and high-wage Canada whupped young, developing, low-wage Mexico in attracting U.S. capital. From 1994 to 1999, for every $1 that U.S. firms invested in Mexico, they sank more than $2 in Canada. For the period, U.S. investment in Canada totaled nearly $53 billion, versus $25.5 billion in Mexico (see Figure 4.4).

The northern predilection of corporate America reflected a number of factors, primary among them the Canadian government's more relaxed

Figure 4.4

U.S. FDI Outflows to Canada and Mexico

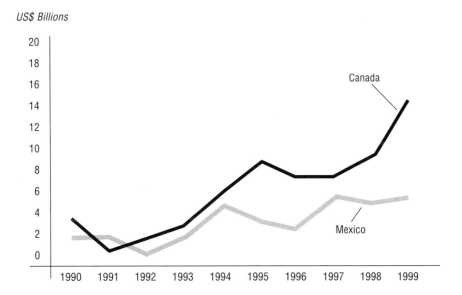

US$ Billions

Source. U.S. Department of Commerce, Bureau of Economic Analysis.

attitude toward foreign participation in the local economy. "There has been a shift in political culture. Canadians to a very great extent have bought the argument that we live in a global economy and it doesn't matter a lot whether companies here are Canadian-owned or U.S.-owned," notes James Laxer, a professor of political science at York University.[2] Hardly a bastion of unfettered capitalism, Canada nevertheless gradually opened a number of key sectors—telecommunications, energy, and financial services—to foreign companies over the 1990s. American firms, in turn, jumped at the opportunity to own parts of Canadian paper companies or telecommunications firms in order to build and beef up their North American capabilities. This new investment came in addition to the massive capital stake that U.S. automakers have steadily built up north of the border.

While second to Canada's, Mexico's investment inflows from the United States in the 1990s were nothing to sneeze at. In fact, among the developing nations, only Brazil attracted more U.S. investment than Mexico in the 1990s. In both nations, the "Lost Decade" of the 1980s gave way to macroeconomic stability and to trade and investment reform in the 1990s. These moves, along with emerging new consumer markets, low manufacturing wages, and an aggressive privatization program in Brazil, catapulted both nations into the top 10 countries for U.S. foreign direct investment in the 1990s.

In Asia, Smaller Is Better

Asia was also at the receiving end of increased U.S. investment in the 1990s, although the region's aggregate total of U.S. investment during 1990–99 ($121.5 billion) lagged other major parts of the world, specifically, Europe and Latin America.

Within the region, the focus of U.S. investment continued to trend away from developed nations and toward developing nations. The three developed nations there—Japan, Australia, and New Zealand—accounted for 70 percent of total U.S. investment in Asia for 1960–69, 60 percent in the '70s and 46 percent in the '80s, before receding to 39 percent in the '90s. Still, Australia, despite having one of the smallest consumer markets in the region, as well as some of the highest wages, maintained its top position as the most attractive market for U.S. investment in Asia. For the 1990–99 period, Australia accounted for just over 20 percent of total U.S. foreign direct investment in the region, placing the nation among the top 10 foreign destinations for U.S. corporations.

Why Australia of all places, whose labor force and consumer market are smaller than those of most U.S. states? One attraction lies with Australia's technological attributes, including a sophisticated, educated, English-speaking labor force. On a per capita basis, the nation is one of the heaviest users in the world of computers and the Internet, which is one key reason why a number of U.S. technology leaders have a local presence. Industry deregulation, notably in energy and telecommunications, has also been a key catalyst attracting U.S. investment. The telecommunications sector was deregulated in mid-1997, and a market that used to be served by just two carriers is now served by more than two dozen domestic and foreign companies. Greater Internet usage has increased the demand for hardware and services of U.S. firms, as has growth in the wireless cellular market and other related market segments. In the utilities sector, U.S. firms are among the most dominant in the country.

Besides Australia, the only other Asian country to make the elite top 10 list was Singapore, among the smallest markets in Asia. In the case of Singapore, the secret to the city-state's allure was location, location, location. Situated in the middle of Southeast Asia, along the prime shipping lanes that connect Europe and the Middle East with the Far East, Singapore has long been the natural regional headquarters and financial center for many multinationals operating in Southeast Asia. U.S. technology firms have been attracted to the city-state's skilled, albeit small, English-speaking labor pool; sophisticated petroleum-refining capabilities have garnered the attention and capital of U.S. energy companies. For all of these reasons, tiny Singapore (population 2.5 million) attracted 28 percent of all U.S. investment in developing Asia in the last decade of the 20th century.

Asia's other city-state, Hong Kong, received more than 22 percent of the total over the same period. The former crown colony lost its number one ranking to Singapore in the '90s when jitters associated with the British handover of Hong Kong to mainland China set in. To some degree, Hong Kong's loss—of both faith and capital—was Singapore's gain, since the latter stood forth as the safer, more stable outpost for American firms in the 1990s. The two combined nonetheless attracted half of total U.S. investment in developing Asia in the '90s, continuing a reign that began in the 1970s.

At the other end of the spectrum lies India. While often viewed as one of the most promising emerging markets in Asia, with its extensive and cheap labor force and huge consumer market, India attracted a mere $1.1 billion of U.S. investment in the 1990s. That was less than half of the U.S. investment in Colombia ($1.9 billion).

Meanwile, Asia's "crisis" economies of South Korea, Thailand, the Philippines, Malaysia, and Indonesia accounted for a combined total of just 3.2 percent of U.S. investment outflows in the 1990s, which acted to minimize the degree of U.S. exposure to these crisis-stricken nations. Total U.S. investment in Taiwan for the decade was less than U.S. outlays to

South Africa. By the same token, U.S. companies invested more in tiny Chile than massive China over the same timeframe.

Having dissected the geographic breakdown of U.S. global investment, now recall the Asian crisis of mid-1997 and the overall impact on earnings of corporate America. Suffice it to say that American firms, based on investment outflows rather than trade flows, were not nearly as exposed to the Asian financial crisis as many people on Wall Street and in the media thought. Yes, by the benchmark of trade, U.S. firms were vulnerable to the Asian shock. And in that Asia's problems spread to other parts of the world, U.S. firms were adversely impacted. But, by taking the benchmark of investment in isolation, the degree of U.S. exposure to Asia's crisis economics was far less than most thought. This becomes evident when the sales of U.S. foreign affiliates are analyzed.

In-Country Sales of Affiliates: The Best Measure of Global Engagement

By the end of the 1990s, and after a half century of foreign expansion, U.S. firms possessed a vast overseas commercial empire that included over 23,000 affiliates strategically positioned around the world. The specific role of affiliates is detailed in the next chapter. The objective here is to examine the sales of U.S. foreign affiliates in relation to U.S. exports. Both serve as a means by which U.S. companies deliver goods to foreign markets, although affiliate sales overwhelmingly are the preferred mode of delivery for American firms.

Over the past 20 years, the ratio of total foreign affiliate sales of goods to U.S. merchandise exports has risen to as high as 3.5:1; for most of the 1990s, the ratio hovered around 2.4:1.[3]

Despite the gulf between what America ships to the world (exports) and what it sells in-country (affiliate sales), policymakers and investors alike continue to cling to exports as the sole barometer of U.S. global engagement. That was all too clear when the Asian crisis struck, triggering a mad scramble to analyze America's trade linkages with the region. Of course, from this vantage point, there was cause for concern: The Asian markets were among the most dynamic in terms of U.S. trade.

However, look closely at the accompanying table (Figure 4.5). The amounts in Column 1 are total U.S. exports of goods in 1997. Column

2 represents exports of goods shipped to U.S. foreign affiliates, with the bulk comprised of exports of U.S. parents to their foreign affiliates; this represents trade within the same firm, or intrafirm trade (discussed in the next chapter). By subtracting intracompany shipments (Column 2) from total U.S. exports (Column 1), one can determine the true level of business between U.S. firms and *foreign* customers (Column 3). As is clear from the table, performing this calculation alters significantly the actual amounts involved but also the ranking of top export markets. Column 4 (foreign affiliate sales) is also adjusted to reflect only sales between U.S. foreign affiliates and foreign customers.

Based on the recalculated numbers in Column 3, the flurry of attention surrounding U.S.-Asian trade during the Asian financial crisis was certainly understandable. Of the top 15 export markets in 1997, 7 were in Asia. Japan ranked number one, followed by South Korea, Taiwan, China, Singapore, Malaysia, and Australia. Using trade to take the measure of global engagement, then, Asia factored heavily into the U.S. equation. Hence the panic on Wall Street when the region crashed in the late 1990s.

But Column 4—local sales of goods by U.S. foreign affiliates excluding sales to parents and other affiliates—reveals a much different story. For starters, note that of the top 15 markets measured by affiliate sales, the developed nations, where U.S. investment roots are deepest, accounted for 11. The United Kingdom, which ranked fourth in terms of U.S. exports, emerges as the largest "local" market in the world for U.S. multinationals, with affiliate sales of $141 billion in 1997, versus U.S. exports of just $23 billion—a ratio of more than 6:1. Anyone looking just at U.S. exports to the United Kingdom would miss the big picture in terms of U.S.-British commercial links. As stated earlier, trade tells one story of U.S. global engagement; investment and affiliate sales, the true measurement of global engagement, tell quite another.

In nearly all developed nations, U.S. foreign affiliate sales surpassed exports and by a wide margin. In Canada, affiliate sales exceeded exports by almost two-thirds. In both Germany and France, affiliate sales were more than six times U.S. exports in 1997. Notice the difference between affiliate sales for both the Netherlands and Belgium, $39.6 billion and $15.7 billion, respectively, versus U.S. exports of $8.5 billion to the Netherlands and $10.4 billion to Belgium. In the case of such countries as Italy, Spain, and Switzerland, while they did not even rank as top export

Figure 4.5

Top 15 Foreign Markets for U.S. Goods, 1997

(US$ Millions)

		Exports					Local Sales to Unaffiliated Persons
		1	**2**	**3**			**4**
		Goods	**Exports to**	**Total (1–2)**			**Local Affiliate**
Rank	**Country**	**Exports**	**Affiliates**	**Exports**	**Rank**	**Country**	**Sales**
1	Canada	151,767	67,626	84,141	1	United Kingdom	141,074
2	Japan	65,549	15,496	50,053	2	Canada	138,851
3	Mexico	71,388	22,057	49,331	3	Germany	102,795
4	United Kingdom	36,425	13,440	22,985	4	Japan	75,475
5	South Korea	25,046	2,174	22,872	5	France	67,530
6	Taiwan	20,366	2,328	18,038	6	Italy	45,190
7	Germany	24,458	8,771	15,687	7	Brazil	44,834
8	Brazil	15,915	4,253	11,662	8	Netherlands	39,600
9	China	12,862	1,745	11,117	9	Australia	35,087
10	France	15,965	4,919	11,046	10	Mexico	25,356[a]
11	Belgium	14,132	3,691	10,441	11	Spain	24,109
12	Singapore	17,696	7,920	9,776	12	Singapore	22,043
13	Netherlands	19,827	11,335	8,492	13	Hong Kong	21,800
14	Malaysia	10,780	2,799	7,981	14	Belgium	15,701
15	Australia	12,063	4,742	7,321	15	Switzerland	12,899

[a]Total affiliate sales to unaffiliated persons.

Source: U.S. Department of Commerce, Bureau of Economic Analysis.

markets for U.S. goods, they emerged as significant global markets for U.S. goods based on affiliate sales, reflecting the large investment ties of U.S. firms with these markets. Even in Japan, a difficult market to crack, U.S. affiliate sales were more than 50 percent greater than exports in 1997.

Closer to home, both Mexico and Brazil are important markets for U.S. firms, but in very different ways. Note that U.S. engagement with Brazil is skewed toward affiliate sales, while that with Mexico is biased toward exports. While Mexico ranks number three in terms of U.S. exports, Brazil ranks eighth. Yet, foreign affiliate sales in Brazil, at nearly $45 billion in 1997, were three-fourths larger than those in Mexico.

The dichotomy reflects the different trade and investment environments of the two Latin countries and the attendant strategies of U.S. firms in penetrating each market. In general, at least up until the early 1990s, import restrictions and nontariff barriers in Brazil acted as a bias against imports. For years, then, U.S. firms that wanted to do business in Brazil had to be there, on the ground. An arm's-length relationship via trade was not a successful and sustainable option. Because of these market realities, U.S. exports to Brazil in any given year are not that impressive—but that is only half the story. Foreign affiliate sales there in 1997 were nearly four times greater than U.S. exports, ranking Brazil as the largest overseas markets in the world for affiliate sales among the developing nations.

In Mexico's case, lower trade barriers and geographic proximity have made it easier for American firms to penetrate the country via investment and exports. Moreover, Mexico is more of an export platform to the rest of the region for U.S. companies than is Brazil; roughly half of total affiliate sales in Mexico in 1997 were affiliate related, and therefore not counted, as opposed to sales to unaffiliated customers.

As for the Asian markets (China, Taiwan, South Korea, Malaysia, and Singapore) that figure so prominently in the ranks of America's top U.S. export markets, and caused nightmares on Wall Street following the region's financial crisis, they are nowhere as significant to U.S. firms in terms of affiliate sales, save Singapore and Hong Kong, ranked 12th and 13th, respectively. Global engagement with many Asian nations entails trade, not investment. Corporate America's greatest involvement and exposure to Asia lies with Australia and Japan, or in developed Asia as opposed to developing Asia. In the latter, U.S. commercial linkages are more "shallow" than "deep."

The critical point here is this: affiliate sales not only are significantly larger than U.S. exports but also are dispersed differently geographically. It should be abundantly clear that analyzing just the trade linkages of the United States with various nations and regions of the world yields a woefully incomplete rendering of America's true level of global engagement.

Revisiting the Asian Crisis

Placed in the context of in-country sales versus trade, the Asian crisis takes on a different tenor. Rewind to mid-1997. On July 2, the government of

Thailand gave in to market forces and allowed the baht to depreciate against the dollar. Other currencies in the region—the won, the rupiah, and the peso—followed, losing luster against the greenback. In the following months, domestic demand seized, investment dried up, imports imploded, and growth came to a halt. The great Asian miracle, so it appeared, proved nothing more than a mirage. Or was it?

Only time will tell. The one clear certainty to emerge from the Asian crisis was that U.S. investors, the media, and the public in general have a very poor understanding of how and where U.S. firms compete and operate in the world economy. There is a general lack of awareness of which countries are important to U.S. companies and which are not. Not surprisingly, many investors drew the wrong conclusions and badly miscalculated the damaging effects on U.S. firms. Corporate America hardly escaped unscathed from the Asian debacle, and there is no mistaking the commercial importance of Asia to U.S. interests. Yet the carnage from one of the most severe global economic crises of the past half century was not nearly as great as many had anticipated. The lesson from the Asian crisis is simply this: global engagement requires an analysis of both trade and investment.

5

ON THE FRONT LINES

The Strategic Role of U.S. Foreign Affiliates

"Superior manufacturers gain a competitive advantage by methodically upgrading the strategic role of their plants abroad."

KASRA FERDOWS, "MAKING THE MOST OF FOREIGN FACTORIES," *HARVARD BUSINESS REVIEW*, 1997.

IN THE ENDLESS discussion over U.S. trade and global competitiveness, foreign direct investment and the role of U.S. overseas affiliates are rarely mentioned, let alone explored in any depth. In the last quarter century, the debate has centered on America's widening and seemingly irreversible trade gap with Japan. In the 1990s, the North American Free Trade Agreement with Mexico and Canada raised new issues on U.S. trade as did America's burgeoning trade deficit with China. As the decade came to an end, attention shifted to the developing nations, notably Asia, where the combination of a collapse in domestic demand and a round of competitive currency devaluations helped push the U.S. trade deficit in goods and services to $167 billion in 1998. As the single engine of global growth in 1998–99, America watched its trade deficit swell to a record $265 billion in the last year of the 20th century.

When the debate moves from trade to foreign direct investment, the common yet misguided lament that surfaces again and again is that U.S. firms continue to shift production—and jobs—to low-wage nations. The result, according to this flawed logic, is not only fewer employment opportunities for American workers but also lower U.S. wages and a rising import bill. Yet, as documented in the preceding chapter, the majority of American investment over the past half century has in fact been destined for the high-wage, wealthy developed nations. Moreover, reinvested earnings of foreign affiliates have long played a major role in U.S. foreign direct investment, countering to a degree the widely held claim that U.S. foreign investment equates to a rising tide of U.S. capital outflows that could be put to better use in the United States. And, while the global activities of foreign affiliates have expanded and diversified over the past few decades, most U.S. parent-company resources remain concentrated in the United States.

Chapter 4 discussed the different means of U.S. global engagement—foreign direct investment versus U.S. trade. This chapter extends the analysis and puts the spotlight on the role and activities of U.S. overseas affiliates. Although exports garner all of the attention among policymakers and the media, affiliates are the true global foot soldiers of corporate America. They carry the burden of penetrating foreign markets and realizing the global strategies of many American transnationals. Despite all of the above, though, the affiliates' overall image does not square with reality.

Affiliates: Neither Outliers nor Outlaws

Foreign affiliates or subsidiaries of U.S. parent companies go by many less than flattering names, among them outposts, outcasts, offspring, and orphans. In the traditional hierarchy of many corporations, affiliates do not carry much rank and are usually perceived as merely following the directions and dictates of corporate headquarters. Even today, accepting a foreign post in many American transnationals can be seen as the death knell for senior U.S. managers.

Externally, the image of affiliates is not much better. Over the years, American affiliates have been the bane of U.S. union officials and various politicians of all stripes who believe that the operations of foreign affiliates rob America of jobs, exports, and income. U.S. companies have been routinely criticized for harming the economic interests of America and the standard of living of its workers by shifting production overseas or pursuing cross-border mergers and acquisitions.

The true role of foreign affiliates cannot possibly be served by a one-size-fits-all description. While some subsidiaries are still nothing more than parent-company appendages and have led to job dislocations in the United States, others are in fact at the forefront of innovation or on the cutting edge of new technological capabilities. General Motors' initiative in Brazil, for instance, dubbed Blue Macaw, is an attempt to build the world's cheapest car by supplanting workers with numerous suppliers capable of delivering entire subassemblies ready to be bolted together. The initiative is expected to help turn a profit in selling small cars and is being adopted in the United States, GM's home market.[1] In Taiwan, General Motors is testing the feasibility of selling autos over the Internet. Going one step further, GM's competitor, Ford Motors, has set up an E-commerce network in the Philippines that links consumers, dealers, manufacturers, and suppliers in one large E-business chain. Given the above, an affiliate's role can range from the mundane (e.g., the simple assembly of parts) to the complex (e.g., undertaking sophisticated production techniques that could very well determine the future prosperity of the company).

When Parents Become Affiliates

In the past decade, many stand-alone companies, which once enjoyed distinct global identities, have been transformed into subsidiaries or affiliates of larger enterprises. Volvo, for instance, was the icon of Swedish industry and one of Europe's premier automobile manufacturers until the company's automobile unit became a subsidiary of Ford Motor Company in 1999. Chrysler, the third-largest automobile manufacturer in the United States, lost its independence when it agreed to join hands with Germany's Daimler-Benz in 1998. Earlier on, Saab of Sweden merged with General Motors. Renault of France assumed control of Nissan's automobile operations, once among the largest in Japan, in 1999. Similarly, famous British car marques such as Rover and Rolls-Royce have been snapped up by foreign owners over the past decade.

The phenomenon extends beyond the automotive sector. Witness Packard Bell's marriage to NEC of Japan and Deutsche Bank's acquisition of Bankers Trust. Until its much-ballyhooed acquisition by British Petroleum in 1998, Amoco was among the most prominent oil companies in the United States. A similar fate befell Atlantic Richfield, also purchased by British Petroleum. Bestfoods was also among the most distinct in its industry until Unilever bought the company in 2000. And Wang, one of the most famous names in U.S. computing history, was brought under the controlling ownership of Dutch-based Getronics in 1999. In short, many high-profile companies in not just the United States but also Europe, Canada, and even Japan started the 1990s with their own distinct culture and brand, only to be transformed into foreign-company affiliates amid the global swirl of mergers and acquisitions that characterized the last decade of the 20th century.

Within this framework, and given the long history of U.S. overseas investment, many American foreign affiliates are more equal than inferior to their parents. They are increasingly looked upon as partners rather than subordinates; innovators as opposed to mere copiers; and leaders rather than followers. More proactive than reactive, affiliates are assuming many of the functions reserved for headquarters. In some cases, affiliates have become headquarters—"overseas parents"—for certain products, with such companies as Monsanto, IBM, and AT&T moving their home bases for some leading products from the United States to Europe.

Gathering market intelligence, monitoring shifts in consumer purchasing behavior, accessing the latest technology capabilities of the local competition, and initiating new research and development were once the traditional domain of the parent company but have since become commonplace among affiliates. In the process, the distinctions between a parent firm and its affiliates are rapidly becoming blurred. Successful transnationals tend now to be built around networks, not hierarchies. As outlined in the accompanying pages, the foreign affiliates of corporate America are more than global bit players.

U.S. Foreign Affiliates: A Lot Like California

When trying to explain the economic clout of California, analysts and economists frequently point to the fact that if the Golden State were an independent nation, it would rank as the seventh largest economy in the world. The state possesses not only an abundance of natural resources but also a large, highly skilled labor force. It is a global leader in many industries—agriculture, entertainment, and above all else, technology—and is a world-class exporter. California, in short, is a global economic power and trendsetter unto itself. So are U.S. foreign affiliates. When considered as a separate but cohesive economic entity, they rank among the most powerful players in the global economy and often act as agents of change in countries around the world.

Collectively, U.S. overseas affiliates rank among the world's largest economic producers. They employ more than 8 million workers worldwide. Their total assets exceeded $3.3 trillion in 1997. Capital expenditures of majority-owned affiliates are rapidly approaching $100 billion a year, with research and development expenditures alone exceeding $14 billion in 1997, greater than the R&D expenditures of many nations. Foreign affiliates are significant exporters in their own right; in fact, in any given year, total affiliate exports ($687 billion in 1997) are equal to or greater than total merchandise exports from the United States, the world's number one trader. Finally, as it relates to the bottom line of many American multinationals, affiliates are a prime source of profits, with foreign sales of many blue-chip companies (Coca-Cola, General Electric, Ford, IBM, United Technologies, Gillette, Citibank) now accounting for the bulk of total annual revenue. What follows is an even closer look at the operations of affiliates.[2]

Dissecting the Functions of U.S. Foreign Affiliates

Gross Product

At the global level, total gross product of majority-owned affiliates reached nearly $520 billion in 1997, an amount that ranks U.S. affiliates as among the largest economic producers in the world, as shown in Figure 5.1.

In certain cases, U.S. affiliates contribute a sizable share to a host nation's gross domestic product. For example, the output of U.S. subsidiaries accounted for 16.5 percent of Ireland's gross domestic product in 1997. Affiliates also have a relatively high share of national output in such nations as Singapore (9.4 percent), Canada (9.2 percent), the United

Figure 5.1

The World's Largest Economic Producers

(GDP at Market Exchange Rates, 1997)

Rank	Country	US$ Billions
1	United States	7,342
2	Japan	5,149
3	Germany	2,364
4	France	1,534
5	United Kingdom	1,152
6	Italy	1,141
7	China	906
8	Brazil	710
9	Canada	570
10	Spain	563
11	U.S. foreign affiliates	520
12	South Korea	483

Source: U.S. Department of Commerce, Bureau of Economic Analysis.

Kingdom (6.8 percent), and Honduras (6.4 percent). Raymond Mataloni of the U.S. Bureau of Economic Analysis traces the relatively high affiliate shares of these nations' GDP to the following: "(1) A common language with the United States, (2) marketing and commercial legal systems similar to those in the United States, (3) geographic proximity to the United States, (4) the availability of a skilled workforce, (5) political stability, and (6) low corporate tax rates."[3]

On a regional basis, the bulk of production of U.S. affiliates is concentrated in Canada and Europe, or in the nations and the region of the world where U.S. foreign direct investment roots are deepest. Canada accounted for nearly 11 percent of total affiliate gross product in 1996, while Europe, led by the United Kingdom and Germany, represented more than 57 percent of the total. In Latin America, Brazil and Mexico are the top countries in terms of affiliate production, while in Asia, affiliate output is concentrated in two nations: Japan and Australia.

Employment

Four distinct features characterize affiliate employment trends. First, while the number of workers employed by U.S. affiliates has increased over the past decade, the rise has not been commensurate with the boom in U.S. overseas investment. Affiliates employed 8 million workers in 1997, an increase of just over 17 percent from the level of 1990 and a rise of only 25 percent from 1983 (see Figure 5.2). U.S. overseas investment, meanwhile, rose 210 percent between 1990 and 1997, and by more than tenfold between 1983 and 1997.

Second, the foreign affiliate workforce remains concentrated in the so-called high-wage developed nations, although their share is steadily declining. In Europe alone, U.S. affiliates employed some 3.3 million workers in 1997, more than the combined U.S. workforce in Latin America and developing Asia. In Canada, some 942,000 workers were on U.S. payrolls in 1997, more than five times the number employed in China. Another 700,000 workers can be counted in Japan and Australia, the two largest markets in Asia for affiliate employment. Overall, U.S. foreign affiliates based in the developed nations employed nearly 5 million workers in 1997, an impressive number but one that is actually declining on a relative basis. Total affiliate employment in the developed nations in 1997 fell to 62 percent of total overseas employment, down from nearly 68 percent in 1990. The steepest decline was recorded in Canada, whose share fell to 11.8 percent in 1997 from 13.6 percent in 1990.

Third, the bulk of hiring by U.S. affiliates in the developed nations has been in the service industries over the past two decades—jobs that are largely nontransferable from the United States. In Europe, for instance, affiliate employment rose by 430,000 workers between 1990 and 1997. Yet, all of the increase was in service employment—total manufacturing workers in Europe declined by 1.6 percent between 1990 and 1997, and by nearly 6 percent between 1983 and 1997.

Figure 5.2

Employment of U.S. Parents and Foreign Affiliates

(Workers in Thousands)

	1983	1990	1997	Change 1990–97
Employment of U.S. Parents				
All industries	18,400	18,430	19,867	1,437
Manufacturing	10,403	9,805	8,623	−1,182
Employment of Foreign Affiliates				
All industries	6,383	6,834	8,018	1,184
Canada	901	932	942	10
Europe	2,649	2,904	3,334	430
Japan	311	402	397	−5
Australia	299	388	304	−84
Latin America	1,243	1,335	1,629	294
Asia (ex. Japan)	542	656	1,135	479
Manufacturing	4,230	4,333	4,593	260
Canada	471	448	402	−46
Europe	1,961	1,876	1,846	−30
Japan	216	254	204	−50
Australia	134	116	148	32
Latin America	887	1,049	1,081	32
Asia (ex. Japan)	413	506	774	268

Source: U.S. Department of Commerce, Bureau of Economic Analysis.

Fourth and finally, the decline in manufacturing employment by affiliates in high-wage developed nations has been offset by an increase in manufacturing employment in the low-wage nations of Latin America and developing Asia. Manufacturing foreign affiliate employment rose by 6 percent between 1990 and 1997, with most of the gains coming from the developing nations. In 1997 of the 4.6 million manufacturing workers employed by U.S. affiliates worldwide, 23.5 percent labored in Latin America, while another 16.9 percent worked in developing Asia. Combined, the two regions accounted for 40 percent of total manufacturing affiliate employment in 1997, up from a share of 36 percent in 1990 and 30.7 percent in 1983.

In Latin America alone, U.S. affiliates employed nearly 1.1 million manufacturing workers in 1997, with roughly 56 percent (605,000) of these workers located in Mexico. In Asia, the most remarkable trend has been the leap in manufacturing employment in China. In 1990, China accounted for less than 4 percent of total affiliate manufacturing employment among the developing nations of Asia, employing fewer than 18,000 manufacturing workers. By 1997, however, U.S. affiliates employed more than 146,000 workers in China, or nearly 20 percent of the total manufacturing workforce of affiliates in developing Asia.

Research and Development Expenditures

At the dawn of the 21st century, the United States reigns as the undisputed champion of technology—although America hardly holds a global monopoly on chips and bytes. U.S. transnationals are directing a small but growing proportion of their research and development efforts abroad, with affiliate research and development expenditures amounting to $14.1 billion in 1997. That represents just over 11 percent of total worldwide R&D expenditures of U.S. parents, a modest share that is nevertheless expected to expand in the years ahead.

Research and development expenditures of affiliates are becoming more important for the simple fact that the world's best and brightest do not necessarily reside in the United States. It is increasingly up to U.S. foreign affiliates to tap into the biotechnology resources of Germany, the advanced medical practices of the United Kingdom, or the cutting-edge research on engine technology and pollution control in Japan. Global success demands that companies leverage and utilize skilled labor from all over the world, leading to rising levels of R&D spending by affiliates.

Given the emphasis on skilled labor, it is not surprising that more than 92 percent of affiliate research and development expenditures were in the developed nations in 1997.

Exports

The primary objective of the majority of U.S. foreign affiliates is to serve their local markets. However, as the value-added functions of these business units have increased over the years, and as production has become more specialized, affiliates have become more integral agents in the global production networks of transnationals. As a consequence, affiliates increasingly sell goods not only to their host country but also to many other markets, acting as world-class exporters in their own right.

Just how potent a force U.S. affiliates have become as exporters is illustrated by the fact that in 1997, the global exports of U.S. affiliates totaled a staggering $687 billion. That figure not only matched total exports from the United States in the same year but also easily surpassed the total exports of several of the world's other exporting powerhouses, including Germany, Japan, France, Italy, China, and Mexico.

Contrary to popular wisdom, the bulk of foreign affiliate exports is not bound for the United States, invalidating the frequent claim that U.S. multinationals, by sourcing lower-cost products from their overseas affiliates, are behind the rising tide of America imports. Less than 30 percent, or $201.5 billion, of total U.S. affiliate exports in 1997 headed to the United States, with the largest portion, $485.7 billion, destined for third countries, mainly within the host country's region. What's more, most affiliate exports do not emanate from low-wage nations such as Brazil, China, or Indonesia; nearly three-fourths of total affiliate exports came from the high-wage industrialized nations in 1997. Eight of the top 10 export platforms of U.S. multinationals in the same year—based on the total value of exports to the United States and to third world countries—were located in the developed nations. Canada ranked number one, followed by the United Kingdom, Germany, France, Singapore, Mexico, the Netherlands, Ireland, Belgium, and Italy.

Whether a U.S. foreign affiliate exports goods to either the United States or a third market depends on the overarching strategy of the parent, as well as the policies and attributes of the host nation. The United Kingdom and Canada offer contrasting examples. The United Kingdom has traditionally been viewed by U.S. multinationals not only as a wealthy market unto itself but also as a gateway to continental Europe. In other words, for many American firms, the road to the European common market runs through the United Kingdom, where the language, legal system, and financial sector are relatively familiar and user-friendly to American firms. U.S. affiliates in the United Kingdom have long operated with one eye on the host nation and one eye on the European common market, with U.S. affiliate exports from the United Kingdom totaling $99.2 billion in 1997. Only 16.7 percent of affiliate exports from the United Kingdom were destined for America in 1997, with most of the remainder presumably bound for the European Union.

Canada is another leader in terms of U.S. affiliate exports, although unlike the United Kingdom, where the majority of exports goes to third markets (the European Union), most affiliate exports from Canada—roughly 90 percent of the total in 1997—are shipped to the United States. Geographic proximity, strong investment linkages between U.S. automakers and their Canadian affiliates, and integrative provisions under the North American Free Trade Agreement (NAFTA) are the main reasons for this disproportionate share of U.S.-bound exports. For many of the same reasons, affiliate exports from Mexico are overwhelmingly geared toward the United States as well.

In the case of both Mexico and Canada, U.S. affiliate trade is conducted largely between the affiliate and the parent. This is known as *intrafirm trade*, a critical yet unappreciated aspect of U.S. global trade and global engagement.

Intrafirm Trade

Put simply, intrafirm trade is international trade that remains in the ambit of a multinational. One business unit of a company, located in Mexico, for example, exchanges or trades goods with another unit in Des Moines, Iowa, or with the parent in Michigan. This type of trade is pervasive: of the total U.S. goods exports in 1997, roughly $182 billion, or 26.3 percent, represented trade between U.S. parents and their foreign affiliates (for example, trade between IBM of the United States and its IBM affiliate in Ireland). In addition, just over 9 percent of the total was intrafirm trade between a foreign-owned subsidiary in the United States and its parent company (for example, trade between Honda USA and Honda Japan). Combined, then, intrafirm trade accounted for more than one-third of total U.S. exports in 1997. In the same year, intrafirm trade accounted for nearly 40 percent of total U.S. *imports*. Yet, whereas intrafirm exports largely consisted of intra-company transactions between U.S. parents and their affiliates, imports are largely composed of transactions between foreign-owned U.S. subsidiaries and their foreign parent. U.S.-based foreign subsidiary imports from their foreign parents accounted for nearly 23 percent of total U.S. imports. Meanwhile, U.S.

parent company imports from their foreign affiliates accounted for nearly 17 percent of total imports. (As a footnote, the figures just cited are from the Bureau of Economic Analysis; intrafirm figures from the Bureau of the Census may vary.)

This means that U.S. trade flows are significantly shaped by the global strategies of transnationals, by U.S. and foreign parents and affiliates, in addition to the traditional determinants of trade, such as exchange rates and competitive endowments. The benefits to a company include the fact that intrafirm trade helps reduce transaction costs relative to arm's-length trade and promotes both economies of scale and global scope. According to William Zeile of the Bureau of Economic Analysis, intrafirm trade "may help an MNC (multinational) to reduce the costs of distributing goods abroad or of acquiring inputs from abroad or to integrate production processes on a global scale. Intrafirm trade may respond differently than trade between unrelated parties to changes in economic conditions; for example, it may—at least in the short run—be more insulated from competitive forces in particular markets or from overall changes in prices, exchange rates, or general economic conditions."[4]

In particular, trade between a parent corporation and its foreign affiliate does not always respond to shifts in exchange rates in the same way as trade between unrelated firms. By their very definition, transnationals operate in various parts of the world, and they often have production, marketing, and distribution facilities in countries on both sides of an exchange rate. This gives a company the necessary flexibility to adjust to a sudden and dramatic swing in exchange rates. For example, a strong dollar, in theory at least, is often associated with a decline in U.S. competitiveness given the adverse impact on export prices. But a company with an extensive overseas investment position, coupled with a dynamic flow of trade between affiliates and the parent corporation, has a built-in buffer that can prevent serious erosion in its overall global competitiveness. In a strong-dollar period, U.S. transnationals are able to ramp up production in existing plants in countries where the currency has depreciated. With little lag time, they can expand output where relative costs are falling and maintain their competitiveness. Companies with production confined to one country, by contrast, are significantly exposed to shifts in both exchange rates and international prices.

Returning to Mexico and Canada, trade flows between the United States and its NAFTA partners increasingly reflect cross-border movement of goods within firms, or intrafirm trade. For instance, of total U.S.

exports to Canada in 1997 ($152 billion), 36 percent were classified as goods shipped from U.S. parents to their affiliates. Coming the other direction, of total U.S. imports of $167 billion from Canada in the same year, 34 percent were between U.S. affiliates in Canada and their American parents. In Mexico, intrafirm exports were over 27 percent of total U.S. exports in 1997, while 28 percent of U.S. imports from Mexico in the same year were intrafirm. (Figures from the Bureau of the Census indicate higher levels of related trade between the United States and Mexico, with related trade accounting for 44.3 percent of total U.S. exports to Mexico in 1999 and a staggering 66.3 percent of imports.) Intrafirm trade also plays a significant part in U.S.-Japan trade flows, a topic that is treated in Chapter 7.

The Bottom Line: So, Where Do Global Profits Come From?

The U.S. overall foreign direct investment position is overwhelmingly concentrated in the developed nations. It follows then that the lion's share of affiliate income is derived neither from Asia, despite the region's stellar growth record up until 1997, nor from Mexico, which emerged as one of the fastest-growing export markets for U.S. goods in the 1990s. Global profits emanate largely from the countries where U.S. investment roots are deepest: Canada, the United Kingdom, Euroland, Japan, and Australia.

That has not always been the case. In 1950, the developing nations accounted for just over 55 percent of total foreign income, with the bulk earned in Latin America, and in such sectors as mining and petroleum. Income from the region totaled $626 million in 1950, representing 35.4 percent of the global total. Venezuela accounted for more than one-third of the regional amount, or $232 million in 1950, just shy of total earnings from all of Europe ($269 million). Canada, however, was the top market in terms of income at the time, representing nearly a quarter of the global total, thanks largely to America's hefty local stakes in the petroleum and oil sectors.

A decade later, in 1960, the developing nations were still holding steady at more than half of total foreign income, with mining and petroleum the dominant sectors. However, the share derived from Latin America had fallen to 27.5 percent, while income from the Middle East, reflecting the rising investment stake of U.S. energy companies in the region, had risen to 20.3 percent in 1960 from 12.4 percent in 1950. Meanwhile, as the U.S. investment base in Europe expanded in the late 1950s, so did income levels. Europe's share of total affiliate income rose from 15.2 percent in 1950 to 21 percent a decade later. Nearly two-thirds of that income derived from manufacturing, with the United Kingdom and Germany as dominant sources of regional revenue. Across the Pacific, the contribution from Japan and developing Asia was still marginal at the start of 1960, amounting to less than 7 percent of the total.

As the flow of U.S. foreign direct investment has shifted over the past decades, so, naturally, have the sources of affiliate income. In 1963, income from the developed nations surpassed income from the developing nations for the first time in the cold war era. The roles reversed the next year, but by 1965, the developed nations had pulled ahead for good. By 1970, they accounted for 56 percent of total affiliate income; in line with the shift in the direction and composition in U.S. foreign direct investment during the 1960s, income earned from manufacturing exceeded that of mining and petroleum.

By 1980, U.S. multinationals derived roughly two-thirds of their foreign affiliate income from the developed nations. At the start of the 1990s, that share was 71 percent. By that point, the United Kingdom was far and away the most important source of affiliate income in not only the region but also the world. Foreign affiliate income from the United Kingdom in 1990, at $8.2 billion, nearly matched the total earnings of Latin America and equaled roughly 85 percent of the total income from Asia. Despite a difficult and tumultuous climate in the 1980s, Latin America still accounted for the largest share of affiliate earnings in the developing nations by the end of the decade: 15 percent of total affiliate income in 1990, versus a 10.3 percent share for Asia.

Throughout the 1990s, the share of income from the developed nations ebbed and flowed, falling to 57 percent of the total in 1992 (reflecting recessionary conditions in Europe) before rising back to an annual range of 60–65 percent over the 1994–97 period (see Figure 5.3). In 1996, the year before the great Asian financial crisis, nearly two-thirds of U.S. overseas profits were made in the developed nations. Of the top 10 sources of affiliate income in 1996, 8 were from the developed nations and 2 (Brazil and Singapore) from the developing nations. Income derived from Asia, excluding Japan and Australia, represented only 13 percent of the total at the time, a

Figure 5.3

Where the Bucks Are Made: U.S. Foreign Affiliate Income by Geographic Region

(Percentage of Global Total)

Country/Region	1996	1997	1998	1999
Europe	47.3	46.9	54.6	51.1
United Kingdom	13.1	12.6	12.8	13.7
Netherlands	10.3	11.9	14.0	12.0
Germany	4.1	3.2	5.3	4.6
France	3.4	2.5	2.7	1.7
Italy	1.4	1.4	2.1	1.7
Switzerland	4.7	4.7	5.9	5.8
Canada	9.9	10.2	9.0	10.4
Latin America (ex. Caribbean)	13.1	13.9	12.2	11.8
Argentina	1.0	0.8	0.7	0.6
Brazil	4.5	4.5	3.4	2.3
Mexico	2.9	3.8	3.5	4.7
Venezuela	0.7	0.8	0.5	0.4
Asia	20.1	18.8	14.0	17.0
Australia	3.0	3.5	2.1	2.2
Japan	3.7	3.4	2.4	3.7
China	0.6	0.8	0.2	0.7
Indonesia	2.1	1.7	1.1	1.2
South Korea	1.0	0.5	0.8	0.7
Taiwan	0.7	0.6	0.6	0.7
Thailand	0.9	0.6	1.3	0.6
Hong Kong	2.4	2.2	1.7	2.7
Singapore	2.9	3.1	2.7	2.4
Philippines	0.6	0.5	0.5	0.6
Malaysia	1.3	1.3	0.2	1.0

Source: U.S. Commerce Department, Bureau of Economic Analysis.

fact lost on many investors who expected the Asian meltdown to crush the global profits of U.S. companies. The share of income from the five crisis economies was less than 6 percent of the global total.

Aggregate affililate income did fall in 1998, with income from Asia plummeting 35 percent from the prior year. Income from Latin America (excluding the Caribbean) also tanked, dropping 21.4 percent. The damage to total affiliate income, however, was not as great and not as bad as many on Wall Street had anticipated, given that the 1997–98 financial crisis was labeled as one of the most severe global economic downturns of the past half century. U.S. foreign affiliate income fell by roughly 13 percent in 1998, hardly a favorable outcome but one made less disastrous by the overlooked fact that Europe accounted for around a half of total global affiliate income during the 1990s. That is another way of saying that U.S. international profits and global exposure are largely determined where U.S. investment roots are deepest—in Europe and the developed nations.

The Different Modes of Foreign Direct Investment

The income or profit of an affiliate is important to the management, employees, and shareholders of any company. After all, the whole idea of investing overseas is to leverage an existing competitive asset or specific ownership advantage for profit. How a company uses this leverage affects not only its bottom line but also the amount of capital available for additional or future foreign investment. Strong income growth from existing foreign operations generates needed investment financing in the form of reinvested earnings. Over the past decades, reinvested earnings have been one of the primary means by which U.S. companies have financed their explosive growth in foreign investment.

Reinvested earnings is one of three modes by which U.S. firms increase their level of overseas investment stock. The other two methods of investment—equity capital and intercompany loans—differ from reinvested earnings in that they represent an actual outflow of capital from the United States. Equity capital represents the capital infusion from a U.S. parent company in a new foreign affiliate, an existing affiliate, or a foreign company. Loans are typically cash infusions from the parent to the affiliate.

Reinvested earnings, by contrast, are profits derived by affiliate operations in the host country that stay in the country in the form of direct foreign investment. In technical terms, reinvested earnings are earnings minus distributed earnings. Earnings are used to expand or build upon the parent's investment stake in the country, while distributed earnings are channeled home to the parent company.

Figure 5.4 details the financing of U.S. foreign direct investment in the past half century. Not unexpectedly, the new investment cycle that began after World War II coincided with a surge in foreign investment

Figure 5.4

	New Equity		Intercompany Loans		Reinvested Earnings	
	US$ Billions	% of Total	US$ Billions	% of Total	US$ Billions	% of Total
1950–59[a]	11.2	54.8			9.2	45.2
1960–69[a]	25.4	60.2			16.8	39.8
1970–79[a]	43.5	35.4			79.3	64.6
1980–89[a]	36.3	21.2			135.6	78.8
1990–99	331.0	41.3	121.7	15.2	349.0	43.5

U.S. Foreign Direct Investment by Mode

[a]New equity and loans combined.

Source: U.S. Department of Commerce, Bureau of Economic Analysis.

in the form of new equity and loans. Even though the share of reinvested earnings was substantial, the first two decades following the war required significant new capital commitment from corporate America in the emerging new world economy. This was notably true of Europe, which quickly became the region of choice among U.S. multinationals. They sank $16.6 billion in Europe over the 1960–69 period, with 71 percent of that foreign direct investment in the form of equity and loans. Worldwide, U.S. foreign direct investment totaled $42.2 billion on a cumulative basis during 1960–69, with new equity and loans accounting for just over 60 percent of the total.

The 1950s and 1960s, then, were a time when corporate America planted the seeds for overseas growth. More than half the level of new foreign direct investment was financed by fresh capital—equity and intercompany loans. During the two decades that followed, U.S. multinationals harvested the fruits of that foreign direct investment. Reinvested earnings as a share of total investment financing rose to nearly 65 percent in the 1970s, up from 40 percent and 45 percent, respectively, over the '60s and '50s. In the 1980s, a period characterized by global recession and the Latin American debt crisis, U.S. firms naturally shied away from new equity investment overseas. Net equity and intercompany flows reversed and even became net inflows in some years during the decade. Reinvested earnings—also weakened by the subpar performance of affiliates in Europe and Canada—became the primary means of funding overseas investment, accounting for nearly 80 percent of investment in the 1980–89 period.

The 1990s were unique in that the global boom in U.S. foreign investment was financed by both strong reinvested earnings of affiliates *and* a bonanza of new equity and debt commitments. The double-barreled funding resulted from the favorable conditions of the time, including healthy earnings of affiliates, robust profit growth among parents, low global interest rates, and rising stock prices. Hefty affiliate income translated into rising reinvested earnings totaling $349 billion in the 1990–99 period, an amount greater than cumulative reinvested earnings for the prior four decades. Meanwhile, strong profit growth among parents, along with the combination of falling global interest rates and rising equity prices, bolstered their ability to make new global capital commitments. These supports provided the necessary equity capital to fund the boom in cross-border merger and acquisitions among U.S. multinationals in the 1990s. As a result, capital outflows of new equity surged to $331 billion, while loans totaled $122 billion. Combined, they hit a height of $453 billion for 1990–99, accounting for 56 percent of total foreign direct investment outflows for the period.

The Strategic Mandate of Affiliates: It All Depends

The primary objective of most U.S. foreign affiliates has not changed dramatically over the past few decades: it is to deliver goods and services to the host market. This long-standing trend is supported by the fact that roughly two-thirds of total worldwide affiliate sales in 1997 were made to customers in the host country, a share virtually unchanged from the early 1980s. The rest of affiliate sales—$687 billion—were considered exports, with the bulk, as previously discussed, destined for markets other than the United States.

This is not to imply that affiliate strategies are static. On the contrary, they are becoming more dynamic and multidimensional as transnationals shift from "simple-integration" strategies to "complex-integration" schemes. Nor are affiliate strategies universal. They differ across countries and regions, shaped by the policies and endowments of the host nation, the capabilities of the affiliate, and prevailing market conditions. The table in Figure 5.5, itemizing the final destination of affiliate sales by region and country, sheds some light on this subject and is summarized below.

Canada

Local sales account for the bulk of total affiliate sales, although as already noted, U.S. affiliates in Canada maintain tight linkages with their home market. Foreign affiliate sales to the United States, 28.3 percent of the total in 1997, were among the highest of the industrialized nations and the world and were concentrated mainly in transportation equipment.

Mexico

Under the provisions of NAFTA, U.S. firms enjoy better access to the Mexican market and operate in an environment more supportive of expanding linkages between U.S. parent firms and their Mexican affiliates. The regional trade agreement, in other words, has changed and broadened the mandate of U.S. affiliates in Mexico. The export propensity of affiliates has increased while trade barriers and disincentives between the United States and Mexico have declined. In 1997, the fourth full year that NAFTA was in operation, sales to the United States accounted for 38.2 percent of total affiliate sales, up from 25 percent in 1992 and 18 percent in 1985. Local sales represented just over half of total sales in 1997, against a share of nearly three-fourths in 1992.

To be sure, Mexico's severe recession at mid-decade contributed to rising exports to the United States, as production that was earmarked for local consumption was redirected toward the U.S. market. But there is little doubt that the rise in affiliate exports is more fundamental than cyclical, as U.S. production facilities in Mexico become incorporated into the wider North America production networks of U.S. multinationals.

European Union

The percentage of local sales to total sales, approximately two-thirds in 1997, is in line with the global average. But what stands out in Europe

Figure 5.5

Destination of Total Sales of Foreign Affiliates

(Percentage of Total, 1997)

	Host Country	Third Country	United States
All countries	65.3	24.5	10.2
Canada	68.7	3.0	28.3
Mexico	53.8	8.0	38.2
European Union	64.3	31.5	4.2
Belgium	46.8	49.5	3.7
Finland	75.2	21.9	2.9
France	71.5	25.3	3.2
Germany	67.2	29.9	2.9
Ireland	21.3	68.3	10.4
Italy	76.7	2.5	20.8
Netherlands	44.1	50.8	5.2
Spain	69.0	28.9	2.1
Sweden	76.6	20.8	2.6
Switzerland	29.6	66.4	4.0
United Kingdom	69.1	25.0	5.2
Latin America and other western hemisphere	65.4	16.3	18.3
South America	84.2	11.8	4.0
Argentina	81.6	17.5	1.0
Brazil	87.9	7.5	4.6
Chile	69.3	25.9	4.9
Venezuela	93.3	4.8	2.0
Asia and Pacific	71.5	18.8	9.7
Australia	83.5	13.3	3.2
China	68.6	19.9	11.4
Hong Kong	62.8	24.2	13.0
India	87.9	7.1	5.0
Indonesia	44.6	50.2	5.2
Japan	92.0	4.8	3.2
South Korea	90.3	6.3	3.5
Malaysia	52.0	20.1	27.9
Philippines	68.2	17.9	13.9
Singapore	42.0	38.0	20.0
Taiwan	77.8	11.7	10.5
Thailand	68.8	25.9	5.3

Source: U.S. Department of Commerce, Bureau of Economic Analysis.

is the tendency of U.S. affiliates to export to third countries, mainly to other markets and U.S. affiliates within Europe. Sales to customers in foreign markets other than the host nation accounted for more than 31 percent of the total, while exports to the United States were relatively small.

U.S. firms have organized their manufacturing operations in Europe not only along local or national lines but along regional lines as well. Lower internal barriers to trade, first under the provisions of the European Economic Community and later under the European Single Market, have encouraged U.S. firms to integrate their European operations. For many American firms with extensive operations in Europe, cross-border exchanges in parts and components are nearly as easy as intrastate exchanges here in the United States. As a result, U.S. firms are often more pan-European than the Europeans themselves. And the introduction of the euro will make cross-border transactions that much easier in the years ahead.

Note that in Europe's smaller markets—Switzerland, Ireland, the Netherlands, and Belgium—sales to the host country represent less than half of the total. The bulk of affiliate sales went to customers in third markets, suggesting that U.S. affiliate strategies in Europe's smaller markets are driven primarily by regional considerations. Many of these nations serve as important distribution centers for U.S. multinationals, with affiliate sales largely reflecting those to neighboring nations.

South America

Given the region's long-standing bias against imports, and national policies that up until the late 1980s promoted investment in import-substitution sectors, U.S. foreign direct investment in South America has long been earmarked for local market transactions. As evidence, local sales accounted for more than 84 percent of total affiliate sales in South America in 1997, well above the global average. In Brazil, the share was nearly 88 percent, clearly indicating that U.S. foreign direct investment in the Latin giant has been overwhelmingly geared toward the local market and not for export.

In Argentina, the percentage of total affiliate sales to the host nation is also high: 82 percent in 1997. However, with the creation of Mercosur—the regional trade agreement among Argentina, Brazil, Uruguay, and

Paraguay—in the early 1990s, American affiliates in Argentina and Brazil have greater incentives and opportunities for rising volumes of cross-border trade. Over time, falling trade and investment barriers under Mercosur will enhance cross-national coordination and production among U.S. affiliates. This will boost their export propensity and promote greater integration among affiliates in the region.

Asia

There is no one strategic thrust for the region. In general, affiliate sales tend to be directed toward the host country, with Indonesia, Singapore, Malaysia, and Hong Kong as notable exceptions. More than half of total affiliate sales in Indonesia are primarily to third markets, particularly for neighboring countries that consume the raw materials and intermediate products provided by U.S. operations in Indonesia. Most of these sales are concentrated in the petroleum industry and shipped to Singapore, which has extensive oil-refining capabilities. In addition, sales in both Singapore and Malaysia are concentrated in electronic goods and components (computer parts, electronic components, etc.), with a significant share destined for the United States.

In the rest of the region, U.S. affiliates usually produce and sell goods for the local market. That is particularly true in Japan, India, and South Korea, where virtually 90 percent or more of affiliate sales are within the nation. Even in China, most affiliate sales are local, meaning that U.S. companies are more interested in selling to the Chinese than using the mainland as a cheap export platform. Hong Kong not only is a sizable local market for affiliates but also serves as a regional distributor of goods. Wholesale trade is the dominant foreign affiliate industry in Hong Kong; sales to third countries (mainly to mainland China) represented nearly one-quarter of the total in 1997.

On balance, the activities of U.S. affiliates are overwhelmingly geared toward the host nation. This is particularly true of most developing nations, a fact that runs counter to the commonly held view that affiliate operations in low-wage nations such as Brazil, China, and India are designed to export goods back to the United States, thereby threatening the employment and wage prospects of U.S. workers. That is true in some cases—for example, Mexico and Malaysia. Ironically, however, U.S. foreign affiliates in the developed nations, namely Europe, Australia, and Canada, have a higher propensity to export than affiliates in the developing nations. This reflects the more advanced and integrated production networks of U.S. firms in the developed nations in general.

The Big Picture: Perspectives on U.S. Parents

The preceding pages emphasize the dynamic role and capabilities of U.S. foreign affiliates. But before leaving the subject, some perspective is in order. U.S. foreign affiliates, to be sure, are influential global economic players and are at the forefront of corporate America's overseas thrust. This does not mean that as the global reach and capabilities of U.S. affiliates has increased over the past few decades, American industry has been left to be "hollowed out," a popular lament of many commentators in the United States. To the contrary, the operations of U.S. parents remain centered on the United States, a fact that is often either overlooked or ignored by critics of American firms with global operations. Moreover, U.S. firms with global operations, rather than being a detriment to the U.S. standard of living, are in reality a significant contributor to America's overall economic well-being.

Figure 5.6 delineates three chief measures—gross product, employment, and capital expenditures—of the parent-affiliate relationship. Note that the share of activity in each category has shifted away from U.S. parents to their overseas affiliates, albeit modestly in each case. Between 1982 and 1997, the worldwide share of affiliate output rose from 22.9 percent to just 24.9 percent, while the share of affiliate employment rose to 24.6 percent in 1997 from 21.2 percent in 1982. Affiliates accounted for 22.3 percent of worldwide capital expenditures in 1997, versus 19.2 percent in 1982.

The flip side to the figures above is this: Despite the aggressive expansion of U.S. firms over the past two decades and beyond, the activities of U.S. global commercial leaders are still oriented toward the United States. More than three-fourths of worldwide parent output, employment, and capital expenditures are in the United States. Moreover, the balance of evidence suggests that U.S. and affiliate activities tend to be more complementary than substitutable, a relationship that contributes to a higher standard of living in the United States. According to scholar Matthew Slaughter, "American companies with global operations contribute in several important ways

---

Figure 5.6

Worldwide Activities of U.S. Parents and Their Affiliates[a]

	Worldwide Total	Parent	% of Total	Affiliate	% of Total
Gross Product (US$ Billions)					
1982	1,019.7	796.0	78.6	233.7	22.9
1989	1,364.9	1,044.9	76.6	320.0	23.4
1994	1,717.5	1,313.8	76.5	403.7	23.5
1997	2,094.4	1,573.5	75.1	520.9	24.9
Employees (Thousands)					
1982	23,727	18,705	78.8	5,022	21.2
1989	23,879	18,765	78.6	5,114	21.4
1994	24,273	18,565	76.5	5,707	23.6
1997	26,358	19,878	75.4	6,480	24.6
Capital Expenditure (US$ Billions)					
1982	233.1	188.3	80.8	44.8	19.2
1989	260.5	201.8	77.5	58.7	22.5
1994	303.4	231.9	76.4	71.4	23.5
1997	398.0	309.2	77.7	88.8	22.3

[a]Numbers are for majority-owned foreign affiliates.

Source: U.S. Department of Commerce, Bureau of Economic Analysis.

to the U.S. standard of living, and this contribution is larger than that of purely domestic firms."[5] These contributions are summarized by Slaughter as follows:

> Investment in physical capital: American companies with global opera-tions undertake the majority—57 percent in most years—of total U.S. investment in physical capital in the manufacturing sector.

Research and development: American companies with global operations perform the majority—between 50 percent and 60 percent—of total U.S. research and development.

Exports: American companies with global operations ship the large majority—between 60 percent and 75 percent—of total U.S. exports. Their foreign affiliates are important recipients of these exports; their share has increased to more than 40 percent today.

Imports: American companies with global operations also receive a sizable share of U.S. imports—roughly 30 percent. These imports benefit the U.S. economy in many ways, including giving U.S. companies access to foreign-produced capital goods and technologies.

He concludes that "All these activities help increase U.S. productivity and thereby the U.S. standard of living."[6]

In the end, U.S. foreign affiliates are pivotal to America's global competitiveness and, by extension, to the economic well-being of the United States. Understanding how U.S. firms engage in global business requires a deeper understanding of the functions of U.S. foreign affiliates. When considering how U.S. companies sell goods—and even services—overseas, one should think more of affiliates rather than exports.

6

WHO ARE US?

Foreign Investment and Foreign Affiliates in the United States

"Breakfast at Dunkin' Donuts. Lunch at Burger King. Grocery shop at Giant Food. Sleep at the Holiday Inn. It all sounds very American. But every one of these companies is British-owned."

DAVID R. FRANCIS, "BUSINESS GOES GLOBAL
AS INVESTMENT BOOMS," *CHRISTIAN SCIENCE
MONITOR*, NOV. 27, 1996.

IN MANY CASES, what is familiar to most Americans is also foreign. All the firms mentioned above are staples of the American landscape. Yet, their home offices lie outside the United States. The same is true of parent companies that peddle such popular items as Lipton tea, Dove soap, Random House books, and Häagen-Dazs ice cream. Bart Simpson and the popular television series *The Simpsons* are also under foreign ownership, as are the Los Angeles Dodgers, of all organizations.

The list goes on and evidences a main tenet of U.S. global engagement: just as U.S. companies are engaged overseas more through direct investment than through exports, many foreign companies compete in the U.S. market in a similar fashion. Sales of foreign-owned U.S. affiliates exceed U.S. imports, just as the sales of U.S. foreign affiliates exceed U.S. exports.

For U.S. firms, then, global engagement is not just about taking the battle for market share and profit to various foreign markets. It's also about defending and competing in the home market against foreign rivals that either want to or have become just as much insiders in the U.S. market as American firms themselves. Again, global engagement is beyond trade.

Like the impressive rise in U.S. outward investment, the inward flow has been even more dynamic over the past two decades; where U.S. affiliates are integral contributors to the economy of the host nation, so too are foreign-owned U.S. affiliates in certain states and sectors of the U.S. economy. The industries, and the top foreign investors in each, are explored in the following pages. This chapter analyzes the role of foreign affiliates in the U.S. economy, starting with a long-term assessment of U.S. investment inflows.

1950–1975: Asymmetrical Investment Flows

U.S. foreign direct investment flows in the quarter century from 1950 to 1975 were primarily one-way: outbound. In 1950, the stock of U.S. foreign direct investment abroad, measured by book value or on a historical-cost basis, was nearly four times greater than inward stock of foreign investment. On a cumulative basis, American firms invested a total of $20.4 billion abroad over the 1950–59 period, while aggregate U.S. inflows amounted to just $3.2 billion, less than 16 percent of outflows.[1]

This investment gap was due in large part to the global economic conditions of the time. Spared the destruction of war in their home market, U.S. firms had the advantage of a healthy economy and the financial wherewithal to expand their overseas operations in the decade following World War II. By contrast, the earlier 1950s were a period of rebuilding and reconstruction for Europe. Before expanding abroad, many European firms had to first resurrect their own plants at home and reestablish their domestic market position. There were plenty of local opportunities that obviated the rush overseas. It was only later in the decade, with the formation of the European Economic Community, that European companies began venturing into their neighboring countries and foreign direct investment became more regional in scope.

Meanwhile, across the Pacific, Japan lay in ruins. The country's crushing defeat all but obliterated its overseas commercial presence. Because capital was scarce, the government imposed strict capital controls on overseas investment through the late 1960s. For the war-torn nation, global engagement meant trade—promoting exports was an overriding objective and the means by which to purchase badly needed imports. Japan would not appear on the radar screen of U.S. foreign direct investment inflows until the mid-1970s.

What investment the United States did receive in the first two decades of the postwar period was relatively concentrated. Canada, the United Kingdom, and the Netherlands accounted for three-fourths of cumulative inflows over the 1950s and for two-thirds over the 1960–69 period. The bulk of Canada's investment was in the manufacturing sector. The Dutch focused on the energy sector, and the British made their imprint on the manufacturing, energy, and financial services sectors.

Over the 1960s, the investment gap—or the ratio of outward to inward U.S. investment—expanded. U.S. firms sent $42.2 billion abroad over the 1960–69 period, more than double the level of the 1950s, while U.S. investment inflows during that time totaled just $5.1 billion. By the end of the decade, in 1969, the stock of U.S. inward foreign investment totaled $11.8 billion, versus an outward investment position of $68 billion. The largest foreign investor by far was the United Kingdom, accounting for 30 percent of total inward stock. Canada ranked second, with a share of 24 percent. The Netherlands (17 percent) and Switzerland (12 percent) ranked third and fourth. Combined, the four countries represented more than 80 percent of total inward foreign direct investment. By industry, manufacturing accounted for 45 percent of the total stock of inward investment; the petroleum sector accounted for 21 percent, while financial services represented 18 percent of the total.

The Mid-'70s and the Beginning of Something Big

The 1970s would prove to be a landmark period in the postwar history of U.S. foreign direct investment inflows. Inflows were robust at the outset of the decade, rising to $1.5 billion in 1970. That marked the highest level of the postwar period, although weak global growth and currency instability caused inbound investment to dip to just $367 million in 1971, and they remained below peak levels in 1972. The tide turned in 1973, when investment flows recovered and surged thereafter: U.S. inflows grew by an average annual rate of 22 percent between 1974 and 1980, nearly three times faster than the average annual growth of just 8.7 percent in the 1950–74 period. Part of this turnaround can be attributed to the significant rise in inflation at the time, although in fact more fundamental and structural forces were at work.

While British, Dutch, and Canadian investment were instrumental to the investment boom of the 1970s, so too were strong inflows from other sources. The industrial leaders of continental Europe were back on their feet, ready and willing, after watching American firms move aggressively into their home markets, to do battle in the United States. By the late 1960s and early 1970s, they had acquired the technological capabilities and built up the organizational strength to enter the U.S. market. In addition, many firms were responding to the challenge laid out by Jean-Jacques Servan-Schreiber in 1967, who warned in his book *The American Challenge* that "Fifteen years from now it is quite possible that the world's third greatest industrial power, just after the United States, will not be Europe, but 'American industry in Europe.' "[2] To counteract America's growing presence in Europe, then, German, French, and other European companies started to build and expand their investment stake in the United States.

Foreign inflows at the end of the 1970s resembled those at the beginning. They were robust because of the combination of a weak dollar, which lowered the cost of U.S. assets for foreign buyers, and a strong U.S. economy. The two factors propelled annual inflows to $8 billion in 1978, an amount roughly equal to the total for the entire 1950–69 period. In the same year, the United States became the largest recipient of foreign direct investment in the world, when its stock of inward investment surpassed Canada's. The United States has maintained this position over the past two decades, meaning that the investment surge at the end of the 1970s was not an aberration. To the contrary, it was the beginning of a long-term boom in inward foreign direct investment that would rebalance the investment gap between the United States and the rest of the world in the 1980s. In the process, the rules of global engagement for corporate America were radically altered.

The Pendulum Swings in the 1980s

At the start of the decade, the foreign investment gap was unequivocally in favor of the United States. Corporate America's overseas investment position totaled $215 billion on a historical-cost basis in 1980, versus an investment stake of $83 billion in the United States. By a factor of over 2.5 to 1, then, U.S. firms enjoyed a global investment advantage over their foreign counterparts.

This gap quickly evaporated in the 1980s, however. In fact, the level of foreign direct investment in the United States (on a historical-cost basis) was roughly equal to U.S. overseas investment by the end of the decade. What happened that would cause America's investment advantage to be neutralized in just one decade?

Part of the explanation is U.S. outflows, which slowed sharply in the first half of the decade. Sluggish economic activity in Europe and Canada, the debt crisis in Latin America, weak earnings of foreign affiliates, all dulled America's appetite for overseas assets and reduced the value and profitability of foreign operations abroad. Outflows rose by just 14.4 percent in the 1980–86 period from the corresponding period of the 1970s. They accelerated at the tail end of the decade, although annual inflows expanded at an even faster clip.

The global recession of the early 1980s also acted to curb U.S. investment inflows. After hitting a peak of $25.2 billion in 1981, inflows fell in 1982 and again in 1983. Notwithstanding this slump, the amount of investment coming into America exceeded that being invested abroad in 1981 and in each consecutive year throughout the decade. Inflows totaled $93 billion for 1980–84 but then rolled on to $245 billion in the second half of the decade. Cumulative inflows of $338 billion for the 1980–89 period were nearly double outflows ($172 billion) and nearly seven times larger than the combined total for 1950–79 (Figure 6.1).

As is often the case in determining investment motives, foreigners' rush to America was occasioned not by one underlying factor but rather by a host of variables. Favorable market attributes in the United States, corporate restructuring that increased the number of domestic candidates for sale, and attractive incentives from many U.S. states and municipal governments all played a part in luring record amounts of foreign investment to the United States over the 1980s. Shifts in U.S. tax laws related to accelerating depreciation schedules are thought to have been another catalyst.

The dramatic depreciation of the dollar in the second half of the decade was still another. The weak buck not only reduced the foreign currency cost of acquiring U.S. companies or building new facilities but also caused the dollar value of wage rates in other major countries to rise

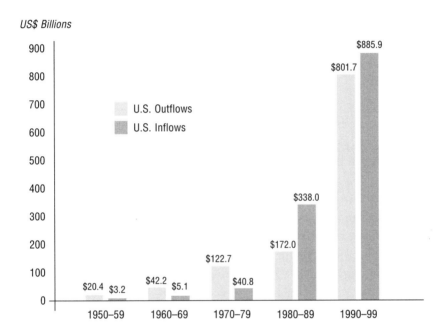

Figure 6.1

U.S. FDI Flows: The Long View[a]

US$ Billions

[a]Cumulative totals in nominal dollars.

Source: U.S. Department of Commerce, Bureau of Economic Analysis.

relative to U.S. wages, making it more difficult to export goods and more attractive to set up shop inside the United States. However, despite the obvious logic that a weak dollar makes producing in the United States more cost effective, a qualifier from Edward Graham and Paul Krugman is applicable: "Whatever the role of the dollar in triggering booms and slumps in FDI, it should be borne in mind that these fluctuations took place around a long-term rising trend. The timing of the surges in FDI may be attributable at least in part to movements in the dollar, but the decline in the dollar cannot explain the whole long-run upward trend in foreign control that began in the early 1970s and lasted through at least the 1990s."[3] In other words, adjustments in the dollar can play a part in influencing investment flows, but a relatively minor part.

Finally, concerns over the rising threat of U.S. protectionism, which increased in proportion to America's lofty trade deficit in the decade, also contributed to stronger investment inflows in the decade. Specifically, the ominous tone from Washington was one variable behind the massive inflow of investment from Japan, whose rising stake in the United States, to the discomfort of policymakers and U.S. executives, increased considerably in the 1980s.

Japan: Better Late than Never

Japanese companies were late entering the U.S. market relative to their European counterparts. Investment inflows from Japan were negligible in the 1950s, and accounted for just 2 percent of cumulative U.S. inflows in 1960–69 and 2.6 percent in 1970–74. On a global basis, Japan was not a significant source of foreign investment in the first quarter century following the war, and what overseas investment Japan did undertake was designed primarily to secure natural resources or to tap the low-cost advantages of its neighbors. Accordingly, outward investment flows were predominantly directed at the developing nations, namely developing Asia and Latin America.

Japan's investment orientation shifted toward the United States in the mid-1970s, a strategic redirection triggered by a number of factors. Like other nations, Japan was attracted to the size and wealth of the U.S. market. Another variable was Japan's rising dependence on the U.S. market (by 1975, the United States accounted for one-fifth of Japan's total exports) juxtaposed against the yen revaluation. The stronger yen, which appreciated by more than 40 percent against the dollar from 1970 to 1978, made it increasingly difficult to effectively serve the U.S. market via trade, prompting the Japanese government to adopt policy initiatives designed to promote foreign direct investment among Japanese firms. The objective was to maintain market access in the United States, and toward this end, the government eased capital controls and foreign-exchange restrictions. Loan programs and other incentives were initiated as well in the 1970s and continued into the next decade.

Japan's rising merchanise trade surplus with the United States, which climbed from $1.3 billion in 1970 to more than $13.6 billion in 1978, was matched by an uptick in protectionist threats from Washington. While just a decade earlier, in the 1960s, Japanese industry was hardly considered a serious competitive threat to corporate America, the mood in Washington shifted as exports from Japan soared in the 1970s. The response from the United States was to establish "voluntary" restrictions on exports in such sectors as ferrous metal, color televisions, and machine tools. Japanese firms responded, in turn, by increasing their investment and in-country presence in the United States as a means to circumvent the ceilings.

Cumulative inflows from Japan totaled $3.4 billion for 1970–79, with roughly half of the amount received in 1978 and 1979. Inflows became even stronger over the next decade. Trade frictions between the United States and Japan only increased in the 1980s, resulting in another round of "voluntary" restraints or quotas. This time Japanese automakers were the primary targets. So, Japanese companies such as Honda, Nissan, and Toyota followed in the footsteps of such firms as Matsushita, Sanyo, Mitsubishi, and other consumer electronics manufacturers in creating production facilities and distribution networks in the United States.

Honda began manufacturing cars in Ohio in 1982, Nissan in Tennessee in 1983, and Toyota in California in 1984. This begat a corresponding rise in investment among Japan's auto parts and component suppliers, which followed their main customers to the United States. In the end, a large part of Japan's rising investment stake in the United States in the 1980s, particularly in consumer electronics and automobiles, was a hedge against rising U.S. trade barriers. The investment wave also reflected such country-specific variables as Japan's soaring current account surplus and the attendant large pool of funds available for investment. Other influences on investment flows between the two countries are outlined in Chapter 7.

Suffice it to say that Japan arrived in the United States in a big way in the 1980s. Japan accounted for 20 percent of total inflows over the 1980–89 period, second only to the United Kingdom. By 1989, the nation's share of total U.S. foreign direct investment had climbed to 27 percent versus less than 6.5 percent in 1979. By then, it was not so much Japan's trade surplus with the United States that provoked Washington's ire. Rather, it was the growing perception that Japan was out to buy the United States on the cheap, that corporate Japan was on the verge of gaining unprecedented control over the U.S. economy. The result was a xenophobic backlash against Japanese investment in the United States over the second half of the 1980s.

"The Selling of America": The Backlash Comes but Quickly Goes

Rising levels of foreign direct investment in the 1980s were matched by mounting concerns in Washington and other parts of the nation that America was selling its economic soul and future to foreign interests. According to many in the media, America was becoming dangerously "addicted" to foreign investment; at stake in "the selling off of America" was none other than America's economic and political independence.

Japan, of course, was singled out as the financial bogeyman, even though Japanese investment inflows ($67 billion) for the 1980–89 period were just 65 percent of inflows from the United Kingdom, the undisputed top investor in the United States in the 1980s. The rising paranoia about Japan was more a reflection of the sudden and dramatic spike in Japanese investment in sectors such as automobiles and consumer electronics, in addition to high-profile purchases of such trophy properties as Rockefeller Center, Pebble Beach, and a host of marquee corporate names.

The seemingly insatiable appetite of Japan prompted a *Newsweek* cover to warn "Your Next Boss May Be Japanese," following Sony's purchase of Columbia Pictures Entertainment for $3.4 billion in 1987. A whole cottage industry sprang to life around the "invasion from Japan," with authors Douglas Frantz and Catherine Collins warning in their book *Selling Out* in 1989 that "It is quite possible that within a decade, the United States will find itself in the position of being a satellite of the powerful industrial machine of Japan."[4]

This dire prediction, and many others like it, were well wide of the mark. The ongoing debate at the time nevertheless signified American ambivalence toward the role of foreign direct investment in the United States. Over the postwar era, America had never before been at the receiving end of so much investment. The nation's customary role as being the world's top home country for foreign investment was turned upside down in the 1980s: the United States not only lost its lead spot as the world's largest overseas investor (albeit temporarily) but also became the largest host nation.

The role reversal greatly intensified the terms of global engagement for corporate America. The competition was no longer an ocean away, but just down the block, as more and more foreign firms contested the U.S. market not only through trade (imports) but also through investment (affiliates).

The sparring between Detroit and Japan rose to the next level. While at the start of the 1980s, there were no Japanese automobiles manufactured in the United States, by the end of the decades, eight major Japanese assembly plants and more than 200 foreign (most Japanese) auto parts suppliers could be counted in the United States and Canada. In the U.S. chemical industry, the growing presence of foreign competition, namely from Europe, was reflected in the fact that by the end of the decade, 37 percent of all chemical employees in the United States worked for foreign-owned firms, versus only 20 percent at the start of the decade. In 1989, of the nation's 10 largest chemical companies, 4 had foreign parents. In the tire industry, 40 percent of all tires produced in the United States in 1989 were manufactured by foreign-owned operations. Fifteen years earlier, there was no significant foreign ownership of U.S.-based tire companies. The same story—the rising presence of foreign companies on U.S. soil—was all too familiar in other U.S. industries, including building materials, petroleum, heavy machinery, and retailers.

The massive investment inflows of the 1980s helped to radically alter the competitive dynamics of U.S. industry. Like other industrialized nations, with Japan the exception, the United States had become both home and host of foreign direct investment.

Inflows in the 1990s: Weak Start, Robust Finish

America's growing angst toward foreign investment, notably asset purchases from Japan, never really reached a dangerous climax because the boom in foreign direct investment came to an abrupt halt in 1990. After hitting a peak of $69 billion in 1989, total inflows fell to $48 billion in 1990. They continued to decline in 1991 and 1992, when annual inflows totaled just $23 billion and $19 billion, respectively. By the end of 1992, the stock of inward investment ($423 billion) had fallen back to 84.3 percent of outward investment ($502 billion).

A number of factors accounted for the marked slowdown early in the 1990s, with the most obvious being the onset of recessionary conditions, first in the United States and then in Europe. The unfavorable turn in the business cycle reduced all three modes of foreign direct investment inflows: new equity flows in 1993 were roughly half the level of 1990; retained earnings of foreign-owned U.S. affiliates were negative in each year from 1990 to 1994, since payments of dividends exceeded earnings; and net lending from parents to their foreign subsidiaries in the United States declined in 1990, turned negative the next year, and were flat in 1992.[5]

With all these forces at work, investment inflows from Europe in 1990 were roughly half the level of the prior year. They gave up another 45 percent and 23 percent in 1991 and 1992, respectively. Meanwhile, fears of Japanese companies' "buying and owning America" dissipated as problems in Japan—slow growth, weak corporate balance sheets, over-leveraged positions—converged to prick the nation's "bubble economy" early in the 1990s. In very short order, Japan lost both its will and its financial ability to aggressively pursue overseas ventures, a development compounded by unprofitable investments in the United States.

Japanese inflows, after reaching a ceiling of $18.8 billion in 1990, slipped to $12.8 billion in 1991. That figure still represented more than half of total U.S. inflows for the year, but that relationship was due more to the free-fall in European inflows than to rising Japanese investment. Thereafter, Japan's share constricted as the nation's investment pool went dry and its earlier investments in the United States, notably in real estate, went sour. Inflows declined to $4.2 billion in 1992 and just $2.9 billion in 1993. They recovered in the second half of the decade but remained below the peak level of 1990.

The "Old World" Invasion

The decline in U.S. inflows did not last long. After hitting a nadir of $19.2 billion in 1992—the lowest annual total since 1983—foreign investment flows more than doubled in 1993, to $50.7 billion. Rising U.S. interest rates in 1994 dampened inflows, but thereafter, foreign investment bound for the United States boomed. The second half of the

1990s will go down as one of the most explosive periods of inward foreign investment in U.S. economic history, ignited not by Japan but by European transnationals. British firms were at the forefront.

If there is one constant of U.S. foreign investment inflows over the century it is the predominant role of companies from the United Kingdom. In the early part of the 20th century, British firms were among the most prominent overseas investors in the United States. By the same token, in the waning decades of the century, and throughout the intervening years, the British were still at the vanguard in pursuing investment ventures in the United States. Between 1980 and 1999, the United Kingdom accounted for almost 30 percent of total inflows, far and away the largest share of any country. Japan ranked second, with a 13 percent share.

Great Britain's attraction to the United States reflects a combination of forces. The most obvious is the relatively robust growth in the United States over most of the past two decades, buttressed by similarities in language, business cultures, and legal systems. In addition, a revival in economic growth in the United Kingdom, along with rising U.K. equity prices, created the necessary credit and cash conditions for U.K. firms to purchase overseas assets.

Besides all of the above, however, there was an even greater force at work promoting two-way investment flows between the United Kingdom and the United States: industry deregulation or market liberalization on both sides of the Atlantic that opened one-time protected industries such as electric utilities and telecommunications to foreign competition. In other words, at the vanguard of global restructuring in the 1980s and 1990s, and the standard-bearers of the Anglo-Saxon model of capitalism, U.S. and British firms found each other's markets not only relatively attractive but, more important, accessible, energizing bilateral investment flows.

Mergers and acquisitions characterized the bulk of U.S. foreign direct investment inflows in the 1990s, with British firms leading the way. Some of the largest deals in 1998–99 were the acquisition of Amoco by British Petroleum for $55 billion; Vodafone's acquisition of Airtouch Communications for $66 billion; and two megadeals in the electrical utilities: Scottish Power's purchase of PacificCorp ($12.6 billion) and Energy Group's acquisition of Texas Utilities. Outside of these three industries—petroleum, telecommunications, and utilities—deals were also announced in industries such as financial services, technology, and consumer products. Given these massive deals, foreign inflows from the United Kingdom skyrocketed to $65.7 billion in 1998 and to a record $116.6 billion in 1999.

Declining flows from Japan and surging inflows from the United Kingdom were two trends that characterized the 1990s. A third was the rising investment position of corporate Germany. Like other transnationals, German firms were quite naturally attracted to the booming U.S. economy and made some mega-acquisitions themselves over the second half of the 1990s. Chief among them were the Daimler-Chrysler deal and Deutsche Bank's purchase of Bankers Trust; the two deals helped boost German inflows to a record $42 billion in 1998, equivalent to Germany's total investment in the United States over the 1980–94 period. German investment slipped to $22.7 billion in 1999, although the country still ranked second largest of foreign investors in the United States over the 1990s.

The size and wealth of the U.S. market, of course, was one propellant of rising capital flows from Germany, with many German firms mindful of the fact that any truly global strategy dictated a presence in the United States. That prompted both BMW and Mercedes-Benz to set up shop in the United States in the mid-1990s, some 10 years after the Japanese had come to the United States. BMW chose Spartanburg, South Carolina, as its main production site, while Mercedes, after a highly publicized search, elected to build its facilities in Tuscaloosa, Alabama.

Other so-called push factors—created by local market and business conditions—were at work in promoting outward flows from Germany. These included rising German labor costs, stifling corporate taxes, and inflexible employment practices, a lethal mix that pushed corporate Germany abroad. Annual investment outflows from Germany, according to U.N. figures, averaged more than $42 billion during 1993–98, versus an annual average outflow of $17 billion for 1987–92. The United States was a chief destination for this capital.

Transnationals from the Netherlands, Canada, and France were not far behind their German, Japanese, and British counterparts in coming to America in the 1990s. Their motivations ranged from a desire to be closer to their U.S. customers to accessing U.S. technology. Acquisitions were the preferred mode of entry, giving firms quick access to the U.S. market, immediate possession of U.S. technology, or both. All totaled, these six nations accounted for more than three-fourths of cumulative

U.S. inflows in the 1990s (a stunning $885.9 billion), with the United Kingdom ranked first, followed by Germany, Japan, the Netherlands, France, and Canada.

The Foreign Direct Position in the United States as a New Century Dawns

"So much of company strategy is driven out of the United States today. No serious player can afford not to have a presence there."[6]

KRISH PRABHU, CHIEF OPERATING OFFICER,
ALCATEL, THE FRENCH TELECOMMUNICATIONS
EQUIPMENT MANUFACTURER

The U.S. foreign direct investment gap—or the ratio of outward to inward U.S. investment—will always expand and contract, but given the sentiment expressed by Alcatel's chief executive, a heavy investor himself in U.S. technology firms, the tremendously unbalanced flow of U.S. foreign direct investment prior to the 1980s is a thing of the past. The United States is likely to remain among the top home and host nations for investment well into the future.

The foreign investment position in the United States is depicted in Figure 6.2. The half dozen countries just mentioned, in addition to Switzerland, accounted for roughly 80 percent of the total stock of U.S. inward investment in 1999, giving effect to the relative concentration of U.S. inflows. The same seven nations accounted for 55 percent of total U.S. investment outflows on a historical-cost basis in 1999.

By industry, the bulk of foreign investment was in the manufacturing sector, accounting for 40 percent of the total in 1999. The next largest share (13.4 percent) was in wholesale/retail trade, followed by insurance (10.3 percent). As it relates to industry, "In some cases, investments by one or two countries dominate certain industrial sectors, suggesting that there is a rough form of international specialization present in the investment patterns of foreign multinational firms."[7]

This country concentration by sector is certainly borne out in the table in Figure 6.3. In the U.S. petroleum sector, for instance, the United

Figure 6.2

___

Foreign Direct Investment Position in the United States, 1999

(by Parent Company Share)

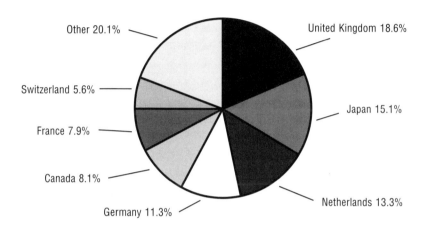

Other 20.1%

United Kingdom 18.6%

Switzerland 5.6%

France 7.9%

Japan 15.1%

Canada 8.1%

Netherlands 13.3%

Germany 11.3%

Source: U.S. Department of Commerce, Bureau of Economic Analysis.

Kingdom and the Netherlands accounted for nearly 80 percent of total foreign investment on a historical-cost basis in 1999.[8] The United Kingdom, France, and the Netherlands accounted for nearly two-thirds of foreign investment in the food and kindred products industry. In chemicals, which includes phamaceuticals, the top investors in 1999 were the United Kingdom, Germany, and the Netherlands, which, combined, accounted for 56 percent of total foreign direct investment. The Dutch held the largest foreign investment stake in the U.S. insurance sector, followed by the Swiss and the Germans.

Japan's presence is significant in such sectors as U.S. machinery and financial services, including banks. Japan also accounts for nearly 45 percent of total investment in wholesale trade, which reflects (1) how the U.S. government classifies overseas investment and (2) the role of Japanese trading companies in Japan's overall investment stake in the United States. The data itself are classified by the United States government according to the major *activity* of the firm. As a result, a large share of Japanese investment

Figure 6.3

Foreign Direct Investment Position in the United States, 1999

(by Sector and Country)

Ranking	All Industries	% of Total	Petroleum	% of Total
1	United Kingdom	18.6	United Kingdom	60.0
2	Japan	15.1	Netherlands	19.8
3	Netherlands	13.3	Canada	5.1

Ranking	Manufacturing	% of Total	Food & Kindred Products	% of Total
1	United Kingdom	17.5	United Kingdom	37.1
2	Germany	15.2	France	16.6
3	Japan	12.1	Netherlands	10.4

Ranking	Chemicals	% of Total	Machinery	% of Total
1	United Kingdom	21.2	United Kingdom	20.6
2	Germany	19.6	Japan	19.0
3	Netherlands	15.3	France	17.5

Ranking	Wholesale	% of Total	Depository Institutions	% of Total
1	Japan	45.4	Germany	25.1
2	Germany	9.2	Netherlands	23.7
3	United Kingdom	8.0	Japan	12.4

Ranking	Finance	% of Total	Insurance	% of Total
1	Japan	33.8	Netherlands	30.1
2	Canada	20.6	Switzerland	15.3
3	United Kingdom	11.6	Germany	10.7

Source: U.S. Department of Commerce, Bureau of Economic Analysis.

in the U.S. auto manufacturing sector has been classified in the wholesale trade category, since this type of investment has been geared more toward distribution than manufacturing.

One final aspect to note about the spending spree in foreign direct investment in the 1990s is that the unprecedented surge produced a collective yawn among American workers and the media at the time. That stands in sharp contrast to the outcry that followed the first wave of investment inflows. To be sure, some observers expressed indignation, such as Ross Perot, who, in describing the growing foreign stake in the United States throughout the 1990s, told the *Wall Street Journal* in late 1998, "I'm just appalled at what doesn't produce outrage today."[9] But Perot was in the minority, with most Americans feeling too confident and secure about the future of the American economy in the 1990s to worry about the rising presence of foreign affiliates.

Strong employment growth, coupled with an extended bull market on Wall Street, proved more than enough to keep American workers not only happy but also largely oblivious to the fact that the corporate owner of Lipton tea and Dove soap is Unilever, the giant British-Dutch consumer products company; that Random House is owned by Bertelsmann of Germany; that Häagen-Dazs and Burger King are part of the portfolio of Diageo of the United Kingdom; that Dunkin' Donuts is held by the British firm Allied Domecq; that Bass of the United Kingdom owns the Holiday Inn and other popular hotel chains; that Giant Food is now part of Ahold, the Dutch grocery giant; and that *The Simpsons* is brought to U.S. viewers by News Corporation, the Australian media giant, which also has a stake in the Los Angeles Dodgers, among other U.S. sports franchises.

Figure 6.4

Selected Data for U.S. Affiliates of Foreign Direct Investors

	Gross Product (US$ Billions)	Employment (Thousands of Workers)	Total Assets (US$ Billions)	R&D (US$ Billions)	Exports (US$ Billions)	Imports (US$ Billions)
1980	70.9	2,034	291	1.9	52.2	76
1985	134.9	2,862	741	5.2	56.4	113
1990	239.3	4,735	1,550	11.5	92.3	183
1995	322.6	4,942	2,389	17.5	135.2	251
1997	385.0	5,164	3,034	19.7	141.0	262

Source: U.S. Commerce Department, Bureau of Economic Analysis.

Affiliate Activities in the United States

U.S. affiliates of foreign companies play only a minor role in the U.S. economy. However, a few finer points need to be made. First, the role of affiliates has grown much over the past two decades. Second, on a micro, or state-by-state, industry-by-industry basis, affiliate activities are significant. Finally, affiliates play a rather large and unusual role in U.S. international trade.

Keep in mind that the bulk of U.S. foreign direct investment inflows in the 1990s reflects the foreign acquisition of existing U.S. establishments (e.g., Vodafone of the United Kingdom purchasing Airtouch Communications) rather than the creation of new establishments (e.g., a Mercedes-Benz plant in Alabama). In other words, the foreign buyer, most of the time, was acquiring U.S. assets, not creating them. Acquisitions accounted for more than 85 percent of total inflows in 1990–99. Accordingly, caution is required when deducing any trends regarding the creation of *new* productive capacity or the creation of *new* employment opportunities by foreign-owned U.S. affiliates. U.S. investment inflows have been more about transferring ownership to foreign companies as opposed to greenfield operations, or creating new capacity and jobs. A summary of the role of foreign affiliates by activity follows.

Gross Product

Output of U.S.-based foreign affiliates totaled $385 billion in 1997, or 6.3 percent of U.S. private-industry gross product (Figure 6.4). That does not sound like much in an $7 trillion-plus economy, and in reality, it is not. The share of affiliate output as a percentage of the U.S. total, however, has grown considerably over the past two decades, rising to 6 percent for the first time in 1994, up from 5.5 percent in 1990, 3.4 percent in 1980, and a share of just 2.3 percent in 1977. Moreover, while the total output of U.S. foreign affiliates is minor in relationship to aggregate U.S. output, the $385 billion accounted for by affiliates in 1997 exceeded the entire output of such nations as Mexico, Taiwan, Russia, and Belgium in the same year.

In other words, U.S.-based foreign affiliates are significant producers in their own right, notably in various sectors of American industry. In the U.S. cement industry, for example, more than 80 percent of the industry is in the hands of European producers. As of late 1999, only 3 of the top 10 U.S. cement producers were actually American. Most were European firms such as Holderbank of Switzerland, Lafarge of France, and Heidelberger of Germany, companies leading the acquisition drive into the U.S. cement market.[10]

It is not surprising that the bulk of gross product of U.S.-based foreign affiliates was accounted for by affiliates whose parent companies are among the largest investors in the United States. Seven countries—the United Kingdom, Japan, Germany, the Netherlands, Canada, France, and Switzerland—accounted for more than 80 percent of the gross product of U.S.-based foreign affiliates.

Employment

At the national level, the total employment of U.S.-based foreign affiliates is relatively insignificant to the rest of the U.S. economy. Affiliate employment has grown along with the rise in foreign direct investment over the past two decades, although foreign affiliates employed only 4.9 percent (5.1 million workers) of the total U.S. private-industry workforce in 1997, down from 5 percent in 1996 and a peak of 5.3 percent in 1991.

At the state and industry levels, however, the scene is quite different. Take the states first, where competition among state capitals to attract foreign investment became so intense that "during the fast-paced investment years of the 1980s, more than 40 states had offices overseas to promote their exports and to encourage foreign investment. At one point, 36 states had offices in Tokyo, primarily to attract Japanese investors."[11]

As a percentage of the total workforce, foreign affiliate employment was the highest in Hawaii in 1997, where 11.4 percent of the workforce toiled for non-U.S. firms. South Carolina (7.9 percent) and North Carolina (7.1 percent) followed. In absolute terms, the states with the largest number of foreign-affiliate workers in 1997 were California, with some 570,000 workers on the payrolls of foreign affiliates in 1997, followed by New York (352,000 workers) and Texas (350,000 workers). Combined, more than 1.2 million employees worked for foreign affiliates in these three states in 1997, yet in all three locations, foreign affiliate employment as a percentage of total private industry was very close to the national average of 4.9 percent in 1997.[12]

As for manufacturing employment, foreign-owned affiliates accounted for 11.5 percent of total manufacturing employment in the United States in 1996 (the last year of available data), basically unchanged from the early 1990s. Regionally, the Southeast accounted for the largest share of foreign manufacturing employment, where foreign affiliates employed 13.2 percent of the manufacturing workforce. In Kentucky, affiliates accounted for 20 percent of total manufacturing employment, the highest share in the nation. South Carolina was not far behind, with foreign affiliates accounting for 18.1 percent of total manufacturing employment.

By industry, foreign subsidiaries accounted for 15 percent of total employment in the U.S. mining industry in 1997, three times higher than the national average. Within various manufacturing sectors, the affiliate share of jobs was even higher, accounting for 34 percent of total U.S. employment in chemicals, 21.2 percent in nonmetallic minerals, and 20.2 percent in electrical equipment, appliances, and components. All totaled, affiliates accounted for more than 10 percent of employment in 12 of the 21 subsectors in manufacturing. In services, affiliate shares were largest in the motion picture and sound recording industries (8.8 percent of the total) and broadcasting and television (8.3 percent). In communications, according to the Bureau of Economic Analysis, affiliate employment rose from less than 2 percent of the total in 1992 to more than 8 percent in 1996, a rise due in large part to foreign acquisitions of U.S. firms.

Research and Development

Research and development expenditures of foreign-owned affiliates are not inconsequential. They doubled between 1989 and 1997, rising from $9.5 billion to nearly $20 billion. The latter is equivalent to 12 percent of total R&D expenditures of all U.S. businesses, not an overly large percentage. However, the $20 billion invested by affiliates in 1997—with the bulk sunk in such sectors as chemicals (pharmaceuticals) and computer and electronic products—is greater than total R&D expenditures of most industrialized nations and exceeds R&D expenditures of U.S. foreign affiliates.

Moreover, as documented by Donald Dalton and Manuel Serapio, "In recent years, R&D expenditures by foreign-owned businesses in the United States have increased at a much faster pace than total R&D

expenditures within the United States by U.S. firms. . . . R&D spending in the United States by foreign-owned companies is now large enough to have an influence on the overall growth rate of total private R&D in the United States. In the high-technology sector, R&D expenditures by foreign companies account for one of every five dollars spent on corporate R&D in the United States."[13]

In general, European-owned affiliates, because they are concentrated in research-intensive industries such as chemicals and pharmaceuticals, tend to outspend their Japanese-owned counterparts. Japan's R&D investment is concentrated in electronics and the automotive industry. In terms of location, foreign R&D facilities are highly concentrated in the United States, with California by far the most popular site, followed by New Jersey and Michigan.

What motivates foreign companies to invest in U.S. research facilities? According to Dalton and Serapio, motivations range from gaining access to U.S. technology to keeping abreast of technological developments. Assisting the parent company in meeting U.S. customer needs is a third variable. Others include following the competition; assisting the parent company in meeting U.S. environmental regulations; and engaging in basic research.

Despite the sizable R&D investment stake of foreign affiliates, foreign transnationals, similar to the strategies of U.S. firms, develop and keep their most important technologies in their home markets.

The Outsized Impact on U.S. Trade

Based on output and employment figures, foreign-owned affiliates command a less than premier position in the U.S. economy. In trade, however, that's not the case. Goods exports of affiliates accounted for 20 percent of total U.S. exports and 30 percent of all U.S. imports in 1997. The former totaled $140.9 billion, the latter $261.5 billion. The difference was a $120.6 billion trade deficit in 1997, equivalent to two-thirds of the total U.S. merchandise trade deficit for the year. Given these numbers, it is clear that foreign-owned affiliates play a significant role in U.S. merchandise trade and in the U.S. merchandise trade deficit (see Figure 6.5).

The dichotomy between the minor influence of foreign-owned affiliates in output and employment on the one hand, and the outsized impact

Figure 6.5

Trade Balances: U.S.-Based Foreign Affiliates Versus Other U.S. Businesses, 1983–1997

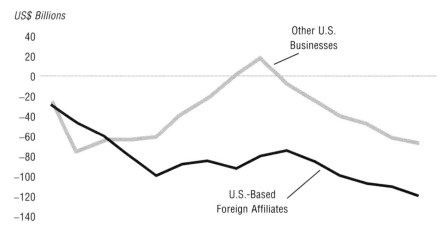

Source: U.S. Department of Commerce, Bureau of Economic Analysis.

in trade on the other, reflects the peculiar nature of affiliate trade. The bulk of the trade deficit for affiliates is accounted for by foreign trading firms, classified as wholesale trade affiliates, rather than as manufacturing affiliates.

Trade of foreign-owned manufacturing affiliates increased sharply over the 1990s, with exports weighted toward chemicals, food and beverages, mineral fuels, and telecommunications equipment. In the majority of cases, affiliate exports were not likely to have originated from the firm's own production. The bulk of imports were comprised of industrial goods such as telecommunications equipment, road vehicles, and office machines and were largely characterized by intrafirm movements. Exports of manufacturing affiliates totaled $70 billion in 1997, versus imports of $99.3 billion. The result was a trade deficit of nearly $30 billion, a sizable shortfall.

But the trade deficit of wholesale affiliates was even larger—more than three times larger, or $92.5 billion—in 1997. Wholesale affiliates have a higher propensity to import than manufacturing affiliates for one simple reason: wholesale operations are in general oriented toward the distribution or marketing of products produced in the home country of the foreign parent. Their main purpose is to serve as a distribution channel for exported and imported goods. By their very nature, then, wholesale affiliates, unlike manufacturing affiliates, provide little value added, with the share of goods for resale without further manufacture almost 90 percent in 1997.

The heftiest deficits among foreign wholesale affiliates were in road vehicles and parts ($44.6 billion), telecommunications and sound equipment ($23.5 billion), office machines ($8.6 billion), and industrial machinery ($3.3 billion) in 1997. For affiliate imports of road vehicles, trading firms or affiliates from Japan, Germany, and Sweden made up the bulk of the total.

By country, the extent of foreign-owned affiliate trade as a percentage of total U.S. exports and imports is quite impressive and generally unrecognized in the United States. For example, Japanese affiliate exports accounted for 52 percent of total U.S. exports to Japan in 1997 and a whopping 80 percent of total imports. These shares are even higher using data based on country of ultimate beneficial owner rather than data based on country of destination or origin. More on that in the next chapter. Besides Japan, foreign-owned affiliates accounted for more than 50 percent of U.S. imports from Switzerland (61 percent), Germany (55 percent), and Sweden (54 percent). Most of these imports came from the affiliates' foreign parent group, testimony to the importance of intrafirm trade, a topic surveyed in Chapter 5.

Given all of the above, suffice it to say that the trade behavior and performance of foreign affiliates are inseparable from the overall equation of U.S. global commerce. Some observers, however, dispute the effect of wholesale affiliate trade, arguing that many of these imports and exports would have been brought into the country by unaffiliated U.S. wholesalers in their absence. While that is a valid point, there's no denying that foreign-owned affiliates in the United States play an outsized role in U.S. trade that few people realize or understand.

Beyond Imports: The Sales of Foreign Affiliates in the United States

In 1997, the United States achieved a milestone: powered by the insatiable appetite of the U.S. consumer, America became the first nation in recorded history to import more than $1 trillion worth of goods and services in a single year.

Yet, as impressive as the import figures were in the waning years of the 20th century, the in-country sales (goods and services) of foreign-owned U.S. affiliates were nearly two-thirds larger than total imports in 1997, the last year of available data. Affiliate sales totaled more than $1.7 trillion in 1997, versus imports of $1.04 trillion, continuing a trend that has been evident since the early 1980s, when the government started to publish the data (see Figure 6.6).

Given data limitations, it is not easy to disaggregate and discern America's top suppliers of imports on the one hand, and top sources of in-country sales of foreign-owned affiliates on the other as presented in Chapter 4. However the accompanying table (Figure 6.7) does succeed in highlighting the principal modes by which foreign firms sell goods in the United States and differentiates between America's top suppliers in terms of imports and affiliate sales.

The left side shows total U.S. imports of goods in 1997. Notice that of the top suppliers of goods to the United States, five are from Asia:

Figure 6.6

U.S. Imports and U.S.-Based Foreign Affiliate Sales, 1983–1997

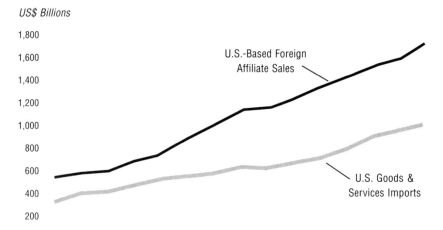

US$ Billions

Source: U.S. Department of Commerce, Bureau of Economic Analysis.

Figure 6.7

Global Engagement: Selling Goods to the United States[a]

(US$ Billions)

Rank	Country	Total Imports	Rank	Country	Total Affiliate Sales
1	Canada	167.0	1	Japan	392.8
2	Japan	121.7	2	United Kingdom	176.7
3	Mexico	85.6	3	Germany	160.8
4	China	62.6	4	Canada	93.0
5	Germany	43.1	5	France	90.2
6	United Kingdom	32.7	6	Netherlands	86.3
7	Taiwan	32.6	7	Switzerland	70.0
8	South Korea	23.2	8	Sweden	28.9
9	France	20.6	9	Belgium	26.0
10	Singapore	20.0	10	South Korea	21.0

[a]1997 data, goods only.
Source: U.S. Department of Commerce, Bureau of Economic Analysis.

Japan, China, Taiwan, South Korea, and Singapore. Half also consist of developing nations—Mexico plus the four Asian states. That being the case, whenever the protectionist debate flares up in the United States, countries such as Japan, China, Mexico, and the developing nations are right in the thick of things due to their commanding rank as importers.

The right side of the table, however, which ranks nations according to affiliate sales, tells a significantly different tale as regards who sells to America and how much. It is not coincidental that the top seven countries in foreign affiliate sales are also the top investors in the United States. Although the United Kingdom has the largest overseas investment stake in the United States, Japan ranks number one in terms of affiliate sales, owing to the strong wholesale nature of Japanese affiliates in the United States. Japan's affiliate sales in 1997 were more than three times as great as Japan's imports to the United States in the same year, although caution must be used in analyzing these data, given the high probability of double counting of imports and affiliate sales. The point is that

Japan's commercial relationship with the United States extends beyond import and trade, the most common measure of global engagement.

Another case in point: Sweden, the Netherlands, Switzerland, and Belgium did not even rank as a top supplier of imports to the United States, although their presence in the United States is strongly evident through investment. Note that U.S. affiliate sales of U.K. firms in 1997 were nearly five times the level of imports from the United Kingdom. A similar gulf between affiliate sales and imports is evident with Germany and France. Conversely, China, Mexico, and the developing nations have very shallow investment ties with the United States and deliver goods to the U.S. market more through trade than investment. South Korea was the only developing nation to rank among the top 10 in both imports and affiliate sales, a function not so much of South Korea's deep investment ties in the United States, but rather of the extensive activities of South Korean wholesale affiliates in the United States.

From this perspective, it's evident that just as U.S. exports can distort the true nature of U.S. global engagement abroad, a singular focus on U.S. imports can misrepresent corporate America's top foreign competitors. As stated in other parts of this book, trade linkages are one thing, investment linkages quite another. Each variable—in isolation and in tandem—needs to be analyzed. Anyone attempting to understand U.S. industry in the context of global competition must look not only at exports and imports, but also at foreign direct investment flows and the operations and sales of foreign affiliates.

America: Some Implications as Host to the World

"How do nation-states exist in an era of transnational corporations?"[14]

SENATOR SAM BROWNBACK OF KANSAS

That question did not preoccupy U.S. lawmakers a quarter century ago. Then, it was common knowledge that the competitive underpinnings and identity of the U.S. economy were closely tied to such corporate giants as General Motors, IBM, and General Electric. The economic interests of the United States in the context of global competition were viewed through the prism of "us" versus "them."

But the answers to "Who is us?" and "Who is them?"—two questions framed and analyzed by scholar Robert Reich—are open to debate following two decades of surging cross-border flows to and from the United States.[15] Over the past decade, the tidal wave of cross-border mergers and acquisitions has blurred the lines of corporate ownership in America. To claim, as Charlie Wilson, the chief executive of General Motors, did years ago that "what's good for General Motors is good for the country" is not necessarily to speak of reality anymore. Today, what is good for the U.S. economy is also determined in part by what is good for Honda, BMW, Unilever, Sony, and hundreds of other foreign companies with significant investment stakes in the United States.

Global competition over the past two decades has moved to the next level for many U.S. firms. Competing at arm's length—through trade—has shifted toward greater in-country competition (a.k.a. investment). According to Graham and Krugman, this shift in the competitive playing field reflects nothing more than the fact that "the United States is simply becoming more normal—that it is becoming, like other countries, a host as well as a home for multinational firms."[16] Evidence of this leaning toward "normalization" is clear from figures compiled by the United Nations showing the stock of U.S. inward foreign direct investment as a percentage of gross domestic product. In 1980, the inward stock of foreign investment in the United States was 3.1 percent of U.S. gross domestic product. The share improved to 4.6 percent in 1985 and to 7.2 percent in 1990. By 1997, the share had claimed 8.4 percent versus a global average of 11.7 percent.

Do foreign-owned affiliates act differently from U.S.-owned firms? That is still under study, although initial research from the U.S. government and other private think tanks shows that foreign affiliates are relatively indistinguishable from other U.S. firms. As Graham and Krugman point out in their research, "U.S. affiliates of foreign firms look quite similar to U.S. firms in the same industries in terms of value added per worker, rates of compensation, research and development. The only noticeable difference between foreign-owned and domestic firms is that the former do on average import more of their production inputs per worker."[17] Certainly, for many U.S. consumers, foreign-owned affiliates are becoming more indistinguishable.

All of this has forced U.S. legislatures to rethink and reexamine their positions regarding American trade policy. For many lawmakers, the threat of a trade war or trade sanctions against, say, Japan or Germany has lost some of its bite now that a sizable percentage of their manufacturing workforce back home is employed by such global firms as Nissan, Volkswagen, and Siemens. Creating jobs—good jobs—is a core task of any politician, and in many states that were relegated to the economic dustbin in the lean 1980s (Ohio, Illinois, Michigan, Indiana, and others), growth in manufacturing employment over the past decade has come largely through foreign-owned affiliates. The effect is that trade legislation is harder to craft with America's widening and expanding foreign investment linkages.

The history of foreign-owned affiliates operating in the United States is relatively new, but there is little doubt that outside of the cyclicality of global investment flows, foreign affiliate operations are here to stay. In the last two decades of the 20th century, the United States became the world's largest host nation to foreign investment, fundamentally altering the terms of global engagement for American business.

PART III

Unique Dimensions of U.S. Global Engagement

T he final section of the book takes a look at U.S. global engagement from the perspective of a country (Japan), an industry
(global services), and a subsegment of the world economy (the
developing nations).

Chapter 7 analyzes U.S.-Japanese commercial relations from the perspective of foreign direct investment. Japan's gigantic trade surplus with
the United States is common knowledge among most Americans and a
perennial concern to lawmakers in Washington. Yet, as this chapter reveals,
it's not Japan's trade imbalance that should have U.S. lawmakers worried.
More threatening to the competitive interests of the United States is the
imbalance in investment flows between the two parties and the attendant
commercial advantage Japan enjoys over the United States. The real battle in this trans-Pacific contest is being fought in terms of foreign direct
investment; and it's a battle Japan is currently winning and one that has
profound implications for U.S.-Japanese trade flows. The good news is that
U.S. access to the second largest market in the world is expected to
improve over the near term. Change does not come easy in Japan, but the
1990s were probably the most wrenching period in Japan's modern economic history. As a result, and more so out of necessity than by design,
the country became more receptive to foreign direct investment in the final
years of the decade. Foreign investment inflows into Japan soared in the
last two years of the 1990s, with U.S. companies leading the pack.

Chapter 8 examines a sector—broadly defined as global services—
that receives little attention in the context of U.S. trade and investment.
Services are often thought of as nontradable, or as being more domestic
than global. This principle, however, like many others in economics,

needs to be updated. Thanks to the proliferation of new technologies, advances in telecommunications, and global industry deregulation, services are rapidly becoming more tradable and mobile. The globalization of services is one of the most exciting elements of the world economy, and a trend that plays right into the strength of many U.S. service leaders. Explosive growth in U.S. service trade in the past decade has been accompanied by a sharp uptick in U.S. foreign direct investment in services; in fact, roughly 61 percent of U.S. investment overseas in the 1990s was in services (including investment of U.S. holding companies) rather than in manufacturing. As a sign of things to come, foreign affiliate sales in services surpassed total U.S. service exports for the first time in 1997. Chapter 8 trains the spotlight on this dynamic and singles out some U.S. service firms that are leading the way overseas. Many—such as Wal-Mart, Fidelity Investment, Yahoo!, and America Online—represent the next wave of U.S. foreign investment and are newly emerging U.S. transnationals in their own right.

The closing chapter examines the unique and evolving relationship between the United States and the developing nations. Think of this relationship as a work in progress. The developing nations emerged as a fourth growth pole in the 1990s, rendering the Triad model of the world economy, revolving around the United States, Europe, and Japan, obsolete. The markets of China, Brazil, and Poland are more accessible today than in the past, with free-market reforms, state privatization, and favorable investment incentives all working to boost U.S. foreign direct investment in all locations. Where the Asian crisis spooked the world's money managers, many U.S. transnationals not only were unswayed but also used the opportunity to purchase distressed Asian assets. However, as the facts make clear, when it comes to investing in the developing nations, U.S. transnationals prefer to stay close to home. Latin America, in other words, remained the top overseas location for American firms in the 1990s, with developing Asia a much distant second. In addition, and contrary to the global norm, U.S. commercial relations with many emerging markets—India, China, and Indonesia, for example—still center on trade rather than investment, although the trend is shifting toward the latter. Meanwhile, in virtually all developing nations, U.S. firms confront intense competition from their European and Japanese competitors. The chapter concludes with a profile of "spheres of influence," or the battle among the world's top transnationals for the markets of tomorrow.

7

JAPAN

Always the Exception

"Foreign investment has fundamentally transformed the U.S.-Japan rivalry into a trans-Pacific contest, one that must be far more carefully assessed if we are to determine why the Japanese sell more in the United States than the Americans sell in Japan."

DENNIS J. ENCARNATION, *RIVALS BEYOND
TRADE: AMERICA VERSUS JAPAN IN GLOBAL
COMPETITION.*

IT SHOULD BE abundantly clear by now that U.S. firms compete more on the basis of foreign investment than international trade. Trade can scarcely be considered the primary benchmark of America's overseas capabilities when the sales of U.S. foreign affiliates are two and a half times the value of U.S. exports. Notwithstanding a chronic and outsized trade deficit, America's global competitiveness is much more formidable when foreign direct investment and the role of U.S. foreign affiliates are penciled into the equation.

America's trade and investment position with Japan, however, is a stark exception to this general rule. While U.S. affiliate sales in Japan exceed U.S. exports to the country, and similarly, the sales of Japanese-owned affiliates in the United States are greater than Japan's exports to America, the commonalities with the rest of the world end there.

One core difference between the United States and Japan is the asymmetrical nature of foreign direct investment flows. Over the past two decades, Japanese companies have built up a towering foreign investment presence in the United States relative to America's investment stake in Japan. As the 1990s came to a close, Japan's foreign investment position in the United States was more than three times larger than America's investment stake in Japan (on a historical-cost basis). The attendant investment gap gives the competitive upper hand to many Japanese firms over their American rivals, evidenced by the fact that Japanese affiliate sales in the United States were nearly four times greater than U.S. affiliate sales in Japan in the late 1990s. In contrast with America's general position with the rest of the world—lagging in trade but leading in investment and affiliate sales—the United States runs second to Japan on both accounts.

This unique dynamic is the subject of this chapter. The following pages sketch the unbalanced nature of investment flows between the two parties, and the respective roles of foreign affiliates. Comparing the Japanese affiliate position in the United States with the U.S. affiliate position in Japan reveals an uneven playing field. A close look at affiliates' activities, and their trade with their parents (intrafirm trade), brings into perspective just how much Japan influences bilateral trade flows with the United States. The chapter ends on an optimistic note—at least for U.S. firms hoping to expand their market presence in Japan. Following the "Lost Decade" of the 1990s, Japan is believed to be on the cusp of momentous change, with greater foreign corporate participation in the Japanese economy expected in the future.[1] The forces of change sweeping Japan are examined, along with the likely effects on U.S. global engagement with the world's second largest economy.

One caveat before we begin: It is not possible to fully dissect the complex relationship between the United States and Japan in just one chapter. Rather, the aim here is to provide a different framework against which to view and analyze one of America's most important bilateral relationships in the world. Too often the U.S.-Japanese relationship—which provokes the fiercest debates among legislatures and other bodies—is assayed solely in the context of trade, which is simply not enough. A more complete analysis must incorporate the foreign investment position of each party. We begin with a brief historical overview of U.S.-Japanese investment linkages.

U.S.-Japan Foreign Direct Investment Linkages: The Long View

U.S.-Japan investment links were established more than 100 years ago. According to Mira Wilkens, "The earliest Japanese direct investments in the United States appear to have occurred in the late 1870s."[2] In 1879, Mitsui & Company opened an office in New York, and just a couple of years later, more than a dozen Japanese trading companies had branches in Manhattan. These companies acted as marketing arms and agents of trade for the home country, exporting steel and other raw materials to Japan, while importing such goods as silk, seafood, and fruit to the United States. In financial services, Yokohama Specie Bank was one of the first Japanese banks to lay stakes in the United States, with the company opening a New York branch in 1880. By the turn of the century, the bank, and other companies as well, had a presence in San Francisco.

Early in the 20th century, Japan's foreign investment in America was concentrated on the east and west coasts (including Hawaii), with the exception of Texas. The lure of the Lone Star State was cotton, a raw material demanded of Japan's textile industry. To help satisfy this need, Mitsui founded the Southern Products Company of Houston in 1911 and began to export raw cotton back to Japan. By the start of the First World War, two more Japanese trading houses had established a presence in Texas.

Japanese shipping companies were also among the first Japanese investors in the United States, with Japanese carriers providing regular service to Hawaii, San Francisco, and Tacoma, Washington, by 1914. Insurance companies were other early entrants. Their investment, similar to Japanese investment in financial services, raw materials, and trade, was designed to help create and promote Japan's international trade. In other words, trade and foreign investment were close complements in Japan. As observed by Wilkens, "The Japanese banks in the United States financed Japanese trade; Japanese insurance companies insured the cargoes; the Japanese trading companies with offices in this country handled the bulk of Japanese commerce (including the movement of intangibles, technology transfer, and assisting American companies in arranging joint ventures in Japan), and Japanese ships transported the goods in both directions. On an even larger scale, Japanese direct investment in the United States provided the business infrastructure for Japanese commerce."[3] The motives behind and composition of Japan's foreign direct investment in the United States changed only slightly over the balance of the century. Although not as prominent and powerful as in early decades, Japan's trading companies—the *sogo shosha*—remain even today among the nation's top foreign traders and investors.

Because Japan was an ally of America in the First World War, the conflict did not severely rupture the investment linkages between the two parties. By 1930, U.S. business investment in Japan was larger than Japanese investment in the United States. Two prominent American investors at the time were Ford Motor and General Motors; Chrysler was also represented in Japan, but through a venture with Kyoritsu Automobile Works. The "Big Three" did not manufacture cars in Japan, but rather assembled "knocked down" kits for the local market. American tire manufacturer B. F. Goodrich was also present in Japan at the time.

By the mid-1930s, a host of local vehicle and parts manufacturers sprang up in Japan, and in order to protect their market positions, both Ford and General Motors applied for licenses to manufacture automobiles. However, their plans for expansion floundered, and their market positions eventually deteriorated, following the decision of the Japanese government to grant licenses only to firms whose shareholders were 50 percent or more Japanese. Toyoda Automotive Loom Works (later renamed Toyota) and Nissan were granted manufacturing licenses, while Ford and General Motors were denied. By the end of the decade, the sales of both U.S. companies had fallen in a pothole. By the early 1940s, rising militarism and nationalism in Japan led to declining sales and investment positions among other U.S. firms operating in Japan, including B. F. Goodrich, Westinghouse, National Cash Register (NCR), IBM, and General Electric.

Again according to Wilkens, "On the eve of World War II, despite the new entries, U.S. direct investment in Japan was barely more than half its 1930 total. Total U.S. direct investment abroad had sunk from $7.8 billion in 1930 to $7 billion in 1940. The worldwide fall was small compared with what was happening in Japan. The reason for the decline of direct investment in Japan lay mainly in the 'domestication' of American manufacturing in Japan."[4]

Foreign direct investment between Japan and the United States was roughly in balance in 1941—Japan's total direct investment in the United States was valued at $35.1 million, versus $32.9 million of U.S. investment in Japan. In the same year, President Roosevelt ordered that Japanese assets in the United States be frozen, and Japan responded in kind. Two-way foreign direct investment flows would not resume until the early 1950s.

Bilateral Investment Flows from 1950 to 1979— Advantage: The United States

Investment flows did revive following the war, although early in the postwar era, the renewed investment linkages were more secondary than primary for both parties. At the onset of the 1950s, America's overseas investment was geared toward Canada and Latin America, with the combined entities accounting for nearly 70 percent of the total stock of U.S. foreign direct investment in 1950. Japan realized just 0.2 percent of total U.S. investment in the same year.

Early in the postwar period, U.S. participation in Japan was conducted more through nonequity arrangements (mostly licensing agreements and subcontracting) than actual foreign investment. As the United Nations report on transnational corporations (TNCs) explained: "United States TNCs played a particularly important role in helping to make Japanese light industries internationally competitive in the immediate postwar period. . . . United States TNCs taught, for example, Japanese apparel makers the needed product design and styling skills and provided them with access to their own marketing channels, in the context of broader opening of the United States market to Japanese exports. In fact, Japan was the first country that served the United States apparel TNCs as their major low-cost labor subcontracting base in the early 1950s."[5]

America's investment stake in Japan did expand in the following decades, although cracking the Japanese market was not easy. Capital controls, trade restrictions, and barriers prohibiting majority ownership all acted as impediments to rising levels of foreign investment. In many sectors, only a limited amount of foreign direct investment was permitted. To expand its market presence beyond wholesaling, IBM negotiated for more than three years with Japan's Ministry of International Trade and Industry in the late 1950s. The company ultimately gained permission to manufacture in Japan, although it had to license its computer patents to other Japanese firms, agree to specific market-share and export targets, and meet a host of other conditions. Many other U.S. firms following in IBM's footsteps, such as Texas Instruments, also faced long, complex negotiations with the Japanese government, which discouraged U.S. firms from building a significant investment base across the Pacific.

Japan's investment climate improved during the 1960s, with Japan's entry into the Organization for Economic Cooperation and Development and the General Agreement on Tariffs and Trade helping to promote more liberalized investment measures. By 1970, the U.S. stock of foreign investment in Japan had increased to $1.5 billion, up nearly fivefold from the prior decade. Thereafter, various phases of capital liberalization, including the elimination of the 10 percent ceiling on foreign share-holdings in existing Japanese companies, and culminating in the government decision in 1979 to codify the investment process, sustained a steady rise in U.S. investment in the 1970s.

On a cumulative basis, American firms sank a total of $4.4 billion in Japan over the 1970–79 period, boosting the stock, or book value, of U.S. foreign investment in Japan to $6.2 billion by 1979. Then, Japan accounted for 3.3 percent of the total global stock of U.S. investment (versus a 1.8 percent share in 1969), a share on par with Mexico's but trailing such nations as Brazil, the Netherlands, Switzerland, France, Germany, and the United Kingdom. In the Pacific Rim, meanwhile, Australia remained the top location of U.S. firms in the 1970s, while Europe—whose share of U.S. overseas investment stood at nearly 45 percent in 1979—emerged hands-down as the favored location of corporate America. Over the 1950–79 period, a noteworthy period in U.S. overseas expansion, Japan accounted for just 3 percent of total U.S. cumulative foreign investment.

Early Japanese Inflows to the United States

As minor as Japan's share in U.S. outflows was in the first three decades following World War II, the value of Japan's investment stake in the United States was even smaller. The amounts were so minute that Japan's investment in the United States was not even published by the U.S. Department of Commerce until 1959. In the 1950s, then, Japan was relegated to the "other areas" category of the investment log. Capital controls, the scarcity of funds, and rebuilding efforts at home combined to impede foreign direct investment outflows from Japan in the first decade following the war. In 1960, according to figures from the United Nations, Japan accounted for less than 1 percent of total global outflows. Early in the postwar period, to the extent that Japanese firms did invest overseas, most of the investment was resource-seeking and stayed within the region. Indonesia became a popular source of raw materials, while Taiwan, South Korea, and Hong Kong became favored locations of Japanese manufacturers in search of low-cost labor.

Japan's foreign investment position in the United States more than doubled between 1960 and 1970, although the total stock of investment in 1970, $229 million, was only 15 percent of America's investment stake in Japan. As a share of total foreign direct investment in the United States, Japan accounted for just over 1 percent in 1970. At the time, the bulk of Japan's U.S. investment was carried out by Japanese trading firms and financial companies, in line with the pattern prior to World War II. Early in the 1970s, Japan's foreign direct investment position in the United States actually turned negative: investment in 1971 was a negative $474 million, a temporary disruption in flows brought on in part by the shift in the exchange rates.

In 1974, the Japanese government reimposed restrictions on overseas investment in response to the spike in world oil prices and the ensuing recession in Japan. These measures, however, did not last long. In fact, the Japanese government removed the last of the capital controls a year later. In the early to mid-1970s, a confluence of factors—more liberal capital controls in Japan, rising protectionist sentiment in the United States due to the rising trade deficit, and the sharp appreciation of the yen against the dollar—set the stage for a jolt in foreign investment from Japan. Manufacturing investment, in particular, rose sharply as one segment of Japanese industry after another decided that manufacturing in the United States was the appropriate strategy in the face of rising U.S. trade protectionism. Investment from Japan's largest electronic manufacturers led the way, with Dennis Encarnation noting, "More Japanese electronics manufacturers invested in local U.S. production between 1978 and 1979 than had invested in the United States for three decades prior to 1978—a claim that could be made by no other Japanese industry."[6]

Sony was one of the first Japanese consumer electronics firms to take the plunge, opening a color-television manufacturing facility in San Diego in 1972. Sony's Japanese competitors followed, with Matsushita Electric Industrial Company (Panasonic), Sanyo, Sharp, and Hitachi all building or acquiring U.S. facilities over the balance of the 1970s. Following a U.S. antitrust suit, NEC and other Japanese semiconductor companies (Toshiba, Fujitsu) adopted a similar strategy at the tail end of the 1970s. Japanese automobile manufacturers, of course, would beat a similar path to the United States early in the 1980s.

Due to both internal and external forces, Japan's foreign investment in the United States spiked in the 1970s from the prior decade, with cumulative inflows totaling $3.4 billion for the 1970–79 period, versus just $90 million in the prior decade. Roughly half of the total was received in 1978 and 1979, which only served as a preview of what was to come next.

Bilateral Investment Flows in the 1980s— Advantage: Japan

At the outset of the 1980s, the investment advantage fell to the United States, whose stock of foreign investment in Japan was nearly one-third larger than Japan's investment stake in the United States. That situation did not last for long, though. U.S.-Japan investment flows would remain asymmetrical over the remaining two decades of the 20th century, but the tables would be turned, with the advantage shifting unequivocally to Japan.

Japan's foreign direct investment in the United States went from a position of insignificance prior to the mid-1970s to one of predominance within less than a decade. The surge in investment in the late 1970s continued unabated in 1980, and one year later the stock of Japan's foreign investment in the United States surpassed America's stake in Japan. In 1984 alone, Japan invested a total of $4.4 billion in the United States, an amount greater than the cumulative investment of Japan over the entire 1950–79 period. That marked an impressive increase, but it was just the beginning. Over the second half of the decade, Japan invested a total of

$55 billion in the United States and emerged, to the consternation of many in the United States, as one of the largest overseas investors in America. In 1989, Japan accounted for more than 27 percent of total U.S. inflows, up from 16.1 percent in 1985 and a share of just 3.6 percent in 1970.

The various forces underlying the run-up in Japanese investment in the United States (and in the world at large) are summarized in Figure 7.1. They range from the relaxation of capital controls in Japan, to the threat of U.S. trade protectionism, to Japan's large current account surplus. At various times, all of the variables outlined, whether alone or in tandem, played a role in boosting Japan's investment position in America.

On a cumulative basis, Japan plowed $67 billion into the United States over 1980–89, nearly 20 times the total for the 1970s. Going in the other direction, U.S. investment in Japan did rise over the same decade, assisted by the abolition of formal capital controls in Japan and other measures that helped promote inward investment. In early 1980, the precondition for foreign direct investment approval switched from a cumbersome and time-consuming licensing-application process to the simple notification of the government. This prompted many U.S. firms— Motorola, General Motors, and Merck, to name just a few—to construct an "inside" presence in Japan. U.S. cumulative foreign investment in Japan equaled $5.2 billion for the 1980–89 period, a rise of 18 percent from the prior decade, but a rise not nearly as robust as the surge in investment from Japan during the same period. U.S. outflows to Japan in the 1980s were less than 8 percent of Japan's investment in the United States over the same period. Moreover, on a historical-cost basis, Japan's investment stake in the United States was more than three times larger than the comparable U.S. level in Japan at the end of the decade. (As a footnote, caution is required when citing investment on a historical-cost basis, since these investments are valued at cost and therefore understate the worth of older U.S. investements.)

The 1990s: The Investment Imbalance Persists

As discussed in the previous chapter, America's angst surrounding Japan's "buying of America" never reached a panic, since the tidal wave of investment from across the Pacific in the 1980s quickly receded in the early 1990s along with that country's fortunes. Japanese inflows peaked at $18.8 billion in 1990 and accounted for nearly 40 percent of total U.S.

Figure 7.1

Variables Influencing U.S.–Japanese Foreign Investment Flows

1970s
- Appreciation of yen
- Resource (raw materials) requirements
- Rising trade surplus
- Increased export dependence on U.S. market
- Relaxed capital controls
- Threat of U.S. trade protectionism; export restraints
- Growing shortage and increasing cost of domestic labor

1980s
- U.S. "voluntary export restraints"
- U.S. anti-dumping investigations
- Desire for U.S. technology
- Yen appreciation (second half of decade)
- Incentives from U.S. state and local governments
- Large current account surplus; excess savings

1990s
- Collapse of "bubble economy"
- Poor U.S. returns; negative reinvested earnings
- Market reform (e.g., financial "Big Bang")

foreign direct investment inflows that year.[7] Inflows from Japan began a rock slide the following year, although, due to an even bigger drop-off of European investment, the country's share of annual U.S. foreign direct investment hit a ceiling of 56 percent in 1991. Just two years later, Japanese investment inflows totaled only $3 billion, a share of U.S. inward investment of just 6 percent.

The dramatic decline reflected the bursting of Japan's "bubble economy," which curtailed not only economic growth at home but also Japan's overseas expansion. Corporate Japan's status as a leading global provider of investment capital was undermined by the lethal mix of a weak stock market, collapsing property prices, an unfolding banking crisis, and sinking corporate profits.

On a global basis, Japan's share of foreign direct investment outflows fell from one-fifth in 1990 to just 3.7 percent in 1998. As discussed in

Chapter 3, global foreign direct investment flows in the second half of the 1990s were driven in large part by burgeoning mergers and acquisitions, with the bulk of these deals more trans-Atlantic than trans-Pacific in nature. It was not until late in the decade that Japan became even remotely involved in the global mergers and acquisitions frenzy.

Japan, nevertheless, still ranked as the second largest foreign investor in the United States on a historical-cost basis as the 20th century came to an end, second only to the United Kingdom. Japan's investment base in the United States was valued at nearly $149 billion in 1999, up from $83 billion in 1990 and less than $5 billion in 1980. Meanwhile, America's investment stock in Japan also increased in the 1990s, rising from $22.6 billion in 1990 to $48 billion in 1999. Corporate America has long been the top foreign investor in Japan. Yet, the U.S. stake in Japan was roughly one-third of Japan's comparable position in the United States as the 1990s came to a close.

From this asymmetrical investment position, Japan derives a commercial advantage over the United States that is largely unrecognized in the United States. While it is Japan's perennial and expansive U.S. trade surplus that makes Washington politicians fume, the same folks would perhaps burst into flames if they knew of Japan's foreign investment advantage—or the difference between Japanese-owned affiliate sales in the United States versus U.S.-owned affiliate sales in Japan. The gap is huge, a point that becomes obvious when comparable foreign affiliate activities are scrutinized.

Profiling Japan's Investment Advantage

The accompanying table (Figure 7.2) delineates Japan's investment advantage over the United States and makes abundantly clear the dichotomy between the in-country presence of corporate Japan in the United States and the position of corporate America across the Pacific.

Beginning with the number of foreign affiliates in each respective market, the first point to note is the lower incidence of majority ownership of affiliates to total affiliates among U.S. transnationals in Japan versus Japanese affiliates in the United States. Of the 990 U.S. affiliates in operation in Japan in 1997, only two-thirds were majority owned, versus an 85 percent majority-ownership share among Japanese affiliates in the United States.

Figure 7.2

Selected Data for U.S.-Japan Foreign Affiliates, 1997

	United States in Japan		Japan in United States	
	MOFAs	**Total**	**MOFAs**	**Total**
Foreign direct investment (US$ billions, historical-cost basis, 1998)	NA	35.6	NA	134.6
Number of affiliates	667	990	2,206	2,587
Total assets (US$ billions)	200	266	541.3	582
Number of workers	178,300	403,900	700,000	812,000
Gross product (US$ billions)	26.6	NA	54.3	62
Affiliate sales (US$ billions)	114.1	204.9	411.6	446.4

MOFAs = Majority-owned foreign affiliates.
NA = Not available.

Source: U.S. Department of Commerce, Bureau of Economic Analysis.

This relatively low level of majority ownership runs counter to the global norm; U.S. transnationals, for purposes of control and execution, strongly prefer majority ownership to minority ownership. In the United Kingdom and Germany, for instance, majority-owned U.S. affiliates accounted for more than 90 percent of total affiliates in 1997. In Japan, however, gaining majority ownership, at least up until the late 1990s, has been difficult because of public and private restrictions, as well as general hostility toward such ownership arrangements.

Turning to total assets, the advantage again falls to Japan. The country's total U.S. assets were valued at $582 billion in 1997, more than double the value of U.S. affiliate assets in Japan ($266 billion). The same lopsided figures are prevalent in employment and gross product: Japan's U.S. affiliates employed 812,000 American workers in 1997, versus

403,900 workers on the payrolls of U.S. affiliates in Japan. Meanwhile, the gross product of U.S. majority-owned affiliates in Japan ($26.6 billion) was half that of Japanese affiliates in the United States.

All of the statistics just mentioned represent the second economic front in America's battle with Japan for market share and profits. As evidenced by Figure 7.3, not only does Japan have the advantage in trade over the United States, with Japan's exports to the United States ($121.7 billion) in 1997 nearly double U.S. exports to Japan, but the advantage extends to investment and foreign affiliate sales as well. Japanese foreign affiliate sales in the United States totaled $412 billion in 1997—towering above the level of U.S. affiliate sales in Japan and Japan's exports to the United States in the same year. The dominance of Japanese affiliate sales over exports in serving the U.S. market has magnified over the past two decades, with the ratio of foreign affiliate sales to exports rising from 2.6:1 in 1983, to 3.5:1 in 1990, to 3.4:1 in 1997, the last year of available data.

Meanwhile, U.S. affiliate sales in Japan in 1983 were roughly even with U.S. exports ($23 billion versus $22 billion). In the intervening years, affiliate sales did outpace exports, although the ratio of sales to exports was just 1.7:1 in 1997. These figures are more in line with ratios with the developing nations, where U.S. investment ties are relatively shallow and still under development.

All told, Japan has a competitive edge over the United States in both forms of global engagement, trade and investment. Moreover, due to Japan's extensive investment network in the United States, and the close ties between Japanese foreign affiliates and their parents, Japan maintains almost unrivaled control over bilateral trade with the United States.[8]

Japan's Stranglehold on U.S. Trade

Japanese affiliates in the United States are very similar to U.S. foreign affiliates in general in that the strategic purpose of both is to serve the local market. Accordingly, local sales represented 88 percent of total U.S. sales of Japanese affiliates in 1997. Another similarity is that just as U.S. parent companies and their foreign affiliates exchange parts, components, and other intermediate goods with each other (intrafirm trade), so do Japanese parents and their overseas affiliates. However, Japan's volume of intrafirm trade with the United States is nothing short of stunning.

Figure 7.3

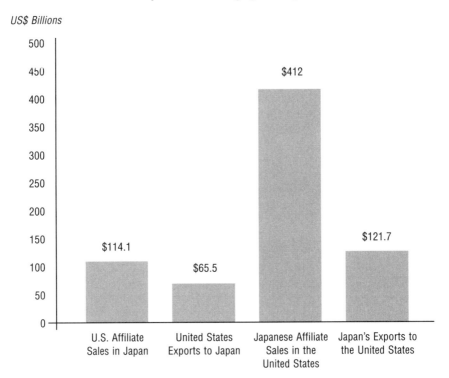

U.S.-Japan Global Engagement, 1997[a]

[a]Affiliate sales of goods and services for majority-owned foreign affiliates.

Source: U.S. Department of Commerce, Bureau of Economic Analysis.

This unique feature of U.S.-Japanese trade is captured in the accompanying table (Figure 7.4). As a substantial export market for U.S. products, Japan consumed more than $65 billion of U.S. exports in 1997 (first column), making it the third largest export market in the world for U.S. goods. That fact is often overlooked in the United States, given America's chronic trade deficit with Japan and the attendant impression that it is very difficult, if not virtually impossible, to sell foreign goods in Japan. In fact, the country represents an attractive export market, but with just one catch: U.S. companies or exporters are not only the ones shipping goods to Japan. Japanese foreign affiliates are significant exporters as well.

Indeed, in 1997 roughly half of U.S. exports to Japan were in the form of intrafirm trade, or trade between Japanese-owned affiliates in the

United States and their parents in Japan. In 1992, Japanese-owned affiliates accounted for a staggering 62 percent of total U.S. exports to Japan. The bulk of these exports comprised agricultural products, beverages, tobacco, and other raw materials required by the parent company.

Japan's control of U.S. imports from across the Pacific is even more impressive. Of total U.S. imports from Japan of $121.7 billion in 1997, more than three-fourths represented Japanese parents providing goods to their U.S. affiliates. The year before, parent-affiliate imports accounted for nearly 84 percent of the total. This suggests that the final market for Japanese imports is first Japanese affiliates, with the job of then distributing parent-company goods in the United States. The bulk of this trade is in automobiles and car parts. The data also suggest how Japanese companies utilize foreign investment as a means to promote trade.

The forces that have allowed Japan to assume near-unrivaled control over U.S.-Japanese bilateral trade have already been touched upon. One is the asymmetrical nature of investment flows, with the imbalance heavily in Japan's favor. Another is the composition of investment. While U.S. investment in Japan, at least up until the 1990s, has been geared toward manufacturing, Japan's investment in the United States has been biased toward services—including wholesaling, financing, and other related activities.

This type of investment has emanated not only from Japan's trading companies but also from the country's more traditional manufacturers such as Toyota, Matsushita, and Sony, which have established their own U.S. wholesalers, distribution arms, and sales outlets over the past few decades.

Commenting on the imbalance in foreign investment, and differing composition of investment, Simon Reich notes: "Japanese firms essentially controlled the bilateral flow of trade between the two countries. Moreover, their large investments in wholesale facilities in the United States, coupled with the private (and any nominal public) sector barriers to trade or investment in Japan, were the conduits for this phenomenon."[9] Also according to Reich, Japan's form of foreign direct investment is more "trade-creating" than "trade-destroying." He contends that Japanese firms "have chosen to pursue a 'trade-creating' strategy that uses their U.S. investment as a conduit for sales rather than a 'trade-destroying' one that substitutes goods produced offshore for exported products." This stands in contrast to the foreign investment nature of the United States, Britain,

Figure 7.4

U.S. Merchandise Trade of Japanese Affiliates in the United States, 1983–1997[a]

(US$ Millions)

	Total U.S. Exports to Japan	Affiliate Exports to Parent Group	Other Exports
1983	21,895	13,991	7,904
1984	23,575	15,775	7,800
1985	22,631	15,779	6,852
1986	26,882	12,322	14,560
1987	28,249	10,866	17,384
1988	37,732	14,463	23,268
1989	44,494	18,856	25,637
1990	48,580	22,420	26,160
1991	48,139	24,394	23,745
1992	47,813	29,551	18,262
1993	47,893	27,974	19,919
1994	53,487	29,312	24,175
1995	64,344	32,906	31,438
1996	67,607	33,315	34,293
1997	65,549	32,533	33,016

	Total U.S. Imports from Japan	Affiliate Imports from Parent Group	Other Exports
1983	41,183	28,323	12,860
1984	57,135	38,688	18,447
1985	68,783	47,863	20,920
1986	81,911	52,248	29,663
1987	84,575	57,356	27,218
1988	89,802	63,903	25,899
1989	93,553	70,904	22,649
1990	89,684	73,085	16,600
1991	91,448	70,699	20,748
1992	97,414	71,152	26,262
1993	107,246	79,323	27,923
1994	119,157	94,309	24,848
1995	123,479	97,801	25,678
1996	115,187	96,594	18,593
1997	121,664	93,158	28,506

[a]Japanese-affiliate exports to and imports from the foreign-parent group account for nearly all of the U.S.-Japan merchandise trade by Japanese affiliates. It would be more accurate to include Japanese-affiliate trade with unaffiliated Japanese persons and to exclude trade with non-Japanese persons in the foreign-parent group, but data for these items tend to be relatively insignificant, and they are not available for every year.

Source: U.S. Department of Commerce, Bureau of Economic Analysis.

and other European investors. A third variable believed to give Japan unrivaled control over U.S. trade is the role of minority-owned affiliates versus majority-owned affiliates. According to Dennis Encarnation, "Because Japan has long hosted a disproportionately large share of minority affiliates, and because these affiliates generally refrain from purchasing U.S. exports (while contributing more to U.S. imports), American multinationals in Japan have contributed a relatively small share of this bilateral trade."[10]

Each one of the variables—asymmetrical investment flows, the dissimilar composition of investment, the role of minority- versus majority-owned affiliates in trade—has given Japan a stranglehold on U.S. trade. However, more research is required on this subject.[11] The point to recognize here is that global engagement between the two parties is far more intricate and sophisticated than most Americans realize. Accordingly, frequent calls for exchange-rate adjustments as the remedy to Japan's looming U.S. trade surplus is a simplistic and naive solution to a very complex relationship.

Rebalancing U.S.-Japanese investment and trade flows necessitates far more than a mere shift in prices. Rather, fundamental and structural change in Japan is required—a tall order for such a tradition-laden and consensus-driven nation. Yet, as the 1990s ended, there was mounting evidence of grass-roots change in Japan.

The "Lost Decade": Reality Overcomes Resistance

There is nothing like a near decade of economic stagnation, depressed profitability, and collapse in asset prices to kindle a rethinking of how to run a country or manage a company. After years of denial and hesitation, the Japanese government sometime in the middle 1990s grudgingly accepted the fact that the much-vaunted Japan model needed an overhaul. It did not have much choice: after expanding by an annual rate of nearly 4 percent in the 1980s, setting the pace among the industrialized nations, Japan's economy stumbled badly in the 1990s, growing by less than 1.5 percent in the 1991–99 period. An economy that rated as the most competitive in the world for most of the 1980s saw its rank as a global competitor decline during the balance of the 1990s. The United States, an economy that was all but counted out at the end of the 1980s, handily stepped into the top spot vacated by Japan.

As Japan's economy wallowed over most of the 1990s—its "Lost Decade"—resistance to change gave way to acceptance of harsh reality. A different mind-set emerged: coddled industries required competition. Overleveraged companies needed to be either consolidated or closed. State-subsidized firms needed to be weaned of public support, since they were a drain on capital. And cheap credit did not produce economic champions, but inefficient firms.

Change does not come quickly in Japan, but it nevertheless became more discernible late in the 1990s. In such service sectors as retail, telecommunications, and financial services, in addition to other industries such as petroleum and chemicals, industry deregulation became the dominant trend. In many cases, barriers to entry for both domestic and foreign competitors were lowered. In telecommunications, the government removed a long-standing ban on foreign companies owning 100 percent of a Japanese telecom carrier, with the exception of Nippon Telephone and Telegraph (NTT), the main telecom operator in Japan. The country's "Big Bang" cracked open the financial services industry, although as in most cases, deregulation is not happening all at once but rather being phased in over time.[12] Other initiatives included tax and pension reform, in addition to new accounting regulations that should lead to improved corporate transparency.

For its part, corporate Japan was also forced into a major reassessment of its business model in the 1990s. At home, the economic slump lingered over most of the decade, culminating with a 2.5 percent drop in output in 1998, one of the weakest periods of economic growth of the postwar era. Not unexpected, various markets of the local economy shrank, compressing sales volumes and profits. Many balance sheets of firms went from bad to worse. Asset values plummeted, dragging many companies deeper into debt. A mountain of nonperforming loans, combined with a fragile banking sector that all but stopped lending money, helped push up the cost of capital for many firms. Once awash in cheap credit, Japanese industry saw funds evaporate in the 1990s. The nation's *keiretsu*—clusters of industrial companies linked by commercial banks and cross-shareholdings—only exacerbated the financial crisis as many Japanese banks, when they did lend money, lent only to favored clients regardless of the credit risks.[13] The *keiretsu* also discouraged labor mobility and domestic competition, prompting Yoshifumi Nishikawa, president of Sumitomo Bank, itself at the center of a powerful *keiretsu*, to intone, "It has been clear for some time that these corporate groups do not work anymore."[14] Finally, industry deregulation meant a new wave of fierce competition and even more intense profit pressures.

Abroad, the U.S. industrial renaissance was for real, evidenced by the ever rising price of U.S. equities and sustained economic growth. U.S. firms were not only well capitalized but also well ahead of their Japanese counterparts in utilizing and leveraging technology. In the pharmaceuticals industry, the combined capitalization of the entire Japanese sector was smaller than that of Merck of the United States at the end of 1999. Many European firms were not far behind their American counterparts and were even ahead in such industries as wireless telecommunications. The frenzy of mergers and acquisitions between U.S. and European firms meant that the global competition was becoming more intense and more formidable at Japan's expense. America and Europe were capitalizing on new technologies and globalization, not Japan. After leading the world in the 1980s, Japan was all but left behind in the decade that followed.

A confluence of causes—industry deregulation, a collapse in profits, a credit squeeze, intense global competition—ultimately forced corporate Japan, and the government, to ponder the unthinkable in the late 1990s: to allow greater foreign participation in the local economy. Global competition had become so acute, the balance sheets of many Japanese companies so precarious, and the economic outlook so grim that Japan was ready to accept foreign involvement as one possible remedy to the nation's multiple ills.

As a result, the door to Japan was gradually but decisively opened, a strategic shift borne out of necessity and survival. As the 1990s wrapped up, the state of mind of the corporate executive in Japan was best summarized by Koji Nishigaki, president of NEC, in an interview with the *Financial Times* in October 1999. Speaking in unusually blunt and direct terms, the head of one of Japan's premier technology leaders said, "It was fine looking at sales growth and market share when the economy was growing and capital seemed inexhaustible. But American business standards are becoming more global, and we need to adopt them to keep up.

If NEC does not change, my successor will not be Japanese."[15] The admission was a sign that the global realities of the time had begun to overcome entrenched local resistance in Japan.

"Open the Market and They Will Come"

"There has never been a shortage of buyers wanting to enter the world's second largest economy. Rather it has been a shortage of sellers. That is changing."[16]

Proclaiming a period of structural change in Japan is a risky endeavor. The last decade was filled with plenty of false starts and spurious hopes, leaving many observers frustrated with Japan's inability to shed the traditional practices of the past.

Even more skepticism surrounds Japan's willingness to embrace foreign transnationals. After all, we are talking about a country whose stock of inward foreign direct investment as a percentage of gross domestic product at the end of the 1990s was on par with Sudan's (see Figure 7.5). This is also a country where the word for "takeover bid" (*nottori*) can also mean "hijack," and where mergers and acquisitions are still viewed in many cases as acts of betrayal of their employees by management. Add to the list Japan's high cost of labor and land, exclusionary business practices, cross-shareholdings, complex distribution system, poor disclosure practices, and lack of labor mobility. It is thus little wonder that many still believe Japan is not serious about accepting foreign transnationals.[17]

The country, to be sure, still maintains a sense of unease with foreign multinationals. (What nation, including the United States, does not?) Yet, despite this ambivalence, the last two years of the 1990s were a time of robust foreign direct investment inflows. U.S. firms alone invested $12 billion in Japan over the 1998–99 period, nearly double the total U.S. foreign investment over 1990–97 and greater than total U.S. inflows over the entire 1950-89 period (see Figure 7.6). The bulk of the investment ($10.6 billion) was recorded in 1999, although many deals were announced in 1998. As a sign of the times, U.S. outflows to Japan in 1999 exceeded comparable U.S. inflows, the first rebalancing of flows since 1979.

The modes of entry of U.S. firms run the gamut—from go-it-alone strategies as exemplified by MCI WorldCom's building its own fiber-optic network through Tokyo, to General Electric's direct purchases of assets and operations from a number of distressed Japanese finance companies. Ford Motor has opted for the middle ground, taking a controlling interest in Mazda, one of a handful of Japanese automakers. General Motors has adopted a different strategy, preferring to construct a web of non-controlling alliances with select Japanese automobile manufacturers. The company bought a 20 percent stake in Fuji Heavy Industries late in 1999, complementing its 49 percent stake in Isuzu Motors and 10 percent share of Suzuki Motors. General Motors had in place a Japanese alliance that claimed 18 percent of the Japanese vehicle market in 1999, second only to Toyota. Moreover, the creation of this alliance not only gives GM market presence in one of the largest car markets in the world but also serves as a springboard to the rest of Asia, where vehicle markets are small but expanding. General Motors is not alone: more and more U.S. firms are leveraging their Japanese relationships to serve both the local market and the greater Asian market.

Figure 7.5

Japan Versus the World

(Inward/Outward FDI Stock as a Percentage of GDP, 1997)

	Inward	Outward
World	11.7	11.9
Developed nations	10.5	13.9
European Union	15.2	18.6
Germany	9.9	14.4
France	10.1	13.6
Italy	7.1	10.9
United Kingdom	21.5	29.1
United States	8.4	10.6
Japan	**0.6**	**6.5**
Developing nations	16.6	5.8
Sudan	0.9	—

Source: UNCTAD.

Figure 7.6

U.S. Foreign Direct Investment in Japan

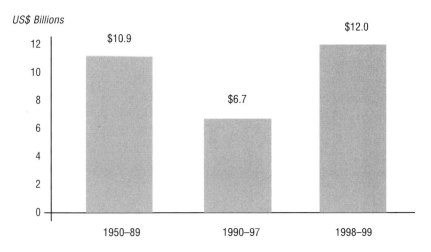

Source: U.S. Department of Commerce, Bureau of Economic Analysis.

Despite the moves of some of America's largest manufacturers in Japan, the most recent advance in U.S. foreign investment has been directed at such service activities as finance, transportation, retailing, and telecommunications, where the ownership advantage of American firms are virtually second to none on a global basis.

Such well-known U.S. firms as Merrill Lynch, Fidelity, Charles Schwab, and GE Capital, the dynamic financial arm of General Electric, have been among the first to take advantage of Japan's "Big Bang" in financial services. These firms, and many others, are vying for a slice of Japan's massive pool of savings (more than $1 trillion) and positioning themselves for the expected boom in the mutual-fund business in the decade ahead. "The Big Bang's opening of financial services will lead to new opportunities and freedom for individual investors," according to GE spokesman Glen Mathison.[18] GE is thought to be the largest foreign financial group in Japan, with the bulk of the firm's $17 billion in assets in Japan acquired in the last two years of the 1990s. The company was joined by a little-known U.S. financial firm, Ripplewood, which, to the surprise of many, made a successful bid to acquire Long-Term Credit Bank in 1999, one of Japan's largest banks. Ripplewood is also eyeing the Japanese hotel market with Marriott International.

In telecommunications, industry deregulation, along with Japan's large market and technological capabilities, prompted market-seeking and strategic asset–seeking investment from such firms as MediaOne and Global Crossing. Not to be left out, AT&T teamed up with British Telecom to acquire a 30 percent stake in Japan Telecom in 1998. The most stunning move in telecommunications came from Cable and Wireless, the telecom group from the United Kingdom, which acquired IDC, a Japanese international telecoms operator. By making a tender offer to shareholders of IDC over the heads of IDC's executives, Cable and Wireless effectively snatched the telecom company from Japan's largest and most powerful telecom giant, NTT. It was an audacious move and the nearest thing to a "hostile" takeover by Japanese standards.

Renault of France engineered an equally bold move. The company took effective control of Nissan, Japan's second largest automobile company, in late 1999, then promptly announced a radical restructuring plan previously unheard of in Japan. Many in the country were shocked when Nissan's first non-Japanese chief operating officer, Carlos Ghosn, nicknamed "Le Cost-Killer," decided to slash 21,000 jobs (mostly in Japan), close five factories, and reduce the number of suppliers by half. The latter move strikes at the heart of Japan's *keiretsu* system of business relationships. In addition, Ghosn plans to introduce stock option bonuses based on achievement; in the future, promotions are expected to be based on performance rather than seniority.

It remains to be seen whether or not "Le Cost-Killer," deploying techniques common to U.S. firms, will be successful in engineering a recovery at Nissan. Overturning decades of corporate tradition in Japan will not be easy or quick. But the fact that such a radical, foreign-driven attempt at corporate restructuring was even made in Japan late in the decade spoke to just how far along the nation had come in accepting, albeit grudgingly, western business practices and the participation of foreign multinationals. In addition, while Japan has been slow to embrace change, the country has proved in the past that once a consensus takes hold, the result can be swift and startling. As the events unfold, the last two years of the 1990s may mark the beginning of a new era in foreign investment inflows to Japan, just as the last two years of the 1970s foreshadowed the stunning rise of Japanese outflows to the United States and the world.

Toward a Level Playing Field

"I think Japan has the chance to be as big as or larger than our total European activities, and it looks as if we will be able to accommodate that in a shorter time than we expected."[19]

DENIS NAYDEN, GE CAPITAL

Given the outsized investment gap between Japan and the United States as the 1990s came to a close, prospects of a level playing field in the near term seem remote. It will take years to rebalance the bilateral flow of investment and trade between the two parties.

That point aside, there is little doubt that as the new millennium begins, Japan represents one of the most important and promising markets in the world for U.S. transnationals. Japan is already hugely salient to the commercial interests of the United States, a point all too clear from the analysis of U.S. exports and affiliate sales in Chapter 4. From an investment base of nearly $50 billion, annual U.S. foreign affiliate income earned in Japan usually ranks in the top 10 in the world and accounts for roughly 15–18 percent of total affiliate income from Asia. Japan versus China? U.S. affiliate income from the former in 1998 was around *10 times* the income earned from China.

The future looks profitable for U.S. firms operating in Japan, a claim supported by two fundamental forces. One is the likely prospect of continued structural reform in Japan: Industry deregulation across a spectrum of sectors will eventually promote greater foreign participation in the local economy. Expanding Internet usage will not only create demand for Internet products but also foster greater e-commerce. Above all else, Internet expansion in Japan will help strip away the layers upon layers of middlemen in Japan, collapsing distribution impediments and costs. This prospect alone will go a long way in creating a more level field for foreign companies in Japan. So too will rising shareholder activism, better corporate governance, and the gradual unwinding of Japan's *keiretsu*; all three, albeit slowly, will help generate more cross-border mergers and acquisitions in Japan in the years ahead.

The second force at work is America's preeminent competitiveness in a number of industries, ranging from software to financial services to entertainment. Numerous U.S. transnationals have firm-specific assets and capabilities that, up until recently, were heavily regulated in Japan. However, as the regulatory grip on Japan loosens and more Japanese firms adopt *some* parts of the so-called American model of doing business, the ownership advantages of many U.S. transnationals will come to the fore in Japan and create new market opportunities for companies willing to operate "inside" Japan. America's global competitiveness is evident around the world through its in-country presence in virtually every major country and its long-term commitment to foreign direct investment. By the same token, a more open Japan, combined with the industrial strengths of the United States, is consistent with a greater and expanding American presence in Japan.

In time, the Japan of the 1990s—difficult, stagnant, and parochial— may very well metamorphose into one of the most explosive, profitable, and dynamic foreign markets in the world for U.S. goods and services this decade. This is not out of the realm of possibilities given the structural forces at work in Japan juxtaposed against America's overriding global capabilities. This mix—a more receptive Japan, and a more interested and competitive corporate America—is mutually reinforcing and could spawn a more cooperative and dynamic relationship between the parties in the years ahead.

8

SERVICES

The New Dynamic of U.S. Global Engagement

"The labour of some of the most respectable orders . . . churchmen, lawyers, physicians . . . is unproductive of any value."

ADAM SMITH, *THE WEALTH OF NATIONS.*

HAD IT BEEN written a few decades ago, this book would not have required a separate chapter on services. Then, services activities were largely immobile and untradable, and few involved cross-border transactions. Not only were services predominantly domestic in nature, but also they were often considered activities with minimal economic value. The lack of significance attached to services is epitomized by their common textbook example: the simple haircut.

Services' image has not changed much since the time of Adam Smith. They are still largely considered poor cousins to manufacturing, although they are anything but. Services have transformed into one of the most dynamic components of the world economy, representing nearly two-thirds of world output by the mid-1990s, according to the World Bank. In countries as diverse as Australia and Mexico, services accounted for roughly 70 percent of total output in 1997. Even in China, a country considered the global manufacturing powerhouse of the 21st century, service-based activities have grown increasingly important to the nation's overall economic health.

In the United States, services account for more than 70 percent of total output, and is home base to such service leaders as Wal-Mart, Charles Schwab, Federal Express, and other prominent U.S. service providers. But not unlike their manufacturing counterparts before them, U.S. service companies are venturing farther and farther from home. In fact, services are one of the most robust elements of U.S. global engagement.

The Globalization of Services

Service activities are rapidly being reshaped on a global basis. Functions that were once considered nontradable (data processing, education, medical services) are now being traded regularly. Activities long classified as domestic endeavors (advertising, legal services, consulting) today easily take place across borders. And industries that were once the domain of the overregulated public sector (telecommunications, insurance, electric utilities) have been privatized and, in many cases, opened to foreign competition. Consequently, service activities have spread globally, igniting market opportunities for U.S. service firms.

Various powerful forces have induced the metamorphosis of services from local to global activities. One is the global sweep of industry deregulation, not only in developed nations such as Germany and Japan, but also in prime developing countries such as Poland, China, and Brazil. In these markets and many others, traditional barriers to entry in major service industries such as transportation, communications, utilities, and financial services are being dismantled.

The process has been slow and laborious, but it is gathering pace as more governments realize that a competitive service sector is becoming a prerequisite to the economic well-being of any nation. In capitals around the world, there is a growing recognition that growth in international trade requires a first-class infrastructure; that a vibrant industrial sector is virtually impossible without a cheap and reliable source of energy; and that an efficient and market-driven financial sector is the best way to allocate credit. Finally, in the age of the Internet, developed and developing countries alike are waking to the fact that they cannot compete globally without both basic telecommunication services and connectivity.

In other words, getting the basics (energy, transportation, communications) right has become paramount among policymakers around the world, launching a global trend toward industry deregulation and privatization in many service sectors.

In Latin America, for instance, Brazil and Argentina privatized such industries as transportation, telecommunications, and electric utilities over the 1990s. In Asia, the financial crisis of 1997–98 exposed the fragile nature of the region's financial services sector and ultimately acted as a catalyst for financial reform and deregulation in the former crisis economies of South Korea, Thailand, and Indonesia, among others.[1] Japan's financial "Big Bang" represents the nation's most intense effort ever to overhaul Japan's malfunctioning financial sector. And across the Atlantic, the European Union, and Switzerland as well, finally opened and deregulated their telecommunications markets at the start of 1998, following on the heels of industry deregulation in such sectors as utilities, financial services, and insurance.

Many of the national efforts to liberalize service activities have been encouraged and advanced in part by supporting multilateral trade agreements. The General Agreement on Trade in Services (GATS), negotiated under the Uruguay Round of Multilateral Trade Negotiations, is chief among them. The agreement, reached in 1995, is the first multilateral deal to provide enforceable rights covering trade and investment in the services sector, and controls such issues as most favored nation status, national treatment, and market access.

Under the auspices of the World Trade Organization (WTO), GATS and two other seminal multilateral deals—the Information Technology Agreement (ITA) and the Basic Telecommunications Agreement—were concluded in the second half of the 1990s. The ITA is designed to eliminate tariffs on a range of information technology products and promote trade in computer hardware, software, and semiconductor manufacturing equipment, analytical instruments, and other products. The Basic Telecommunications Agreement is the first multilateral telecommunications trade package ever reached and was signed by 69 nations, which account for more than 90 percent of world telecom revenue. Specifically, the agreement addresses market access and national treatment for suppliers of telecommunications services; it grants foreign investment in telecommunications services and facilities, with foreign participation varying by country, and includes procompetitive regulatory principles essential to ensure that market access is fully realizable. The upshot of this, according to the U.S. government, has been falling international calling prices and more choices for customers.

Combined, the Information Technology and Basic Telecommunications agreements will accelerate the construction of the global information highway of the 21st century. In the process, the mobility and tradability of services will increase and help propel the globalization of services.

Technology and the "Death of Distance"

Also recasting the role of services is the accelerating pace of technological change. In many regions of the world, technological advances have appreciably lowered the cost of communications, making it more feasible and efficient to retrieve, process, and disseminate multiple forms of information worldwide. Just as container ships made the physical export of goods possible in the past, fiber-optic cables will make it possible to export more data, information, and other knowledge-based services (education, legal services, banking) that used to be considered nontradable. As the World Bank notes: "Communications technology increasingly allows service firms to split and disperse parts of service production to foreign affiliates or outsource labor-intensive activities, such as data entry in the Caribbean or software writing in India."[2] Such service activities as research and development, computing, inventory management, accounting, marketing, and advertising have all become more mobile and less bound to the home market.

As communication costs fall, and as the information infrastructure expands and the proliferation of the Internet continues unabated, the tradability of knowledge-based services will only rise, promoting greater trade and foreign investment in services among multinationals. Financial services ranked among the first service-related activities to experience a leap in global business due to improving technological capabilities, and other service-related activities are poised to follow along.

The general shift from manufacturing-dominated activities toward more service-related activities the world over has been another impetus to the globalization of services.[3] As the accompanying table (Figure 8.1) attests, the transition to service-based activities is not unique to the developed nations; it is well under way among many developing countries. In Russia, Brazil, Mexico, and South Korea, for example, services accounted for more than half of total output in 1997. In all, the rising service-intensity of these countries, and others like them, coupled with technological advances and industry deregulation, implies greater market opportunities for many U.S. service providers with a global reach.

Figure 8.1

The Role of Services in the Industrialized and Developing Nations

(Services as a Percentage of GDP, 1997)

Industrialized Nations	1980	1997
Australia	58	71
United Kingdom	55	67
Finland	51	62
Italy	55	66
Netherlands	NA	70
France	62	72
United States	64	71
Japan	54	60
Developing Nations		
India	36	45
China	21	32
Indonesia	34	41
Philippines	36	49
Thailand	48	49
Russia	37	55
Brazil	45	57
South Africa	43	57
Malaysia	30	41
Mexico	59	69
Argentina	52	61
South Korea	45	51
Hong Kong	68	84
Singapore	61	65

Source: World Bank.

Finally, leading transnational manufacturers themselves have been behind the growing global role of services. As they have extended their global reach, U.S. companies have generally demanded the same services they are accustomed to receiving in their home market. Often, local suppliers lack the technological skills and sophistication to handle large accounts that span different markets and time zones, and are therefore unable to provide the type of service to which firms are accustomed in their home markets. Several global service providers have stepped in to exploit this discrepancy, among them: Federal Express, which, by offering reliable global shipping capabilities, has become a strategic necessity for U.S. multinationals; Citigroup and its financial services counterparts, which offer advice and capital to U.S. firms around the globe; U.S. airline carriers, such as American and United Airlines, which have added international routes as the number of U.S. global business travelers has steadily risen; and miscellaneous providers such as the security firm Pinkerton (now under foreign ownership), which today safeguards the operations of U.S. multinationals worldwide. As a result, global opportunities are cropping up in a wide variety of service activities, from insurance to car rentals. More and more U.S. service companies have figured out that in order to increase their global sales, they should follow their best customers (manufacturers) abroad. As such, it is not solely the service providers themselves that are instigating the broad-based, secular trend toward greater service activities. Traditional manufacturers are driving the process as well.

Industry deregulation, propitious multilateral trade agreements, technological advances, the diffusion of the Internet, the availability of more service-based activities, the global spread of U.S. manufacturers—all have come together in the past decade to make service activities more tradable and contestable. This confluence has resulted in both a pronounced rise in U.S. exports of services and a marked increase in U.S. foreign direct investment in various service-related activities.

U.S. Trade in Global Services

As a starting point, it is important to define service exports. The conventional breakdown features five main categories: travel; passenger fares; other transportation, including freight and port services; royalties and fees; and other private services. Travel and other private service exports are the two largest based on value, accounting for nearly two-thirds of total service exports in 1999. Royalties and fees ranked third, followed by exports of other transportation and then passenger fares.

Travel exports consist of receipts earned from foreigners traveling in the United States. Every time a foreign citizen comes to the United States and purchases food, lodging, recreational items, entertainment, or any other type of good or service, that is considered a U.S. export. Since the United States is one of the prime destinations in the world for business travelers and tourists, it is little wonder then that travel exports count among the largest exports of the United States. Owing to the Asian crisis, however, 1998 was not at all a typical year for U.S. travel exports, which actually fell for the first time in more than a decade. Harsh economic conditions in Asia and later Latin America curbed international travel in the afflicted nations, although travel receipts did rebound in 1999.

Passenger fare exports also declined in 1998 for the same reasons before recovering the following year. As defined by the Bureau of Economic Analysis, these exports "consist of fares received by U.S. operators for transporting foreign residents between the United States and a foreign country and between foreign countries."

Other transportation exports include transactions for freight and port services for the transportation of goods by ocean, air, and truck to and from the United States. Exports are earned when a U.S. carrier transports U.S. goods for export or between two foreign ports. Port service receipts, again according to the definition of the Bureau of Economic Analysis, are the value of the goods and services procured by foreign carriers in U.S. seaports and airports. Also included under this category are U.S. trucking firms' freight receipts, earned largely by cross-border trade between the United States and Canada and, to a lesser degree, Mexico. While travel and passenger fare exports are dictated by the movement of people, exports related to other transportation are determined by the movement of goods and closely track general trends in U.S. exports and imports.

Exports of royalties and fees represent receipts and payments on such intellectual property rights as patents, trademarks, and copyrights. Broadcast rights also fall under this category, as do the rights to distribute, use, and reproduce computer software. Unfortunately for both U.S. movie and software producers, copyright infringements are all too common in many parts of the world, penalizing not only the companies involved but also

U.S. exports. These problems notwithstanding, royalty and licensing export receipts more than doubled in the 1990s, rising to nearly $37 billion in 1999, exceeding total U.S. exports of civilian aircraft, which is often cited as America's largest-single export.

One of America's most dynamic exports is also one of the least understood and recognized. When is the last time you heard a trade analyst or someone in the media extolling the competitive strengths of U.S. exports of "**other private services**"? Yet, these exports, representing a basket of knowledge-based activities (see Figure 8.2), have zoomed over the past decade as more and more U.S. firms exploit the globalization of services by leveraging their competitive strengths outside the home market.

America's export capabilities go well beyond traditional goods such as heavy machinery and chemicals. U.S. export growth increasingly reflects brains, not industrial brawn. Private service exports include activities that most people do not even consider as exports. One is education exports, which have elevated owing to America's first-class university system and expertise in management and technical training. Another is financial services exports, which totaled nearly $14 billion in 1998.

More impressive has been the heady growth of exports under the category of business, professional, and technical services, a subsegment under "other private service" exports. They have been among the fastest growing U.S. exports of the past decade, expanding by a compound annual average rate of nearly 15 percent in the 1986–98 period.[4] Leading the way were accounting (up 26.2 percent on a compound annual average basis over the period), advertising (up 16.3 percent), construction and engineering (15.0 percent), legal services (31 percent), and management consulting (15.1 percent). Aggregated, business, professional, and technical service exports topped $24 billion in 1998, producing a handsome surplus of nearly $16.6 billion.

As for total "other private service" exports, they advanced to $92.1 billion in 1998, rising by an annual rate of more than 7 percent in the face of difficult economic conditions. In 1999, they reached nearly $97 billion, well in excess of America's traditional exports such as chemicals ($72 billion), machine/transport equipment ($81 billion), and motor vehicles ($17 billion).

Total U.S. service exports topped $270 million in 1999. To put that number into perspective, what America earns just in service exports in a

Figure 8.2

U.S. "Other Private Services" Exports[a]

	Total, 1998 (US$ Billions)	Compound Average Annual Growth, 1986–98 (%)	Trade Balance, 1998 (US$ Billions)
Total "Other Private Services"	92.1	10.8	44.4
Education	9.0	8.2	7.5
Financial services	13.7	12.6	9.9
Insurance	2.8	6.2	4.1
Telecommunications	3.7	6.0	−4.4
Business, professional, and technical services	24.3	14.5	16.6
Accounting	0.3	26.2	0.0
Advertising	0.6	16.3	0.4
Computers and data processing	2.0	6.2	1.6
Construction and engineering	4.1	15.0	3.4
Legal services	2.5	30.9	1.8
Management consulting and public relations	1.7	15.1	0.8
Medical services	1.2	7.8	NA[b]

[a]Components do not add up to the respective totals since some categories have been omitted.
[b]Not available given absence of imports data for medical services.

Source: U.S. Department of Commerce.

given year is greater than the total exports of most nations, including upcoming exporting powerhouses China and Mexico. Save for exports of capital goods, services represent the largest category of U.S. exports. And on a global basis, the U.S. reigns supreme as the world's top service exporter, accounting for 18.1 percent of total world service exports in 1998. The United Kingdom was a distant second, with a global share of 7.7 percent.

More important perhaps than the foregoing statistics is that while the United States runs a chronic trade deficit in goods with the rest of the world, services have consistently generated trade surpluses for years. From a modest level of just $100 million in 1985, the U.S. trade surplus in services rose to $28 billion in 1990 and to a peak of $92 billion in 1997. In 1998, for the first time in more than a decade, the surplus fell modestly, to $80 billion, due to the global downturn related to the Asian crisis. The surplus totaled $80.6 billion in 1999. The service surplus is significant for two reasons. First, the surplus represented nearly a quarter of the deficit in goods in 1999 and was critical in stanching the deterioration in the overall U.S. balance of trade. Second, it substantiates the importance and contribution of a generally overlooked mode of U.S. global engagement—trade in services. Equally as important is U.S. foreign direct investment in services.

U.S. Foreign Direct Investment in Global Services

Almost nothing produces more anxiety among U.S. lawmakers than another announcement by another large U.S. company that it is closing a plant or facility in the United States and shifting production overseas. The ripple effect can entail displaced American workers, in addition to mounting fiscal pressures on municipalities and, more often than not, demands from local politicians and union officials alike that Washington "do something."

Washington cannot do much in a global marketplace where the production of transnationals knows no geographic boundaries. And besides, the composition of U.S. foreign investment in the 1990s was not geared toward manufacturing, the popular image conveyed by the media, but rather was overwhelmingly encompassing of services. Over the 1990–98 period, manufacturing foreign investment accounted for 32.5 percent of the total, while investment in petroleum constituted another 6.1 percent. The rest of U.S. investment outflows—more than 60 percent of the total—were composed of services. Even after adjusting for service investment by large U.S. holding companies, which inflates aggregate numbers, services still accounted for nearly 43 percent of total outflows, well beyond the share of manufacturing. In other words, *the great boom in U.S. foreign investment in the last decade of the 20th century was led primarily by service-based activities, with U.S. service giants and leading U.S. manufacturers showing the way* (see Figure 8.3).

U.S. service firms have ventured farther afield for many of the same reasons that directed American manufacturers overseas decades ago. At home, saturated markets have slowed the pace of industry growth, while cutthroat competition—both foreign and domestic—has squeezed profit margins. Abroad, market opportunities for U.S. services have improved for all the reasons previously discussed, turning many well-known U.S. companies, still considered domestic entities, into unlikely global pioneers.

One such pioneer has been Wal-Mart, which is more American than apple pie. But mature markets at home, in addition to rising hostility in

Figure 8.3

U.S. Manufacturing and Services FDI Outflows, 1983–1998

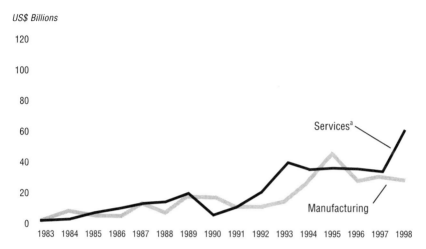

US$ Billions

aExcluding investment of U.S. holding companies.

Source: U.S. Department of Commerce, Bureau of Economic Analysis.

many parts of the United States to the company's overwhelming market dominance, prompted the Arkansas retail giant to think and act more globally in the 1990s.

Wal-Mart's foreign crusade was commenced in 1991, and as with other U.S. companies before it, the firm's initial overseas foray was close to home. Mexico and Canada were early targets. Thereafter, other stakes were claimed in a few parts of Asia, including South Korea and China. Europe became the strategic focus of the company over the second half of the 1990s for the simple logic expressed by Jay Fitsimmons, Wal-Mart senior vice president: "In order to be big globally we have to be in Europe."[5] The company executive was echoing the thoughts of many U.S. firms, and off to Europe Wal-Mart went.

The retailer's initial thrust into Europe was directed at one of the region's most difficult markets to crack: Germany. The allure of Germany rested on its large and wealthy consumer market, Europe's largest. But juxtaposed against this and other attributes were numerous barriers to success: one was tight zoning regulations that prohibited Wal-Mart from building a retail chain from the ground up. Rather, entering and expanding in Germany required acquisitions, a strategic route not often deployed by the company. Another hurdle was restrictive operating hours that forced Wal-Mart to open and close according to the timetable of the government. Finally, many of the traditional practices of Wal-Mart, the bedrock of the company's success in the United States, were either forbidden or frowned upon in Germany. For instance, the company is prohibited from promising customers a refund for any item sold for less elsewhere. In addition, German workers have been turned off by some of the company's work practices, with reported "cases of some workers hiding in the company toilets because they find the company's traditional morning ritual—involving chanting the company name—embarrassing."[6]

Wal-Mart's venture into Germany was followed by a major move into the United Kingdom two years later. Again, entry was via acquisition, in acknowledgment of the difficult and prohibitive retail environment of the host nation. To clear this hurdle, Wal-Mart made a cash offer for the Asda Group in 1999, the third largest supermarket chain in the United Kingdom, giving the company immediate access to the British market. This move, along with the nearly 100 stores in Germany, established a solid beachhead for Wal-Mart in Europe as the decade ended. It also positioned the company to achieve its strategic objective of generating more profits from abroad; specifically, the company expects its international operations to contribute roughly one-quarter to one-third of total earnings in five years, up from less than 10 percent at the end of the 1990s. In addition, Wal-Mart's expanding foreign presence is expected to enhance the company's already mighty clout with its suppliers and allow the company to gain greater economies of scale.

Wal-Mart has seen the future, and it lies abroad. The same is true for other U.S. service leaders such as AT&T, Charles Schwab, and America Online. All three have become more globally engaged, realizing that future success and growth are increasingly dependent on leveraging their strengths in overseas markets.

The global sweep of deregulation in the telecommunications sector presents all sorts of market opportunities for AT&T and other U.S. telecom companies such as MCI WorldCom, Quest, and Sprint. One ripe and ready market is Japan, one of the largest telecom markets in the world, where AT&T, in conjunction with British Telecom (BT), has moved aggressively in establishing a market position. After taking a 30 percent stake in Japan Telecom in 1998, Ma Bell and BT teamed up again and acquired a 33 percent share of Rogers Cantel, Canada's top mobile phone operator, in 1999. The deal, among other things, will allow AT&T to provide wire and wireless service throughout North America. The linchpin of the AT&T and BT alliance lies with the $10 billion global venture in Concert, a venture that combines the cross-border assets and operations of both companies. Not confined to the developed nations, telecommunications deregulation has also spread over emerging markets such as Brazil, Argentina, Hungary, and Poland, among other countries, creating a plethora of new market opportunities for not only U.S. telecommunications leaders but also leading European telecommunications providers.

In financial services, the U.S. discount broker Charles Schwab has joined the ranks of such service giants as Citigroup and American Express in venturing abroad. Japan has been one of the main attractions of Schwab's foreign push, where the company hopes to capitalize on the financial reform churning through the nation. Other on-line brokerages have followed, forging positions and partnerships in not only Japan but also Europe.

Even U.S. Internet companies such as America Online (AOL) and Yahoo! have joined the rush overseas. As growth in U.S. subscribership slows or levels off, these companies and others are looking elsewhere—to Europe, Japan, and a number of emerging markets—where computer access and Internet usage are just beginning to accelerate. With skilled labor at a premium in the United States, many American Internet firms have expanded their labor forces beyond the United States. AOL's workforce now includes cheap, English-speaking workers in the Philippines, which, according to the *Far Eastern Economic Review*, answer some 10,000 to 12,000 technical and billing inquiries a day, most of which are from the United States.[7] The company has also established several alliances and joint ventures (Mitsui in Japan, China.com in Hong Kong, and Cisneros in Venezuela) to extend its global reach. Yahoo!, meanwhile, is steadily making inroads in Asia, notably Japan, where the company has created a joint venture (Yahoo! Japan) with Softbank, one of Japan's leading Internet investment companies. Hoping to facilitate the spread of a global Internet culture is none other than Microsoft, another U.S. global pioneer with foreign investments and strategic alliances in such nations as Mexico, Brazil, China, and the United Kingdom.

All totaled, many leading U.S. service companies, from various sectors of the economy, have stepped beyond the confines of the local market and become more globally engaged over the past decade. This helped alter the composition of U.S. foreign direct investment in the 1990s. Also at work has been the updraft in service investment by U.S. manufacturing companies.

The Service Activities of Global U.S. Manufacturers

"As machines and components become more like commodities, the real competitive advantage for companies will come in having the service capabilities to make the products work effectively."[8]

EBERHARD REUTHER, CHAIRMAN OF KORBER, ONE
OF GERMANY'S LARGEST ENGINEERING COMPANIES

Not all of the rise in U.S. foreign investment in services can be attributed to actual U.S. service companies. Bolstering foreign service investment have been American manufacturing champions such as Ford Motor, United Technologies, IBM, and General Electric, whose composition of foreign investment often belies the true nature of the affiliate's operation.

Over the past few years, for instance, Ford Motor has acquired the auto operations of Sweden's Volvo and sunk millions of dollars in bricks and mortar in Brazil. Both foreign investment deals were typical of Ford: the Volvo acquisition embellished Ford's product line at the high end of the market, while the in-country presence in Brazil theoretically positions Ford to grow in one of Latin America's largest and most promising auto markets.

Also typical of Ford and its counterparts is foreign investment in various service-related activities. As the preceding quote implies, global success requires not only a superior product but also the financing and after-sales services mandated to close deals and sustain overseas relationships. Toward this end, Ford, which owns one-third of Mazda of Japan, extended its reach in Japan by buying Mazda's financing affiliate, Mazda Credit, in 1999. The objective is to offer Mazda customers better financing options and terms, thus helping the bottom line of both Mazda and Ford. In the same year, Ford Credit, the financing arm of the massive parent company, bought Sahasin Finance, a finance company in Thailand, in a move to complement and embellish Ford's truck assembly plant in the country. And in the United Kingdom, the company bought Kwik-Fit, one of Europe's largest independent aftermarket service chains, in a bid to expand the company's presence in the aftermarket.

Ford's global thrust has clearly gone beyond manufacturing. The company's foreign investment applies increasingly to services: expanding dealerships and financing operations, and establishing after-sales parts and components capabilities. This service-based emphasis complements and fortifies Ford's global manufacturing capabilities and underpins the company's overarching strategic objective of becoming the "world's leading consumer company for products and services," according to Jacques Nasser, CEO of Ford.[9]

Ford is not alone. Building and selling an elevator is one thing Otis Elevator, a division of United Technologies, does better than virtually any other company in the world. But the company's overriding profitability and long-term global success depend more on after-sales servicing, which is one reason it has opted to set up its own national outlets in China rather than relying on local agents. Caterpillar, one of the world's leading manufacturers of construction equipment, confronts a similar competitive dynamic and has invested heavily in overseas maintenance and after-sales support facilities. General Electric has manufacturing and assembly facilities all over the world, although GE Capital, the giant financial service arm of the company, is among the most aggressive global investors within the GE family. Other examples abound.

Complementary service activities (distribution, after-sales maintenance, wholesaling, financing) thus are assuming greater importance to the global success of U.S. manufacturers and U.S. investment outflows. Foreign investment and affiliate activities of companies such as Ford Motor extend well beyond traditional manufacturing and assembly-type operations. In fact, often significant differences lie between the activities of the U.S. parent and those of the foreign affiliate, with scholar Matthew Slaughter observing, "Within many American companies with global operations, affiliates and parents do different things. . . . A key reason manufacturing parents establish affiliates is to perform service activities, such as wholesaling and distribution, retailing, and after-sales maintenance."[10]

Figure 8.4

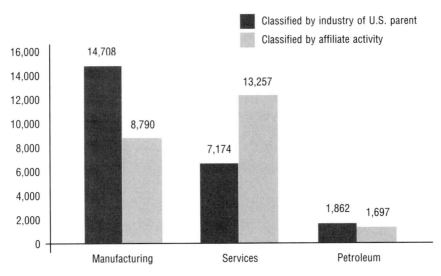

Total U.S. Foreign Affiliates by Sector, 1998

Source: U.S. Department of Commerce, Bureau of Economic Analysis.

That is apparent from the accompanying chart (Figure 8.4). When U.S. foreign affiliates (majority-owned) are classified by their parents' sector, the majority, or 62 percent of the total in 1998, are considered in manufacturing. Service affiliates number nearly 7,200 out of a total of 23,700 affiliates. However, when affiliates are classified by sector of activity, the share of manufacturing drops to 37 percent, while the number of affiliates considered in services rises to more than 13,200, or 55.8 percent of the total.

The upshot is that traditional service firms are not the only U.S. companies leveraging expanding growth opportunities in global services activities. So too are many U.S. manufacturing companies, whose profitability and staying power in any foreign market increasingly depend not only on selling a quality product but also, in many cases, on providing the financing and after-sales service once the product is sold. Foreign investments in manufacturing and services, in other words, go hand in hand for Caterpillar, United Technologies, Ford, General Electric, and many other American manufacturers with large foreign operations.

Sales of U.S. Foreign Affiliates: The Preferred Mode for Delivery of Services

U.S. companies deliver services to foreign customers in the same way as they sell goods: either through exports or through foreign affiliates. However, the gulf that exists between U.S. exports of goods on one hand and affiliate sales of goods on the other does not exist in services, at least not yet.[11]

Remember, the roots of U.S. foreign direct investment in manufacturing and energy are deep; those of U.S. investment in services, in contrast, are relatively shallow. Global opportunities for U.S. services firms have materialized with any significance only within the past two decades. However, as America's global investment position in services increased in the 1990s, so did affiliate sales, which soared by more than 165 percent between 1990 and 1998. Service exports, while relatively robust, expanded at a much slower pace over the same time frame, by 78 percent. In 1997, affiliate sales exceeded service exports for the first time, with the former totaling $270 billion, versus $257.2 billion in U.S. service exports (see Figure 8.5). As a warmup for events to follow, the gap between affilate sales ($323.9 billion) and service exports ($263 billion) widened in 1998.

By region, U.S. affiliate sales in services closely resemble affiliate sales in goods. They are greatest where investment roots are deepest. That is in Europe, which accounted for nearly 60 percent of total affiliate service sales in 1998. Within the region, the United Kingdom stands out. There, the pace of industry deregulation, corporate restructuring, and adoption of new technologies such as the Internet has far exceeded trends in not only Europe but also the rest of the world for that matter. Add to this a common language and legal system, and the result has been burgeoning market opportunities for U.S. firms. Affiliate sales of $97.1 billion in the United Kingdom in 1998 represented nearly 30 percent of the global total. Canada and Japan were distinct runners-up, with a global share of 8.4 percent and 7.3 percent, respectively.

Looking forward, the trend is clear: as industry deregulation continues around the world, and as technological capabilities proliferate, both U.S. trade and investment in services will continue to rise. However, in concert with the competitive dynamics of the global marketplace, where proximity to the customers is paramount in delivering either a good or

Figure 8.5

U.S. Sales of Services to Foreigners, 1990–1998

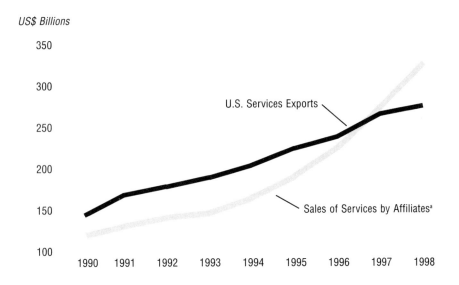

^aMajority-owned.

Source: U.S. Department of Commerce, Bureau of Economic Analysis.

service, more U.S. service firms, like their manufacturing counterparts before them, will opt, where possible, to deliver their products through local affiliates rather than arm's-length transactions. The demands of global competition favor one form of engagement over the other. Service exports will remain integral to the overall trade picture of the United States. But in the future, affiliate sales should continue to expand at a faster pace than exports and unequivocally become the primary means of U.S. global engagement in services.

9

UNFINISHED BUSINESS

U.S. Global Engagement with the Developing Nations

"Increased integration and faster growth in China, India, Indonesia, Brazil, and Russia—five countries that today account for half the world's labor force but only 8–9 percent of its GDP or international trade—will likely redraw the economic map of the world over the next quarter century."

—GLOBAL ECONOMIC PROSPECTS AND THE
DEVELOPING COUNTRIES

THE CENTRAL THEME of this book is that American firms deliver goods and services to their overseas customers more through foreign affiliates than through arm's-length transactions, or trade. Another premise is that these customers are concentrated in the developed nations, which, therefore, account for the majority of U.S. international corporate profits.

That said, even though the global bias of corporate America was toward the developed nations as the new century began, that hardly portends the same picture 50 years from now. Recall that the developing nations' share of total U.S. foreign investment was more than 50 percent in 1950.[1] In the 1990s, moreover, the investment climate in the developing nations was uniquely hospitable for transnationals, with trade and investment reform at the top of many governments' policy agendas. Add to this favorable secular dynamics in such emerging markets as Poland, Argentina, and India (i.e., young populations, rapid growth in new households, great infrastructure needs) relative to the mature economies of Japan, Canada, and Germany (i.e., elderly populations, a decline in number of households, mature markets), and all of the above suggests greater U.S. investment flows to the developing nations in the years ahead.

This final chapter analyzes U.S. global engagement with the developing nations. Think of this relationship as a work in progress, best illustrated by the fact that while U.S. foreign affiliate sales of goods to the developed nations were more than triple U.S. exports in 1997 (an indicator of deep integration), the ratio of affiliate sales to exports was just 1.4:1 for the developing nations (shallow integration). In some large and strategic markets such as China, India, and Russia, or those "likely to redraw the economic map of the world," it was trade, not investment, that formed the basis of U.S. engagement with these nations as the new century commenced.

Despite the media hype and swollen expectations surrounding the collapse of the Berlin Wall and the sweep of free-market reforms that followed, the 1990s did not in fact herald a surge of *new* U.S. investment in the developing nations. Integration and penetration in many of these markets remains a painstaking endeavor for U.S. transnationals, with many firms leaving it up to their foreign affiliates to do the heavy lifting. This chapter highlights that challenge and provides a snapshot of which countries were in or out of favor with U.S. transnationals in the 1990s. Another topic centers on regional spheres of influence and the intense rivalry among the world's top transnationals for market share in the developing nations. The last section examines the level and mode of U.S. global engagement with a variety of developing nations. We begin with the strategic shift of the world economy from the so-called Triad powers—the United States, Europe, and Japan—to the emergence in the 1990s of a fourth pole of global growth comprising the developing nations.

The "Triad" Plus One

"This Triad is where the major markets are; it is where the competitive threat comes from; it is where new technologies will originate. . . . The prime objective of every corporation must be to become a true insider in all three regions." [2]

KENICHI OHMAE

In the mid-1980s, well-known management consultant Kenichi Ohmae of McKinsey and Company popularized a grand thesis that many corporate executives seized upon. The thesis was straightforward: Any company with global ambitions and hopes for world-class status had to become an "insider" in what he dubbed the Triad—or the tripolar world of the United States, Europe, and Japan. While recognizing the importance of the developing nations, Ohmae's main contention was that successful global engagement required that a company become a "Triad power." "The Triad," as Ohmae explained, "is where the main action is. Corporations still wrapped up in the 'United Nations' approach, seeking a market presence in each of the 150 countries of the world, often find their resources suddenly depleted." [3]

Ohmae's book was written during the first half of the 1980s and published in 1985, a time when his thesis was generally relevant and constructive, given market conditions in the developing nations. Latin America was in the throes of a debt crisis and offered scant market opportunities for transnationals. Central and eastern Europe remained under lock and key to the Soviet Union, and off-limits to western firms. Following the second "oil shock" in the early 1980s, and the attendant collapse in world commodity prices, the Middle East went bust. The same fate befell most of Africa. The primary exporting nations of Southeast Asia—notably Thailand, Malaysia, Indonesia, and the Philippines—were also adversely affected by plunging world commodity prices, creating budgetary pressures and balance-of-payment woes.

China had yet to emerge at the time Ohmae's *Triad Power* was published. India remained an outlier even among the developing nations. Asia's emerging economic stars, meanwhile, were wrestling with their own problems: South Korea was buffeted by recession and periodic bouts of political unrest over the first half of the 1980s; Hong Kong was rattled by the 1984 Sino-British Accord, which created a formal time line for handing back the crown colony to the mainland; and Singapore, following a disastrous wage policy that helped undermine the city-state's global competitiveness, slipped into recession in 1985, the first in the nation's short history.

In these circumstances, market opportunities in the developing nations at the time Ohmae penned his bestseller were less than encouraging, which helped validate his grand proclamation that the markets and profits were to be found in the Triad. Why bother with the risky and volatile developing nations? U.S. firms, for their part, seemed to agree: the developing nations accounted for only a quarter of total U.S. overseas investment stock in 1985, half the level of 1950.

The Emergence of a Fourth Global Growth Pole

Prior to the 1990s and during most of the cold war era, growth in the developing nations was closely aligned with that of the industrialized nations. Domestic demand in the mature and wealthier nations, especially the United States, was a bellwether not only for the export-dependent manufacturing economies of Asia but also for global commodity exporters. Hence, as the saying went, when the United States sneezed (or experienced a marked downturn in economic growth), the developing nations caught a cold, or followed the U.S. and the industrialized nations into recession.

Early in the 1990s, the United States, as well as Europe, did sneeze, but the developing nations did not. In fact, they remained relatively immune to decelerating domestic demand in America and Europe, and continued to expand on their own. While growth fell by nearly 1 percent in the United States in 1991, and by 0.4 percent in Europe in 1993, the developing nations cruised on. Collectively, they grew by roughly 5 percent in 1991, with growth accelerating to an annual rate of 6.4 percent in 1993, more than four times faster than the rate among the industrialized nations.[4] The developing nations, to a large degree, had become "decoupled" from their mature and wealthier brethren. And in a stunning case of role reversal, robust import demand in such nations as Mexico, Chile, Poland, Malaysia, and China actually helped cushion recessionary conditions in the industrialized nations early in the 1990s.

Rising demand from the developing nations became one of the most powerful forces of the global economy in the 1990s. Demand was mobilized in large part by climbing per-capita incomes and the steady rise of middle-class consumers in such diverse markets as China and the Czech Republic. The global reintegration of central Europe and Russia alone translated into millions of new potential consumers for western transnationals. By conservative estimates, the combined middle class of India and China was estimated to be in the neighborhood of 400–500 million people, nearly twice the size of the total U.S. population and larger than that of the entire European Union. In Latin America, the break from hyperinflation early in the decade helped put more disposable income into the pockets of consumers, and resurrected middle-class consumers in Chile, Argentina, Mexico, and Brazil. Motivating all of the above was globalization—unfettered capital flows, market liberalization, and trade and investment reform—which brought these new consumers within striking distance of transnationals. In this setting, John Pepper, chief executive of Procter & Gamble, claimed in 1997 that the number of consumers within reach of the company had increased from 1 billion to 4.5 billion in a decade.[5]

The developing nations proved to be both buyers and builders in the 1990s. Billions of dollars were spent on massive capital projects throughout developing Asia and, to a lesser degree, Latin America and central Europe. With the objective of upgrading overburdened and creaky infrastructures, governments poured billions of dollars into new roads, airports, and power-generation plants. And the developed nations were the principal suppliers of the hardware, the capital goods needed for such large infrastructure initiatives.

With these demand dynamics in place, the "sucking sound" that Ross Perot ominously intoned about in the mid-1990s did in fact emanate from the developing nations. But it was not the sound of U.S. capital and jobs being sucked from America, as Perot famously argued during the heated debate over the North American Free Trade Agreement. Rather, it was the resonance of soaring import demand in the developing nations. Their imports from the industrialized nations climbed from $502 billion in 1989, the year the Berlin Wall fell, to more than $1 trillion in 1995. Then, the developing nations accounted for 34 percent of world imports, up from 27 percent in 1989. More important, they posted a massive trade *deficit* with the industrialized nations to the tune of $134 billion in 1995, a bold leap from the modest surplus of $2.4 billion in 1989 and $16.4 billion 10 years earlier.[6]

This shift in global trade highlighted the pent-up demand and market opportunities of the developing nations. It was also emblematic of the seismic tilt in the world economy. A fourth global growth pole emerged as Latin America recovered from its "Lost Decade"; developing Asia moved into a new and dynamic phase of industrialization, slowed temporarily, to be sure, by the severe cyclical economic downturn beginning in mid-1997; and Russia and central Europe "opened" for business and embraced free-market reform measures. This "pole" accounted for nearly 45 percent of world output by the middle of the decade.[7] Transnationals thus were obliged to rethink the logic of the Triad model.

Many U.S. firms have done just that over the past decade. But the rethink, contrary to popular wisdom, has not triggered a rash of new U.S. investment to the developing nations. Rather, the process—global engagement between U.S. transnationals and the developing nations—has moved at more of a cautious than a breakneck speed and has been more erratic than even. Despite all of the positive commentary about robust growth in Thailand, the availability of cheap labor in China, market reform in Poland, greater regional integration in South America, and other favorable attributes of the developing nations, transnationals have been rather slow to invest in the developing nations' favorable long-term growth story.

Some Perspectives on U.S. Foreign Investment in the Developing Nations

As established in Chapter 4, the 1990s marked one of the most explosive periods of U.S. foreign direct investment in history. U.S. firms invested more than $800 billion abroad over 1990–99, more than the entire amount of the prior four decades.[8]

However, that global thrust of corporate America was notably concentrated in the "mature" markets versus the "less than mature" markets (see Figure 9.1). Of total investment outflows for the decade, roughly two-thirds were directed at the developed nations, primarily Europe, which chalked up for just over half of the global total. More telling, equity

Figure 9.1

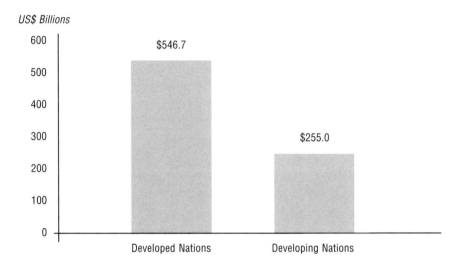

Developed Versus Developing Nations: U.S. Foreign Direct Investment Outflows in the 1990s

(Cumulative Outflows, 1990–1999)

Source: U.S. Department of Commerce, Bureau of Economic Analysis.

capital investment was even more skewed toward the developed nations. Representative of new capital inflows, equity investment soared in the 1990s, although nearly three-fourths of the total went to the developed nations, with the developing nations receiving only a 27 percent share. Similarly, the developed nations accounted for the lion's share of total intercompany loans (nearly 76 percent), a second form of new foreign investment, reflecting fresh parent-company investment in affiliates.

Affiliates Do the Heavy Lifting

U.S. foreign direct investment in the developing nations in the 1990s rose more than sixfold from the prior decade. But here's the catch: the majority of this investment was not in the form of new capital or loans from the parent. Rather, the bulk of the investment outlays came from the foreign affiliates themselves, through reinvested earnings, the third source of foreign investment (Figure 9.2). Reinvested earnings were nearly 45 percent greater than equity capital investment for the 1990–99 period and accounted for just over half of total investment inflows. Similarly, over the 1982–89 period, reinvested earnings in the developing nations were more than double the amount of U.S. equity investment and represented more than 70 percent of total foreign flows.[9]

In other words, the majority of U.S. foreign investment in the developing nations over the past two decades has been funded indigenously, or out of the profits of foreign affiliates. So, foreign affiliates, rather than U.S. parents, have been the chief investment conduits to the developing nations. Accordingly, the better the market conditions in the host country, the better the profitability of affiliates, and therefore the larger the amount of capital (reinvested earnings) available to make new acquisitions, expand existing operations, or increase share in an ongoing strategic alliance. In this case, macroeconomic stability, trade and investment reform, and accelerating growth in the developing nations coincided to rejuvenate many operations of U.S. foreign affiliates over the 1990s. This in turn helped generate stronger levels of U.S. foreign direct investment in the form of reinvested earnings.

Preferred Destinations: Close to Home

The 1990s brought the collapse of communism and the attendant opening of new markets in Russia and central Europe. It was a period when developing Asia assumed its stance as one of the most dynamic regions of the world economy, notwithstanding the sudden downturn in growth in mid-1997. Yet, whatever the hype, however attractive both regions appeared to U.S. companies in the 1990s, Latin America remained the preferred overseas destination of corporate America among the developing nations.

The bias toward America's "backyard" was incontrovertible, with Latin America accounting for 61 percent of the total $255 billion invested by U.S. firms in the developing nations over the 1990–99 period. Geographic proximity, restored growth-cum-decelerating inflation, aggressive state privatization initiatives, and the formation of regional trade agreements (NAFTA and Mercosur) helped heave U.S. foreign investment in Latin America to $156.8 billion in the 1990–99 period, roughly a five-

Figure 9.2

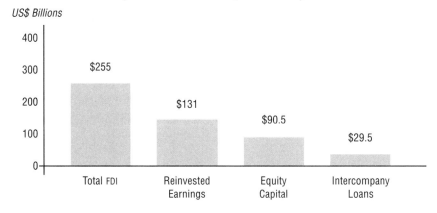

U.S. FDI to the Developing Nations: Modes of Investment[a]

(Cumulative Outflows, 1990–1999)

US$ Billions

[a]Figures for the modes of investment do not add to total due to rounding and the fact that data was unavailable for some countries.

Source: U.S. Department of Commerce, Bureau of Economic Analysis.

fold increase from the prior decade. Also contributing to the rise in investment was the improved performance of U.S. foreign affiliates, which led to a corresponding increase in reinvested earnings of affiliates. The bulk of U.S. investment was market- and efficiency-seeking, in contrast to resource-seeking investment of earlier periods. On a global basis, Latin America's share of U.S. foreign investment advanced to 20 percent in the 1990s, up from 19.1 percent in the 1980s.

Latin America versus Asia? Figure 9.3 makes it clear where corporate America has more at stake, a fact lost on many Wall Street investors when Asia plummeted into crisis in mid-1997. Investors rushed to the exits not realizing that the primary commercial risks to U.S. firms among the developing nations lay more in Latin America than in Asia. Even after adjusting for U.S. outflows to the offshore financial centers of the Caribbean ($46.7 billion over 1990–99), U.S. foreign direct investment to Latin America was still nearly 50 percent greater over the decade than flows to developing Asia. Some 3,345 U.S. foreign affiliates were located in Latin America in 1998, versus 2,600 in developing Asia. In the same year, total

Figure 9.3

The Long View: U.S. FDI Outflows to Latin America Versus Developing Asia

(Cumulative Outflows)

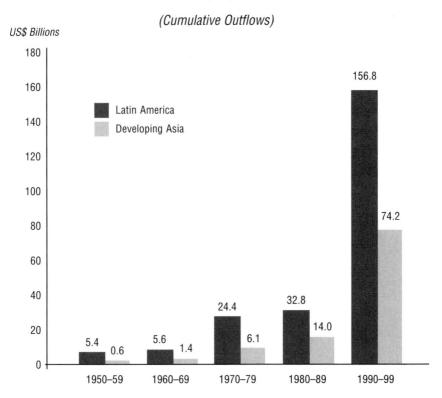

US$ Billions

Source: U.S. Department of Commerce, Bureau of Economic Analysis.

affiliate assets were $434 billion in Latin America, relative to Asia's $235 billion, while more than 1.4 million manufacturing workers were on U.S. affiliate payrolls in Latin America, versus 859,000 in Asia. In terms of affiliate income, Latin America accounted for 17 percent of the global total in the 1990s, against a global share of 10 percent for developing Asia. Based on these measures of relative exposure, a political event in Brazil typically has a far more dramatic effect on U.S. business interests than a political event in South Korea. Similarly, a currency crisis in Thailand is not the same as a currency crisis in Mexico, assuming, of course, that the financial contagion does not spread to other emerging markets. Thailand's malaise was unique in that it did spread and ultimately engulfed most of Asia and then other developing nations, notably Russia and Brazil. Whether this contagion becomes the global norm remains to be seen.

While developing Asia's global share of U.S. investment (9.7 percent) edged higher in the last decade, totaling $74.2 billion for 1990–99, it still significantly lagged Latin America's share in both dollar and percentage terms. In the end then, and despite all of the hoopla about new consumers and new opportunities in markets just opened to U.S. firms, the 1990s were no different from the decades that preceded them, with U.S. investment out-flows to developing Asia trailing investment flows to Latin America. In fact, the amount U.S. firms invested in developing Asia—home to roughly 2.5 billion and accounting for more than one-quarter of world output—in the 1990s only slightly exceeded the total U.S. investment in Brazil and Mex-ico combined. This dynamic duo, by a wide margin, represented the top destinations among the developing nations for U.S. investment in the 1990s.

Top 10 Destinations Among the Developing Nations

Brazil and Mexico combined accounted for more than a quarter of total U.S. investment in the developing nations over the 1990s (see Figure 9.4). By a slim margin, **Brazil** ranked as the favorite developing country loca-tion for American firms, accounting for 13.3 percent of total U.S. invest-ment in the developing nations. Roughly half of this investment took the form of reinvested earnings, which rebounded as Brazil recuperated from the "Lost Decade" of the 1980s and a brutal period of hyperinflation in the early 1990s. Economic growth in Latin America's largest economy began to recover in 1993, and as the macroeconomic climate improved in Brazil, so did the operations and profits of existing U.S. affiliates, gen-erating more investment in the way of reinvested earnings.

Also aiding strong investment inflows to Brazil were radical yet favor-able policy initiatives. Beginning in the late 1980s and continuing into the next decade, traditional import-substitution measures were replaced with market-reform measures that included trade liberalization and indus-try deregulation, notably the privatization of several state-owned compa-nies. Custom duties fell from an average of 80 percent in 1985 to around 14 percent by the mid-1990s, while other protectionist trade legislation,

Figure 9.4

Preferred Destinations of U.S. Transnationals Among the Developing Nations in the 1990s[a]

(FDI Outflows, Cumulative Total, 1990–1999)

Rank	Country	Total (US$ Billions)	% Total to Developing Nations	% Total to World
1	Brazil	34.0	13.3	4.2
2	Mexico	33.6	13.2	4.2
3	Singapore	20.8	8.2	2.6
4	Hong Kong	16.6	6.5	2.1
5	Argentina	11.0	4.3	1.4
6	Indonesia	8.7	3.4	1.1
7	Chile	8.0	3.1	1.0
8	Venezuela	7.4	2.9	0.9
9	China	7.2	2.8	0.9
10	South Korea	5.4	2.1	0.7

[a]Excluding Panama.

Source: U.S. Department of Commerce, Bureau of Economic Analysis.

such as laws restricting imports of computer equipment, were amended. Similar to other Latin America countries, state privatization in some of Brazil's industries, ranging from iron and steel to telecommunications, led to new equity capital investment inflows over the 1990s. So did the formation of Mercosur, the regional trading bloc consisting of Argentina, Brazil, Uruguay, and Paraguay, which, along with Brazil's own large market, attracted large volumes of market-seeking investment. Greenfield investment in the automobile industry shifted into high gear as Ford Motor and General Motors joined other global manufacturers (e.g., Mercedes, Volkswagen) in establishing a local production presence in one of the largest auto markets in the western hemisphere.

These developments helped boost U.S. investment flows to Brazil from an annual average of $1.4 billion in 1985–89 to roughly $3.4 billion in the 1990s.[10]

Mexico ranked a close second to Brazil as the preferred developing nation destination in the 1990s. U.S. investment inflows to Mexico accelerated in the late 1980s and early 1990s due in large part to Mexico's successful debt-equity conversion program, which led, among other things, to a reduction in inflation and rising confidence among foreign investors. U.S. flows averaged $536 annually over the 1985–89 period; investment flows were actually negative in 1986 (minus $339 million) but recovered thereafter. In the run-up to the North American Free Trade Agreement, U.S. investment in Mexico topped $2.5 billion by 1993. The following year, U.S. investment in Mexico hit a record $4.5 billion, bolstered by Mexico's successful entry into NAFTA, which generated new capital investment as U.S. companies, particularly in automobiles and electronics, moved to take advantage of better market access to Mexico and (largely) tariff-free trade between Mexico and its two North American partners. The decade ended on a sweet note, with U.S. firms exhibiting their underlying confidence in Mexico and approval of NAFTA by investing $5.4 billion south of the border in 1999. For the decade, annual U.S. outflows averaged roughly $3.3 billion, more than six times the level of the second half of the 1980s. Looking ahead, the surprise presidential election of Vincent Fox in July 2000 is expected to further strengthen the trade and investment ties of NAFTA.

Elsewhere in Latin America, **Argentina**, ranked fifth among the developing nations, was another favored Latin location in the 1990s for U.S. firms. Although annual U.S. investment inflows averaged less than $100 million over the 1985–89 period, the combination of macroeconomic stability, privatization, and debt-equity swaps under the Menem government helped lure more American firms to Argentina in the 1990s. The 1991 Convertibility Plan, which pegged the peso to the dollar, helped break the back of hyperinflation and restore investor confidence in Latin America's second largest economy.

Argentina's aggressive privatization plan, with parts of the telecommunications sector privatized as early as 1990, was also integral to attracting more investment. So too were special incentives in the automotive sector, as well as Argentina's participation in the creation of Mercosur. The latter granted privileged access to neighboring Brazil and helped attract both market- and efficiency-seeking investment from the United States. Annual U.S. flows to the nation averaged $1.1 billion for the 1990–99 period, more than a tenfold increase from the second half of the 1980s, and were concentrated in such sectors as telecommunications, energy, financial services, chemicals, food processing, and automobiles.

Although one of the smallest markets in the region, **Chile** has an open and outward economic orientation, in addition to a stellar growth record (average real annual growth was slightly over 8 percent during the 1988–97 period), making it one of the most attractive overseas locations for corporate America. Privatization measures in the telecoms sector opened the window of opportunity for such U.S. firms as BellSouth and Qualcomm. American energy firms (e.g., Duke Power) were also drawn to Chile's more liberal industry environment, although in some instances, U.S. firms were outbid or outmaneuvered by foreign investors from Europe. Spain, in particular, became one of the largest foreign investors in not only Chile but also all of Latin America in the 1990s.

U.S. investment to **Venezuela** varied tremendously year to year over the 1990s but nevertheless totaled $7.4 billion for the decade. Investment inflows averaged $740 million annually, which stands in sharp contrast to the various years of U.S. disinvestment over the 1980s. U.S. participation in Venezuela's privatization program, combined with a rebound in reinvested earnings, helped raise inflows relative to the prior decade. Such plum sectors as telecommunications, steel, refining, tourism, and banking were opened to foreign investment during the decade. Limits remain in place on investment in the all-important oil sector although the government did liberalize investment activities in certain areas of this industry. The natural gas industry also became more open to foreign investment.

Across the Pacific, **Singapore** and **Hong Kong** remained the top Asian choices of U.S. foreign direct investors in the 1990s, a preference that dates back to the 1970s. Among the developing nations, Singapore ranked as the third most popular destination of U.S. investment last decade, with Hong Kong standing fourth. With some of the highest per-capita incomes in the region, both city-states are important markets unto themselves and attracted market-seeking investment in financial services, telecommunications, and pharmaceuticals in particular. U.S. investment was also motivated in part by each entity's strategic location. For many U.S. companies, Singapore and Hong Kong serve as gateways to other regional markets— Singapore to the rest of Southeast Asia, and Hong Kong to greater China, namely relatively affluent and sophisticated Guangdong Province. In addition to this regional focus, more and more American firms, notably in Singapore, are using Asia's city-states as global procurement centers.

In both locations, the composition of U.S. investment has shifted from labor-intensive, low-tech production to higher-end manufacturing and service operations. Low-end functions have been moved to other sites, while more U.S. investment has gone into higher-valued activities such as research and development, product design, process engineering testing, and market research over the past decade. The bulk of U.S. investment in Singapore was funded locally, or through affiliates. Reinvested earnings were also important to Hong Kong, but rapid growth in mainland China, in particular across the causeway in Guangdong Province, motivated U.S. firms to commit more new equity capital in Hong Kong ($5.6 billion over 1990–98 versus $1.6 billion in Singapore).

Indonesia (ranked 6th) and **China** (9th) were also among the preferred developing countries of U.S. firms. As one of five so-called crisis economies, U.S. investment to Indonesia slumped to just $21 million in 1997, although lost confidence among U.S. investors quickly returned: U.S. foreign investment in Indonesia rose to $360 million in 1998 and then barreled to $2.4 billion in 1999.

Indonesia lifted numerous restrictions on foreign investment in such service activities as distribution and retail operations in 1998. In the same year, the government amended its 1992 Banking Law, paving the way for full foreign ownership of banks. A sizable share of U.S. investment in Indonesia is in the oil and gas sector, where the United States is the leading investor. Specifically, the number one oil producer in the nation in 1998 was Caltex. In the mining sector, U.S. firms Freeport McMoRan and Newmont Mining Company are among the largest foreign investors. Other top U.S. multinationals, including General Electric, General Motors, and Heinz, have significant investment positions in Indonesia.[11]

"Opened" to western investment and influence since 1978, China only recently showed up on the radar screens of U.S. corporations. For instance, from 1980 to 1992, annual U.S. investment flows to China averaged less than $100 million. However, following new efforts at economic reform and Deng Xiaoping's celebrated 1992 trip to south China urging a faster pace of market liberalization, U.S. investment flows jumped to $556 million in 1993. The next year, they doubled, to $1.2 billion. U.S. capital flows to the country averaged $1.1 billion annually over the second half of the 1990s (1995–99), versus an annual average of $386 million the first half. Roughly two-thirds of this investment was directed at the manufacturing sector, principally in industrial machinery and electronic equipment. In the future, the mainland's entry into the World Trade Organization should open the gates to greater U.S. investment in such service activities as telecommunications, financial services, and insurance.

In terms of motivating U.S. investors, the bulk of U.S. investment in China is market seeking, or geared toward the local market, rather than for export, as is commonly assumed. Of total U.S. foreign affiliate sales in China in 1997, roughly 69 percent went to the local market, slightly above the global average of 65.3 percent, while only 11.4 percent represented sales or exports back to the United States, versus the global average of 10.2 percent.

These figures confirm the findings of a survey conducted by the U.S. embassy in Beijing, with assistance from the Gallup Organization, of American investors in China in 1998. The primary reason for investing in China was local market opportunities, according to results of the survey. Just 10 percent of the American companies polled utilized China as an export platform. In terms of the bottom line, 52 percent of the respondents reported that they had achieved a positive return on their initial investment, while 57 percent reported that they were currently earning a profit. On the downside, the lack of legal transparency, high cost of doing business, laborious customs procedures, and foreign exchange risks and regulations were cited as among the most frustrating aspects of investing in China.[12]

The mainland remains one of the most vexing markets in the world for U.S. firms to navigate. China, as characterized by the U.S. embassy in Beijing, is "rich in contradictions for U.S. firms. The world's most populous nation, China covers an area larger than the United States. Yet, the Chinese market is small and concentrated in a few areas along the eastern seaboard. China is one of the world's oldest civilizations . . . yet, the People's Republic is a mere 50 years old, and most of the laws and regulations governing business and trade have been written in the past 20 years. China is a communist country . . . yet, over the past 20 years, China has moved from a planned to a market economy and is now in many ways more capitalist than communist."[13] Working with and through these contradictions is the primary challenge for U.S. firms in the years ahead.

South Korea, a reluctant convert to foreign direct investment, rounds out the top 10 list. Like other countries in the region, South Korea capitulated to greater economic reforms, including investment liberalization, in the wake of the Asian financial crisis. To a degree, the nation did not have much choice—the $58 billion IMF package negotiated during the depths of the crisis was conditioned on market-opening measures in such sectors as financial services, telecommunications, and energy. President Kim Dae-Jung, elected in December 1997, has been another catalyst for reform, which, despite fierce local opposition, has continued to push ahead with market-opening initiatives. Gradually, indigenous hostility toward foreign direct investment in general and foreign mergers and acquisitions in particular has given way to a more positive attitude toward greater foreign participation in South Korea.

Specifically, foreign companies in the telecommunications sector can now own up to 49 percent of a Korean basic telecom services company. In the oil-refining and retail gas sectors, unlimited foreign investment is allowed. Beginning in May 1998, the Korean stock market was opened to foreign investors. Real estate restrictions have been removed as well. In July 1999, restrictions were still in place on 21 industrial sectors, compared to constraints on more than 120 industries in 1996, or prior to the great Asian finanical crisis. For their part, U.S. firms responded by investing a record $1.2 billion in South Korea in 1999, more than the total U.S. investment for the entire first half of the decade.[14]

Notable Absentees from the Top 10 List

One specific developing nation missing from the top 10 table is **Taiwan**, among the largest and most dynamic developing economies in Asia and the world. Taiwan represents significant export markets for U.S. goods with U.S. exports to Taiwan totaling $20.4 billion in 1997, twice the value of exports to Italy and greater than the total U.S. exports to France.

That does not mean, however, that Taiwan is a larger market for U.S. goods than either France or Italy. In fact, the opposite is true, as Figure 9.5 makes clear. U.S. global engagement with Taiwan is "shallow" and is anchored in trade, not foreign investment and affiliate sales. The opposite is true of France and Italy, where foreign affiliate sales in excess of exports illustrate a deeper form of U.S. global engagement. Figure 9.5

Figure 9.5

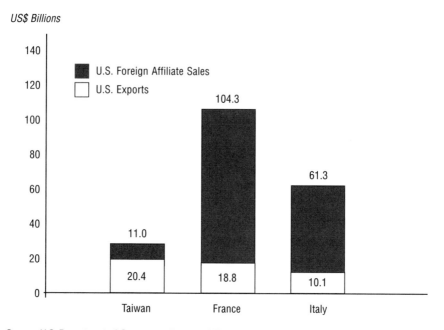

U.S. Global Engagement: U.S. Exports Versus U.S. Foreign Affiliate Sales, 1997

Source: U.S. Department of Commerce, Bureau of Economic Analysis.

then, not only illustrates the difference in total U.S. sales to Taiwan relative to France and Italy but also corroborates how misleading U.S. exports can be when viewed in isolation.

U.S. investment in Taiwan has trailed that in the rest of Asia over the past decade; traditionally, the role of foreign direct investment has been secondary to indigenous industrial development, with government-led strategies directed more toward the development of local capabilities. However, there is no mistaking the fact that Taiwan has become more amenable to foreign participation since the Asian currency crisis of mid-1997. The government launched structural-reform efforts that have led to greater foreign participation in such sectors as finance, telecommunications, energy, real estate, and transportation, to name a few. In addition, investment and industry reform related to Taiwan's accession to the World Trade Organization has created a more favorable investment backdrop for U.S. firms.

Also absent from the elite list of preferred destinations are the countries of central Europe, including **Russia**. Despite all of the excitement surrounding the end of the cold war era and country-specific efforts in attracting and promoting greater foreign participation, U.S foreign direct investment in the region over the 1990s—roughly $10 billion—was less than total U.S. investment in Belgium during the same period. Hungary, one of the early reformers in the region, was the preferred location of U.S. transnationals, attracting roughly $2.5 billion over the decade. Poland, also an early reformer and home to one of the largest markets in the region, ranked second, with U.S. investment inflows nearly $2 billion in the 1990s. Both countries have been leaders in establishing a solid legal framework that protects property rights and investments, and allows for the repatriation abroad of profits.

Depressed economic growth, corruption, political instability, currency volatility, a rickety legal framework—all of these problem areas and others largely kept U.S. firms at bay from Russia in the last decade. In fact, total U.S. investment in Russia ($1.5 billion) was less than total investment in Peru in the same period, testimony that to many U.S. firms, the many risks surrounding Russia's investment climate outweighed the potential rewards (copious natural resources, a large consumer market) over the 1990s. All tallied, preliminary estimates suggest that central Europe and Russia attracted less than 1.5 percent of total U.S. investment outflows in the 1990s, a rather paltry amount in light of the historic opening and outward thrust of the former Soviet Union and its empire.

Finally, one of the most populous nations in the world, **India**, is also absent from the top 10 list. India's near decade of economic reform in the 1990s did not yield much in the way of U.S. foreign direct investment, with U.S. investment totaling just $1 billion over 1990–99, representing only 0.4 percent of total investment to the developing nations. Dampening U.S. enthusiasm for one of the largest markets in the world are India's uncertain politics, overburdened infrastructure, and distrust of foreign ownership. U.S. sanctions on India following the nation's nuclear testing in 1998 have also complicated matters for American investors. Adding fuel to the fire in the late 1990s, the entire Indian subcontinent went on nuclear alert following Pakistan's own nuclear testing, which did little to stimulate investor confidence in South Asia as a whole.

The nuclear controversy aside, future U.S. investment flows to India may look different from the past as a result of the nation's progress in deregulating and opening various sectors of the economy (electricity generation, financial services, telecommunications) to foreign participation. As part of the nation's wide-reaching economic-reform movement begun in 1991, investment proposals have been simplified, exchange-rate controls have been amended, corporate tax rates have been cut, and the ban against using foreign brands and trademarks has been lifted. These initiatives are just a sampling of India's more hospitable investment climate for global transnationals, and stand in stark contrast to the stifling and restrictive policies prior to 1991. "It's a different ball game altogether," according to AT&T managing director Virat Bhatia, who hopes to successfully position the American telephone giant in India's rapidly expanding telecommunications sector.[15] Over the past decade, companies such as Exxon, Coca-Cola, and IBM, all three of which pulled capital out of India prior to the economic-reform measures announced in 1991, have returned and recommitted capital to the nation. Meanwhile, U.S. technology leaders such as Texas Instruments, Intel, and Microsoft have increased their investment positions in and around the software hub of Bangalore.

In summary, there is no mistaking the fact that the 1990s represented a pronounced period of economic reform for not just India but also other developing nations. In countries as diverse as Chile and China, policies became more uniform, featuring lower trade barriers, greater foreign investment incentives, increased industry deregulation, rising regional integration, more privatization initiatives, and active participation in multilateral agreements. The upshot was a favorable global investment backdrop for U.S. transnationals. But outflows were concentrated, with the top 10 preferred destinations of U.S. firms accounting for nearly 60 percent of total investment outflows to the developing nations.

Meeting the Microchallenges

While all of the macrofactors mentioned made for great headlines and great expectations, numerous microvariables that are often overlooked and discounted have slowed the pace of U.S. transnational penetration in the developing nations. Perhaps the most significant microchallenge that transnationals have faced in entering these newly opened economies is finding real markets and consumers for their products and services. That may sound disjointed, since roughly 85 percent of the world's 6 billion humans reside in the developing nations. There should be roughly 5 billion people salivating over a Coke, a hamburger from McDonald's, an automobile from General Motors, or a computer from Dell, right? Perhaps not.

As successful U.S. firms have quickly come to realize, the consumer markets of the developing nations are a great deal smaller than general population figures suggest. In many countries, the real markets are made up of purchases by government enterprises, foreign transnationals, and expatriate workers, not the greater populace. Indigenous consumer purchases make up only a small percentage of the total and are typically concentrated in urban areas. In China, for instance, there is no national market, but instead various regional markets divided by buying patterns, demographics, infrastructure, and political climate. Regional characteristics also define the large markets of India and Brazil. In such locations as Thailand or Chile, national spending power and national income is concentrated in just one city—Bangkok in the case of Thailand, and Santiago in Chile. The chief consumer markets of Russia are concentrated in Moscow and Saint Petersburg.

Many developing nations in Asia are more rural than urban, making it tough for U.S. companies to reach and penetrate markets. Extra effort is required and is exemplified by Colgate-Palmolive's strategy of sending promotional vans equipped with videos, educational materials, and samples into rural areas of India. The company even holds dental clinics in vans or on trains, and has had to package various products in several languages. The ultimate goal for the company is to build brand and product awareness among consumers who typically use charcoal or salt to clean their teeth instead of toothbrushes.

In this respect, advertising is key, yet many firms have found, to their dismay that the most powerful medium for selling is their greatest liability. In Shanghai, for instance, Pepsi watched its bestselling soft drink, 7-Up, founder until the company realized that in the local dialect, the product name means "death through drinking." The Marlboro man is almost synonymous with Philip Morris, but in Hong Kong, local adjustments were required because the cowboy reminded locals of a coolie. And of course the story of initial dismal sales in Latin America of the Chevy Nova, with the Spanish translation "doesn't go," is a legend in the annals of international consumer marketing.

Consumer affordability is another hitch for many U.S. firms hoping to sell their goods in the developing nations. In many parts of the world, disposable diapers are still considered a luxury, as are foreign cigarettes and beverages, and eating at McDonald's is reserved for special occasions. Often, premium brands come with a corresponding price beyond the reach of the mass market. Purchasing an automobile remains a dream for many consumers. In addition, while global consumption patterns are converging, firms that specialize and customize their products for the local market are more apt to succeed than firms that do not. Demand, in other words, can be more heterogeneous than homogeneous. That means that in India, Ford Motor's Ikon, the first passenger car designed with the Indian consumer in mind, was built with extra legroom in the back, since many Indian car owners use chauffeurs. The cars also come equipped with an extra-powerful air conditioner and an extra backseat vent to counter the sweltering heat of the subcontinent.

Another microchallenge for U.S. investors lies with overtaxed and underdeveloped infrastructures of the developing nations, which in some cases can prevent a company from leveraging its ownership advantages abroad. For instance, overnight or express service, in addition to worldwide electronic tracking capabilities, represent the core competencies of U.S. package delivery company Federal Express. However, in China and other parts of Asia, making prompt, scheduled deliveries is difficult due to the poor state of the infrastructure. That is one reason why Federal Express's business in China is pretty much confined to the major cities.

Dell, the U.S. computer manufacturer, has high hopes for the Brazilian market and even plans to export computers and accessories from its Brazilian hub. However, managing a tightly controlled logistics chain, selling directly, and ordering on-line, all relatively simple functions in the United States and central to Dell's operating success, may prove to be far more difficult in Brazil and other developing nations. In particular, online purchases of Dell computers as well as other goods will not become a profitable proposition in Brazil or other developing countries until the cost of both owning a computer and logging on to the Internet declines.

The good news is that both costs are coming down in the developing nations, but the rate is just not fast enough for eager U.S. firms.

Intense competition and excess capacity pose yet another challenge to transnationals. In various markets around the world, firms have sometimes overestimated demand (the number of actual consumers), while underestimating supply (local and foreign competition). Remarking on the market dynamics of Brazil, Jean-Nicolas Ludwig of Ford Motor told the *Wall Street Journal*: "What we have learned is that Brazil has really become an open, competitive market. It used to be that there was more demand than supply. Now it's the reverse."[16] Brazil and China are two of the largest automobile markets in the developing nations, but that does not ensure profitable foreign ventures, since virtually every major automobile manufacturer in the world has streamed into both countries, creating a glut of supply.

The fierce competition is not restricted to autos. Technology product and service providers are facing selling pressures in the major developing markets as well. In Brazil, America Online is in intense competition with local favorite Universo Online International (UOL), the largest Internet service provider and portal in Brazil. In China, Microsoft faces serious competition from local Chinese software producers, while in computer hardware, IBM, Compaq, and Dell, to name just a few U.S. brands, are going head-to-head with Legend Corporation, a company barely recognized in the United States but a household name in China. "We plan to be among the top 10 PC manufacturers in the world by 2000," Yang Yuanqing, general manager of Legend Computer Systems, told *Business Week* in 1998.[17] By the end of the 1990s, Legend had surpassed IBM and others as the leading market supplier of computers in China.

Meanwhile, consumer product firms such as Coca-Cola and RJR Nabisco have also found indigenous brands to be stalwart competitors, forcing the duo, and other transnationals like them, to de-emphasize their global brands in favor of acquiring or establishing local brands. In India, therefore, Coca-Cola's success does not derive from the "real thing," but from Thumbs Up, the firm's bestselling indigenous product. In Russia, RJR Nabisco has had more success marketing and selling the local brand, Peter I, than either of the global brands Winston or Camel.[18]

In addition, Procter and Gamble confronts intense indigenous competition in Brazil from Natura, a direct-sales cosmetics company voted one of Brazil's most admired companies. And in the Philippines, and other locations in Asia, McDonald's faces a formidable competitor in fast-food chain Jollibee.

These few examples embody an often overlooked facet of U.S. global engagement with the developing nations: local competition is fierce in most sectors, notwithstanding the size, ownership advantages, distribution capabilities, brand awareness, and capital strengths of most U.S. firms. As underdeveloped and untapped as many markets may seem, offering the prospect of almost limitless growth for many global leaders, they are nevertheless hotly contested by domestic producers. This underscores the need for many U.S. firms to go beyond trade and serve these markets through foreign investments and affiliates. In addition, U.S. transnationals confront an equal if not more potent competitive threat in the form of transnationals from Europe and Japan.

Regional Spheres of Influence

The rivalry among U.S. firms and their counterparts in Europe and Japan is not confined to the Triad, or to each other's home market. Rather, the rivalry has extended to the fourth global growth pole of the world economy—the developing nations. Eastman Kodak's global battle with Fuji Films, for example, is being played out not only in the United States and Japan, the respective home markets of each company, but also in China, where only 15 percent of households own a camera, versus more than 90 percent ownership in both the United States and Japan.[19]

In Latin America, Wal-Mart is vying against French retail giant Carrefour, with the latter holding a decided edge in Brazil, Latin America's largest market. In other parts of the developing world, it is Boeing against the European consortium Airbus; Procter & Gamble against Unilever (Dutch-Anglo); or Heineken (Dutch) and Fosters (Australia) against American brand Pabst Blue Ribbon. It is Citigroup versus Commerzbank of Germany in Poland. Or Ford Motor competing against Japan's Suzuki Motor in India. In the fastest growing market in the world for toilets, China, it is American Standard of the United States versus Toto of Japan.

U.S. foreign investment in the developing nations, in short, is motivated by more than just traditional variables such as economic growth, market size, labor costs, and macroeconomic reform. Global competition is another important motivator. Companies such as Ford Motor, United Technologies, and IBM, can little afford to allow such markets as Mexico, India, and Russia to go uncontested. New consumers, new resources, and new opportunities to expand and leverage global production networks are at stake, all of which can determine the long-term success of one transnational versus another. Hence the intensifying battle among transnationals for the markets of the developing nations. Too important to be waged through trade alone, this battle is being fought increasingly through foreign direct investment.

On a regional basis, American investment interests are most dominate in Latin America, while in developing Asia and central Europe, the U.S. maintains significant footholds in several strategic markets.

Think of Latin America as America's sphere of influence, with expanding trade and investment ties binding the markets of the region closer together. However, the continued dominance of the United States is far from assured. European investors, in particular Spanish firms, aggressively expanded their investment stake in Latin America in the second half of the 1990s, in some cases becoming the top foreign investors in such sectors as energy, telecommunications, and financial services. Acknowledging the incursion by European firms into America's turf and the complacency on the part of the United States, the *Wall Street Journal* headlined a 1997 article "In Backyard of the U.S., Europe Gains Ground in Trade, Diplomacy."[20] The Spanish presence became so great at the end of 1999 that many in the region began to talk of the "reconquest."[21]

Using its collective might, the European Union has concluded a free-trade agreement with Mexico. Europe hopes for the same in South America, where rising European investment may culminate in a far-reaching free-trade deal between the European Union and Mercosur, South America's largest regional market. The deal, no doubt, would challenge the commercial supremacy of corporate America in the western hemisphere. "Latin America is a natural market for BellSouth. It's in our backyard," stated Robert Myer, the company's director of Business Development for Latin America.[22] But for BellSouth and plenty of other U.S. companies, the level of competition in America's backyard is rapidly being elevated.

In Asia, the U.S. investment presence is imposing, although U.S. firms confront stiff competition from their European and Japanese counterparts in nearly every country. In China, for instance, General Motors and Ford Motor face a competitive challenge from Volkswagen of Germany, which enjoys a 65 percent market share. Meanwhile, the French telecommunications equipment manufacturer Alcatel dominates the market in telephone switching equipment. Both Volkswagen and Alcatel were early entrants in China and have a leg up on their American competition.

Japanese manufacturers represent another tough competitive challenge in Asia, with Japan ranked among the top foreign investors in nearly every country in the region. So dominant was Japan's investment presence in Southeast Asia in the second half of the 1980s and into the 1990s, that many spoke of the "keiretsu-ization" of Asia at various points during the decade. Despite its own economic woes, Japan remains a dominant investor in Asia, although the Asian crisis and the subsequent collapse in asset prices triggered a spike in foreign investment from both the United States and Europe.

U.S. investment in central and eastern Europe is also quite prominent, but just as Japan ranks among the most dominant regional foreign investor in Asia, so German firms and other European companies are among the most prevalent foreign investors in central Europe, their own backyard. Of the region's three most promising markets—Hungary, Poland, and the Czech Republic—Germany was the number one investor in two (Hungary and the Czech Republic), with the Netherlands ranked number one in Poland in 1998. Based on total inward foreign investment stock, Germany was the single largest investor in the region at the end of the 1990s, according to figures from the United Nations.[23]

Looking forward, the competitive backdrop for U.S. firms operating in central Europe is not expected to become any easier if the European Union ultimately allows various nations of central Europe (the Czech Republic, Cyprus, Estonia, Hungary, Poland, and Slovenia, in addition to Bulgaria, Latvia, Lithuania, Malta, Romania and Slovakia) to join the European Union. Accession would only pull eastern Europe further into the sphere of influence of western Europe and potentially tilt the competitive balance away from U.S. corporate interests.

Overall, regionalization has figured heavily in investment flows to the developing nations, with the majority of inflows originating from a single nation, usually in the same or a proximate geographical region. This framework has created clusters or spheres of influence, with U.S. commercial interests superior in Latin America, Europe entrenched in many parts of eastern and central Europe, and Japan strategically positioned in various Asian states. Each sphere, however, is being hotly contested. European firms are encroaching on U.S. interests in Latin America. U.S. and

European firms are muscling their way into attractive markets in Asia. And U.S. and Japanese companies are taking aim at central Europe. Up for grabs are the emerging markets of Africa. So too is central Asia, where the interests of geostrategic politics and oil meet, in addition to such promising individual markets as Turkey, Israel, Saudi Arabia, and Egypt to name just four. Following a decade of trade and investment reform in the developing nations, the campaign is just starting and promises to become more intense in the years ahead.

Trade Versus Investment: Taking Stock of U.S. Global Engagement with the Developing Nations

While foreign affiliate sales are the primary means by which U.S. companies deliver goods to the developed nations, the same cannot be said of the developing nations, where the modes of delivery (trade or exports versus investment or affiliate sales) are mixed. That is clear from Figure 9.6, which portrays the degree of U.S. global engagement with 15 developing nations.

This table is similar to the presentation in Figure 4.5. (Country data on central Europe were not available.) The amounts in Column 1 are total U.S. exports of goods in 1997, the most common benchmark of global engagement. Column 2 presents exports to U.S. foreign affiliates in the same year, which are subtracted from Column 1 to determine the true level of business between U.S. firms and *foreign* customers (Column 3). Column 3 yields some interesting results: One, Mexico remains the largest U.S. export market among the developing nations, even after some $22 billion in exports to affiliates is excluded from total exports. Two, after subtracting exports to affiliates, U.S. exports to Hong Kong were just one-third the original total in 1997 ($5.2 billion versus $15.1 billion), highlighting the intrafirm nature of U.S. exports to Hong Kong. And three, after adjusting for affiliate trade, of which there was little, South Korea and Taiwan retained their status as the largest export markets in Asia for U.S. goods in 1997.

Column 4, sales of goods by U.S. foreign affiliates to foreign customers, and Column 5, the ratio of affiliate sales to exports, reveal even more compelling aspects of U.S. global engagement with the developing nations.

Figure 9.6

U.S. Global Engagement with the Developing Nations

(U.S. Exports and Affiliate Sales in Goods, US$ Billions, 1997)

Country	1 Goods Exports	2 Exports to Affiliates	3 Total Exports (1 - 2)	4 Local Affiliate Sales to Unaffiliated Persons	5 Affiliates Sales/Exports (%)
Mexico[a]	71.4	22.1	49.3	25.4	0.5
Brazil	15.9	4.3	11.7	44.8	3.8
Venezuela[a]	6.6	1.6	5.0	6.8	1.4
Chile	4.4	0.6	3.7	4.6	1.2
Argentina[a]	5.8	1.5	4.4	14.1	3.2
China	12.9	1.7	11.1	7.2	0.6
Hong Kong	15.1	10.0	5.2	21.8	4.2
Singapore	17.7	7.9	9.8	22.0	2.3
South Korea	25.0	2.2	22.9	6.9	0.3
Taiwan	20.4	2.3	18.0	7.3	0.4
Malaysia[a]	10.8	2.8	8.0	8.0	1.0
Philippines	7.4	1.3	6.1	4.4	0.7
Thailand	7.3	1.5	5.9	8.1	1.4
Indonesia[a]	4.5	0.4	4.1	4.2	1.0
India	3.6	0.2	3.4	2.0	0.6

[a]Total affiliate sales to unaffiliated persons.

Source: U.S. Department of Commerce, Bureau of Economic Analysis.

Note, as laid out in Chapter 4, that U.S. engagement with Brazil is largely defined by affiliate sales ($45 billion in 1997) while that with Mexico is pretty much exports. Based just on exports, Mexico is the most important developing market in the world for U.S. goods; however, measured by affiliate sales, Brazil is clearly the top market. Affiliate sales in Brazil were nearly four times greater in 1997 than U.S. exports, significantly above the global average. In Mexico, the ratio of affiliate sales to exports was 0.5:1 ($25.4 billion versus $49.3 billion), a rather "shallow" level of integration considering the heightening in U.S. foreign direct investment in Mexico over the past decade. However, keep in mind that nearly half of U.S. affiliate sales in Mexico are destined for the United States and third markets, and are not included in the sales figure in Column 4.

U.S. global engagement with Argentina is similar to the situation with Brazil in that affiliate sales in Argentina, $14.1 billion in 1997, were more than three times larger than exports (just $4.4 billion) in the same year. By contrast, U.S. engagement with the two largest markets in the world—China and India—is relatively shallow, hinging more on trade than investment. Note that total U.S. merchandise exports to China and Brazil (Column 1) were roughly equal in 1997 and identical once adjusted for affiliate trade (Column 3). However, of the two markets, and based on affiliate sales, there is no mistaking Brazil's overriding importance to the commercial interests of the United States versus America's interests in China. Based on affiliate sales, Argentina is a much larger market than China as well. Meanwhile, with U.S. foreign affiliate sales of just $2 billion in 1997, India represents one of the largest untapped markets in the world for U.S. firms. Finally, America's relatively shallow investment linkages with developing Asia as a whole are made clear by the fact that in 5 of 10 Asian markets listed (China, South Korea, Taiwan, the Philipines, and India), the ratio of affiliate sales to exports was less than 1. Hong Kong and Singapore, where U.S. investment roots are deeper, were notable exceptions.

In the end, there is a lack of uniformity in how U.S. companies deliver goods to the developing nations. Engagement in many vital markets still centers on trade, while in other nations, it is investment and foreign affiliate sales that matter most. In some cases, notably in many large markets, the primary modes of delivery (trade and investment) remain either independent or substitutes for each other. Yet, as barriers to entry fall, as trade and investment reform takes hold, as greater regional cohesion materializes in such places as South America and Southeast Asia, as new market opportunities arise, and as U.S. transnationals strive to integrate more developing nations into their global production networks, trade and investment are likely to become more intertwined, following the pattern established long ago in the developed nations.

As stated at the outset, U.S. global engagement with the developing nations remains an important work in progress. A primary challenge for many American firms in the decade ahead is to become more integrated—through trade and foreign investment—with the fourth growth pole of the world economy.

EPILOGUE

THIS STUDY PRESENTS a different framework by which to view and analyze how U.S. firms actually compete in the world economy. The aim was
to isolate and explore foreign direct investment as the primary means of
U.S. global engagement, and to make the case that global competition
goes well beyond the cross-border exchange of goods, or trade. As the evidence in the preceding pages makes all too clear, U.S. exports and imports
are neither representative of America's global linkages nor indicative of
how U.S. firms compete at home and abroad. In other words, there is a
great deal of global commerce missing from the U.S. trade figures. Global
engagement is more about foreign direct investment than trade.

Yet American policymakers and investors alike still view global competition through the lens of trade and through the theoretical framework
established some 200 years ago by Adam Smith and David Ricardo. The
common assumption from this vantage point is that exports are good,
imports are bad. A trade deficit is a sign of national weakness, a flash
point that something is amiss with the industrial underpins of the economy relative to the rest of the world. Against an otherwise stellar economic backdrop, America's perennial trade deficit—a record $265 billion
in 1999—is often singled out as the principal soft spot in the world's most
dynamic economy.

Explanations for the persistent U.S. trade deficit run the gamut.
America buys more from the world than it sells in return because America's global competitiveness is in decline. Others point to unfair trade practices and market restrictions overseas as the root cause of the trade deficit.

Another explanation lies with shifts in exchange rates, or the price competitiveness of U.S. goods and services. Whatever the validity of these arguments, more important and pertinent to the dialogue on trade is what is missing from the ongoing discussion.

Absent from the debate is the fact that given a choice, U.S. firms prefer to sell goods and compete abroad via foreign affiliates (foreign investment) as opposed to exports (trade). In developed and developing nations alike, being an "insider" is critical to the long-term success of any company, whether it's IBM penetrating a market in Asia or a Japanese manufacturing hoping to capture a slice of the U.S. market. Also absent from the debate is an awareness of the linkages of U.S. trade on the one hand and U.S. foreign investment on the other, or the fact that a significant share of U.S. trade takes place within firms. Finally, the debate is missing the recognition that imports are not the sole means by which foreign companies sell goods in the United States; indeed, they are secondary to the sales of foreign-owned affiliates operating in the United States. Foreign direct investment, in other words, cuts both ways.

All three examples represent just the tip of the iceberg in terms of what is missing from the debate on U.S. global competitiveness. The trade-oriented mentality of U.S. policymakers and the general public at large is fraught with danger in that it ignores the fundamental basis of global competition. Trade alone as a scorecard of international competitiveness is not enough in a world in which more than 23,000 U.S. foreign affiliates are scattered around the world. It is the extraterritorial reach of corporate America, whose roots date back to the late 19th century, that is the hallmark of U.S. global engagement and the single most important variable underwriting America's global strength. Similarly, the level of foreign competition in the United States has become even more intense as European, Japanese, and other firms complement their trade-led strategies with investment-led initiatives. As a result, a new and different playing field has emerged over the past few decades.

Does that mean the U.S. trade imbalance and the current account deficit—the broader measure of America's global engagement—are nothing more than dangerous obsessions? The answer is unequivocally "no." The current account deficit, to be sure, represents the net financing needs of the United States, which, to say the least, are ominous. It is not, however, an indicator of an economy in duress or lacking the competitive wherewithal to compete. Consider prostrate Japan over most of the 1990s, with its massive current account surplus, versus the dynamic U.S. economy burdened with a mirroring current account deficit.

One of the gravest risks on the U.S. trade front lies with equating the trade deficit and massive current account deficit to a loss of global competitiveness or to unfair trade practices, circumstances that in turn could elicit a protectionist mood or backlash from U.S. policymakers, which in turn triggers similar policy initiatives around the globe. At risk is not only the global trading system. Also exposed are the thousands of U.S. foreign affiliates and the billions of dollars invested overseas by U.S. firms over the past decades. Before it is to late, then, to avoid stumbling into policy errors, it is time to rethink and recalibrate how countries exchange goods and services with each other. A new scorecard is needed since the current one—the trade balance—offers a dangerously inaccurate picture of U.S. global engagement.

Also needed is a better understanding of U.S. foreign direct investment flows. The image of U.S. foreign direct investment remains frozen in time. The common assumption is that cost variables (i.e., wages) dictate where U.S. firms decide to invest abroad. By extension, then, American firms prefer to invest in low-wage nations at the expense of American workers, and often use these cheap production platforms to export goods back to the United States. Reality, as analyzed in the preceding chapters, is quite different.

Shedding a different light on U.S. trade and investment is the primary objective of this study. It is an attempt to reshape the understanding of how U.S. firms actually compete in the world economy. It became all too evident during the Asian crisis that many people in the United States were oblivious to U.S. trade linkages on the one hand and U.S. foreign investment linkages on the other, or the differences between the underlying modes of global engagement. The Asian crisis, in other words, served as my own personal wake-up call and was the catalyst for this book.

There is no better time to rethink U.S. global engagement given the reemergence of globalization in the 1990s and the attendant surge in both U.S. foreign direct investment outflows and inflows. At mid-year 2000, the global boom in foreign direct investment showed little signs of a slowdown. Global integration continued unabated, with the United States center stage.

From present trends, foreign investment as the primary means of U.S. global engagement is likely to push trade further into the background. That is encouraging in that foreign direct investment is a catalyst for change, for growth, for integration. Just as U.S. investment outflows have helped jump-start economic growth and development in various parts of the world, so have foreign investment inflows helped revitalized various parts of the U.S. economy over the past two decades. The downside is that the lines of global competition are becoming increasingly blurred. The spread of global production networks by the world's leading transnationals have greatly complicated global commerce. Confusion over how U.S. firms actually compete in the world markets is only likely to mount against this backdrop, raising the risk of policy mistakes or a backlash against transnationals in general.

As we enter the 21st century, then, a strategic priority for America is to better grasp the true meaning of U.S. global engagement. Corporate America has never been more fit to compete on a global basis, although you would never know it looking at the mountainous U.S. trade deficit. The disconnect lies with the way we keep score of global competition. But isn't it time to update Adam Smith–era statistics?

NOTES

Chapter 1

1. Angus Maddison, *The World Economy in the 20th Century* (Organization for Economic Cooperation and Development, 1989).

2. "Globalization in a Historical Perspective," *World Economic Outlook*, May 1997, (International Monetary Fund): 112–16.

3. *World Investment Report 1994: Transnational Corporations, Employment, and the Workplace* (New York/Geneva: United Nations Publications), 120.

4. Ibid., 121.

5. Ibid.

6. Maddison.

7. Peter Dickens, *Global Shift: The Internationalization of Economic Activity*, 2nd ed. (Guilford Press, 1992), 16.

8. Ibid.

9. See various editions of the semiannual *World Economic Outlook*, published by the International Monetary Fund.

10. The best source of these data is the United Nations, which publishes an annual report on global foreign direct investment flows.

11. *World Investment Report 1999: Foreign Direct Investment and the Challenge of Development* (New York/Geneva: United Nations Publications), 9.

12. *Globalization of Industry: Overview and Sector Reports* (Organization for Economic Cooperation and Development, 1996), 20–21.

13. Daniel Yergin and Joseph Stanislaw, *The Commanding Heights: The Battle Between Government and the Marketplace That Is Remaking the Modern World* (New York: Simon & Schuster, 1998), 13.

Chapter 2

1. John Dunning, *Multinational Enterprises and the Global Economy* (Wokingham, England: Addison-Wesley, 1993), 58.

2. Ibid.

3. Overview to *World Investment Report 1998: Trends and Determinants* (New York/Geneva: United Nations Publications).

4. Ibid., 114.

5. Ibid., overview section.

6. Stephen H. Hymer, 1960, "The International Operations of National Firms: A Study of Direct Foreign Investment," doctoral dissertation, Massachusetts Institute of Technology (Cambridge, Mass.: M.I.T. Press, 1976).

7. Raymond Vernon was a leading U.S. scholar on multinationals and published such seminal works as *Sovereignty at Bay* (1971), *Storm over the Multinationals* (1977), *Beyond Globalism* (1989), and *In the Hurricane's Eye* (1998). The Harvard scholar has also published numerous articles; his work stands at the top of the list as required reading.

8. Dunning, *Multinational Enterprises*; and "Location and the Multinational Enterprise: A Neglected Factor?" *Journal of International Business Studies*, 1st quarter, 1998.

9. Clay Harris, "International Mergers and Acquisitions: On Course to Topple the Record," *Financial Times*, September 22, 1999.

10. *World Investment Report 1999: Foreign Direct Investment and the Challenge of Development* (New York/Geneva: United Nations Publications), 98.

11. Kenichi Ohmae, *The Borderless World: Power and Strategy in the Interlinked World* (HarperBusiness, 1990), 114.

12. *World Investment Report 1998*, 23.

13. For more on this subject see Debra Sparks, "Partners: Special Report," *Business Week*, October 25, 1999: 106; and Stefan Wagsty, "When Even a Rival Can Be a Best Friend," *Financial Times*, October 22, 1997: 12.

14. Gary Hamel and C. K. Prahalad, *Global Strategies: Insights from the World's Leading Thinkers* (Harvard Business Review Book, 1994), 17.

15. Edward M. Graham, "Foreign Direct Investment in the World Economy," *International Monetary Fund, Staff Studies for the World Economic Outlook*, September 1995, 130.

16. For more on this subject see Edward M. Graham, *On the Relationship Among Direct Investment and International Trade in the Manufacturing Sector: Empirical Results for the United States and Japan* (Washington, D.C.: Institute for International Economics, April 8, 1997).

17. *World Investment Report 1996: Investment, Trade, and International Policy Arrangements* (New York/Geneva: United Nations Publications), 79.

Chapter 3

1. Eric R. Peterson, "Surrendering to the Markets," *Washington Quarterly*, autumn 1995.

2. Mira Wilkens, *The Emergence of Multinational Enterprises: American Business Abroad from the Colonial Era to 1914* (Cambridge, Mass.: Harvard University Press, 1970).

3. *World Investment Report 1994: Transnational Corporations, Employment, and the Workplace* (New York/Geneva: United Nations Publications), 137.

4. Ibid., 138.

5. For more on favorable returns of multinationals see "Everybody's Favorite Monsters: A Survey of Multinationals," *The Economist*, March 27, 1993; and "Big Is Back: A Survey of Multinationals," *The Economist*, June 24, 1995.

6. Christopher A. Bartlett and Sumantra Ghoshal, "What Is a Global Manager?" in *Global Strategies: Insights from the World's Leading Thinkers* (Harvard Business Review Book, 1994), 77.

7. The index of transnationality has been compiled by the United Nations since 1990 and is among the best variables in determining the true global scope of firms.

8. The United Nations is the best source for global foreign direct investment flows. For an excellent summary of the dynamics of global business see the *Financial Times* 10-part series "Mastering Global Business."

9. *World Investment Report 1991: The Triad in Foreign Direct Investment* (New York/Geneva: United Nations Publications), 31.

10. Katharine Campbell, "The Minnows' Fight Against the Sharks," *Financial Times*, October 24, 1997: 12.

11. G. Pierre Goad, "Mexican Wave," *Far Eastern Economic Review*, November 11, 1999: 10.

12. Sharon R. King, "A High-Definition Gambit," *New York Times*, April 1, 1999: C20.

13. For more on Asian and global capital flows see the Institute's outstanding website—www.iif.com.

14. "Leading Multinationals Vote Their Confidence in Asia," United Nations Conference on Trade and Development, May 1998.

15. General Electric annual report, 1998.

16. For more on Brazil's rise as a major recipient of foreign direct investment see *World Investment Report 1998: Trends and Determinants* (New York/Geneva: United Nations Publications), 248.

17. *World Investment Report 1999: Foreign Direct Investment and the Challenge of Development* (New York/Geneva: United Nations Publications), 69.

18. *World Investment Report 1995: Transnational Corporations and Competitiveness* (New York/Geneva: United Nations Publications), 91.

19. Victor Mallet, "The Ravaged Continent," *Financial Times*, December 1, 1999: 16.

20. See Joel Bergsman and Xiaofang, "Foreign Direct Investment in Developing Nations: Progress and Problems," *Finance and Development*, December 1995.

21. Murray Weidenbaum and Samuel Hughes, *The Bamboo Network: How Expatriate Chinese Entrepreneurs Are Creating a New Economic Superpower in Asia* (New York: Free Press, 1996).

22. Ibid., 65.

Chapter 4

1. Figures in this analysis are from the Bureau of Economic Analysis. For more information see the following U.S. Department of Commerce publications—For historical information, "U.S. Business Investments in Foreign Countries: A Supplement to the Survey of Current Business," 1962; and "International Direct Investment: Global Trends and the U.S. Role," 1988 ed. For more current information related to U.S. investment figures see *Survey of Current Business*: "Direct Investment Positions on a Historical-Cost Basis," July 1996, p. 45; "Direct Investment Positions for 1998: Country and Industry Detail," July 1999, p. 48; "U.S. Multinational Companies: Operations in 1997," July 1999, p. 8; "U.S. Multinational Companies: Operations in 1996," September 1998, p. 60; and "Direct Investment Positions for 1997," July 1998, p. 35.

2. Edward Alden, "U.S. Companies Go on Spree in Canada's Bargain Basement," *Financial Times*, July 7, 1999: 5.

3. Data for foreign affiliate sales are sourced from the Bureau of Economic Analysis. One problem with the data is the lag in reporting time, with statistics available only through 1997 in 2000.

Chapter 5

1. Peter Fritsch and Gregrory L. White, "Latin Formula: Even Rivals Concede GM Has Deftly Steered Road to Success in Brazil," *Wall Street Journal*, February 25, 1999: 1.

2. For an excellent overview of the evolution of U.S. multinationals see Louis T. Wells Jr., *Conflict or Indifference: U.S. Multinationals in a World of Regional Trading Blocs* (Organization for Economic Cooperation and Development, 1992).

3. U.S. Department of Commerce, "U.S. Multinational Companies: Operations in 1997," *Survey of Current Business*, July 1999: 22. Additional *Survey of Current Business* articles—"Real Gross Product of U.S. Companies' Majority-Owned Foreign Affiliates in Manufacturing," April 1997, p. 8; and "Operations of U.S. Multinationals: Preliminary Results from the 1994 Benchmark Survey," December 1996, p. 11.

4. U.S. Department of Commerce, "U.S. Intrafirm Trade in Goods," *Survey of Current Business*, February 1997: 23. Also see Marco Bonturi and Kiichiro Fukasaka, "Globalization and Intra-Firm Trade: An Empirical Note," OECD *Economic Studies*, no. 20, spring 1993.

5. Matthew J. Slaughter, *Global Investments, American Returns. Mainstay III: A Report on the Domestic Contributions of American Companies with Global Operations* (Washington, D.C.: Emergency Committee for American Trade, 1998), 2.

6. Ibid.

Chapter 6

1. See U.S. Department of Commerce, "Selected Data on Foreign Direct Investment in the United States, 1950–79," December 1984.

2. Jean-Jacques Servan-Schreiber, *The American Challenge* (New York: Atheneum House, 1968).

3. Edward M. Graham and Paul R. Krugman, *Foreign Direct Investment in the United States*, 3rd ed. (Washington, D.C.: Institute for International Economics, January 1995), 46.

4. Douglas Frantz and Catherine Collins, *Selling Out: How We Are Letting Japan Buy Our Land, Our Industries, Our Financial Institutions, and Our Future* (Chicago: Contemporary Books, 1989), 9.

5. For more on this subject see the following articles from the U.S. Department of Commerce, *Survey of Current Business*—"Foreign Direct Investment in the United States," June 1997, p. 42; "Foreign Direct Investment in the United States," July 1996, p. 102; "Foreign Direct Investment in the United States: Detail for Historical-Cost Basis and Related Capital and Income Flows, 1995," September 1996, p. 69; "Foreign Direct Investment in the United States," June 1998, p. 39; "Foreign Direct Investment in the United States: Preliminary Results from the 1994 Benchmark Survey," August 1999, p. 21; and "Foreign Direct Investment in the United States," June 1999, p. 16.

6. *Financial Times*, September 3, 1999.

7. James K. Jackson, "Foreign Direct Investment in the United States: Setting New Records," *CRS Report for Congress*, March 7, 1997.

8. Gordon Cramb, "Off to New Amsterdam," *Financial Times*, July 21, 1999: 13.

9. Jacob M. Schlesinger and Christina Duff, "As Foreigners Again Gobble Up U.S. Firms, Where's the Outrage?" *Wall Street Journal*, December 15, 1998: 1.

10. Jeremy Grant, "Investment in Roads Reinforces Cement Groups," *Financial Times*, September 7, 1999: 18.

11. Jackson, 9.

12. For a closer examination of employment trends among foreign-owned affiliates in the United States see *Investing in American Jobs*

(Washington, D.C.: Organization for International Investment, November 1999); and *The United States and Europe: Jobs, Investment, and Trade* (Washington, D.C.: European-American Business Council, 1998).

13. Donald H. Dalton and Manuel G. Serapio Jr., "Foreign R&D Facilities in the United States," Douglas P. Woodward and Douglas Nigh, Eds., *Foreign Ownership and the Consequences of Direct Investment in the United States, Beyond Us and Them* (Westport, Conn.: Quorum Books), 163.

14. Gerald F. Seib, "Can We Find U.S. Companies in Global Village?" *Wall Street Journal*, September 30, 1997.

15. See Robert Reich, "Who Is Us?" *Harvard Business Review*, January-February 1990, and "Who Is Them?" *Harvard Business Review*, March-April 1991. Also see Robert Reich, *The Work of Nations: Preparing Ourselves for 21st-Century Capitalism* (Alfred A. Knopf, 1991). For a counterargument to Reich see Laura D'Andrea Tyson, "They Are Not Us: Why American Ownership Still Matters," *American Prospect*, winter 1991: 37–49.

16. Graham and Krugman, 31.

17. Ibid., 4.

Chapter 7

1. For an excellent overview of Japan see "Restoration in Progress: A Survey of Business in Japan," *The Economist*, November 27, 1999.

2. Mira Wilkens, "Japanese Multinationals in the United States: Continuity and Change, 1879–1990," *Business History Review*, December 22, 1990: 3.

3. Ibid., 9.

4. Mira Wilkens, "American-Japanese Direct Foreign Investment, 1930–1952," *Business History Review*, winter 1982: 435.

5. *World Investment Report 1995: Transnational Corporations and Competitiveness* (New York/Geneva: United Nations Publications), 240.

6. Dennis J. Encarnation, *Rivals Beyond Trade: America Versus Japan in Global Competition* (Ithaca, NY: Cornell University Press, 1992), 121–122.

7. For more information on Japanese global investment flows see the various white papers on trade and investment prepared annually by the Japan External Trade Organization.

8. See David E. Weinstein, "Foreign Direct Investment and Keiretsu: Rethinking U.S. and Japanese Policy," working paper no. 122, Columbia Business School, June 1996.

9. Simon Reich, "Intrafirm Trade and USFDI," Douglas P. Woodard and Douglas Nigh, Eds., *Foreign Ownership and the Consequences of Direct Investment in the United States, Beyond Us and Them* (Westport, Conn.: Quorum Books), 119–162.

10. Encarnation, 31.

11. For starters see Andrew D. M. Anderson and Kazuo Noguchi, "An Analysis of the Intra-Firm Sales Activities of Japanese Multinational Enterprises in the United States: 1977 to 1989," *Asia Pacific Journal of Management* 12, no. 1: 69–89.

12. Gillian Tett and Alexandra Nusbaum, "Busting the Broker's Cartel," *Financial Times*, October 1, 1999: 7.

13. Paul Abrahams and Gillian Tett, "The Circle Is Broken," *Financial Times*, November 9, 1999: 18.

14. Paul Abrahams, "Great Asset Now Being Derided as Liability," *Financial Times Survey*, December, 17, 1999: II.

15. Paul Abrahams, "Visions Replace Old Delusions: Foreign Investment in Japan," *Financial Times Survey*, October 19, 1999: I. For more on Japan's rising acceptance of foreign direct investment see "Japan Restructures, Grudgingly," *The Economist*, February 6, 1999, p. 63;

and Henny Sender, "Predator to Prey," *Far Eastern Economic Review*, June 4, 1998, p. 70.

16. Abrahams, "Visions."

17. See Bill Spindle, "Travelers, Nikko Union Is Many Things; Easy Is Not One of Them," *Wall Street Journal*, May 19, 1999: 1.

18. Gillian Tett, "GE Capital Hits $17 Billion Mark in Japanese Deals," *Financial Times*, December 2, 1999: 22.

19. Ibid.

Chapter 8

1. See Carlos A. Primo Braga, "The Impact of the Internationalization of Services on Developing Countries," *Finance and Development*, March 1996.

2. *Global Economic Prospects and the Developing Nations* (Washington, D.C.: World Bank, 1997), 47–48.

3. For an overview of the rising importance of services see Andrew Wyckoff, "The Growing Strength of Services," OECD *Observer*, June 1996.

4. See Carol Gentry, "A Surprisingly Popular Export: Managed Care," *Wall Street Journal*, December 20, 1999: B1.

5. *Financial Times*, June 15, 1999.

6. *Financial Times*, June 23, 1999: 22. Also see Jeremy Kahn, "Wal-Mart Goes Shopping in Europe," *Fortune*, June 7, 1999, p. 105; and Kerry Capell, "Wal-Mart's Not-So-Secret British Weapon," *Business Week*, January 24, 2000, p. 132.

7. G. Pierre Goad, "At Your Service," *Far Eastern Economic Review*, September 2, 1999: 8.

8. Peter Marsh, "At Your Service," *Financial Times*, May 12, 1999: 14.

9. Tim Burt, Nikki Tait, and John Griffiths, "Ford's Full Service," *Financial Times*, August 9, 1999: 11.

10. Matthew J. Slaughter, *Global Investments, American Returns: Mainstay III: A Report on the Domestic Contributions of American Companies with Global Operations* (Washington, D.C.: Emergency Committee for American Trade, 1998), 34–35.

11. For statistical data on U.S. services activities see the following—U.S. International Trade Commission, "Recent Trends in U.S. Services Trade, 1998 Annual Report," publication 105, May 1998; "Manual of Statistics of International Trade in Services," draft, November 5, 1999; European Commission, International Monetary Fund, Organization for Economic Cooperation and Development, United Nations, World Trade Organization; and U.S. Department of Commerce, "U.S. International Transactions in Private Services: A Guide to the Surveys Conducted by the Bureau of Economic Analysis," March 1998.

Chapter 9

1. For historical investment data see *International Direct Investment: Global Trends and the U.S. Role*, 1998 ed. (Washington, D.C.: U.S. Department of Commerce).

2. Kenichi Ohmae, *Triad Power: The Coming Shape of Global Competition* (New York: Free Press, 1985), 121.

3. Ibid., 27.

4. For economic statistics on the developed nations versus the developing nations see various semiannual editions of the International Monetary Fund's *World Economic Outlook*.

5. Richard Tomkins, "Fallen Icons," *Financial Times*, February 1, 2000: 12. On a similar subject related to global brands see Richard Tomkins, "Selling to the Sated," *Financial Times*, March 22, 2000: 12.

6. International Monetary Fund, *Direction of Trade*, various editions.

7. *World Economic Outlook: October 1999* (Washington, D.C.: International Monetary Fund, 1999).

8. See various sources of U.S. foreign direct investments listed under Chapters 4–6.

9. Figures for reinvested earnings are from the Bureau of Economic Analysis.

10. Figures for Brazil and other countries mentioned are from the Bureau of Economic Analysis.

11. Company information was sourced from "Country Commercial Guide, Indonesia," published by the U.S. & Foreign Commercial Service and U.S. Department of State, Washington, D.C., 1998. These reports are prepared by the U.S. embassies in the host nation and are invaluable sources of information for U.S. concerns.

12. For a good article examining the difficulties of doing business in China see Constance L. Hays, "It Seemed So Easy: Sell Shampoo to the Chinese," *New York Times*, October 17, 1999, p. C1. See also Dexter Roberts, "A Hard Sell for Microsoft," *Business Week*, November 1, 1999, p. 60; and Craig S. Smith, "Multinationals Rethink Chinese Joint Ventures," *Wall Street Journal*, October 26, 1999, p. A18.

13. "Country Commercial Guide, China, Fiscal Year 2000," U.S. & Foreign Commercial Service and U.S. Department of State, Washington, D.C., 1999.

14. "Country Commercial Guide, South Korea, Fiscal Year 2000," U.S. & Foreign Commercial Service and U.S. Department of State, Washington, D.C., 1999. For an overview of American investment in Asia see "U.S. Investment in Asia," *Far Eastern Economic Review*, May 9, 1996.

15. Jonathon Karp, "India Again Is Alluring to Foreign Telecoms," *Wall Street Journal*, February 10, 2000: A13.

16. Matt Moffett, "Bruised in Brazil: Ford Slips as Market Booms," *Wall Street Journal*, December 13, 1996: A10.

17. Dexter Roberts, "Is Legend the IBM of China?" *Business Week*, December 21, 1998.

18. For a good article examining the difficulties of doing business in Russia see "It's Tough But We're Staying, Say Companies," *Financial Times*, August 28, 1998, p. 3. For the experience of McDonald's in Russia see Andrew Jack, "McDonald's Relishes Its 10 Years in Russia," *Financial Times*, February 1, 2000. For an article on the troubles of doing business in the developing nations see Jeffrey E. Garten, "Troubles Ahead in Emerging Markets," *Harvard Business Review*, May-June 1997, p. 38.

19. William J. Holstein, "All the Film in China," *U.S. News and World Report*, July 6, 1998: 53; and Craig S. Smith, "Kodak, Fuji Face Off in Neutral Territory: China's Vast Market," *Wall Street Journal*, May 24, 1996: A1.

20. Matt Moffett and Helene Cooper, "In Backyard of the U.S., Europe Gains Ground in Trade, Diplomacy," *Wall Street Journal*, September 18, 1997.

21. Mark Mulligan and Ken Warn, "Return of the Conquistador," *Financial Times*, June 29, 1999: 13; and Ken Warn and Jonathon Wheatley, "Counterattack in Cyberspace," *Financial Times*, March 8, 2000: 20.

22. Teresa Mears, "BellSouth Goes South," *Latin Trade*, July 1997: 24. For other articles related to U.S. firms expanding in Latin America see John Barham, Ken Warn, and Andrea Mandel Campbell, "Online Invaders from a Neighbor to the North," *Financial Times*, November 17, 1999: 12.

23. For more on this subject see *World Investment Report 1999: Foreign Direct Investment and the Challenge of Development* (New York/Geneva: United Nations Publications), 72.

Bibliography

Barber, Benjamin R. 1995. *Jihad Versus McWorld: How Globalization and Tribalism Are Reshaping the World*. New York: Ballantine.

Barnet, Richard J., and John Cavanagh. 1994. *Global Dreams: Imperial Corporations and the New World Order*. New York: Touchstone.

Barnet, Richard J., and Ronald E. Muker. 1974. *Global Reach: The Power of the Multinational Corporations*. New York: Simon and Schuster.

Bartlett, Christopher, and Sumantra Ghoshal. 1989. *Managing Across Borders: The Transnational Solution*. Boston: Harvard Business School Press.

_____. 1998. "Organizing for Worldwide Effectiveness: The Transnational Solution." *California Management Review* 31, no. 1.

Belous, Richard S., and Rebecca S. Hartley, eds. 1990. *The Growth of Regional Trading Blocs in the Global Economy*. Washington, D.C.: National Planning Association.

Boyd, Gavin, and John H. Dunning, eds. 1999. *Structural Change and Cooperation in the Global Economy*. Northhampton, Mass.: Edward Elgar Publishing.

Bryan, Lowell, Jane Fraser, Jeremy Oppenheim, and Wilhelm Rall. 1999. *Race for the World*. Boston: Harvard Business School Press.

Buckley, Peter J., and Mark C. Casson. 1976. *The Future of the Multinational Enterprise.* London: Macmillan.

Cantwell, John. 1989. *Technological Innovation and Multinational Corporations.* Oxford: Basil Blackwell.

Caves, Richard E. 1982. *Multinational Enterprise and Economic Analysis.* Cambridge: Cambridge University Press.

Chimerine, Lawrence, Andrew Z. Szamosszegi, and Clyde V. Prestowitz Jr. 1995. *Multinational Corporations and the U.S. Economy.* Washington, D.C.: Economic Strategy Institute.

Dickens, Peter. 1992. *Global Shift: The Internationalization of Economic Activity.* 2nd ed. New York: Guilford Press.

Drucker, Peter F. 1986. "The Changed World Economy." *Foreign Affairs* 64: 768–91.

_____. 1986. "The Changed World Economy." *McKinsey Quarterly,* autumn.

Dunning, John H. 1993. *Multinational Enterprises and the Global Economy.* Wokingham, England: Addison-Wesley.

_____, ed. 1998. *Globalization, Trade, and Foreign Direct Investment.* Kidlington, Oxford: Elsevier Science.

Dunning, John H., and Khalil A. Hamdani, eds. 1997. *The New Globalism and Developing Countries.* New York: United Nations Press.

Encarnation, Dennis J. 1992. *Rivals Beyond Trade: American Versus Japan in Global Competition.* Ithaca, N.Y.: Cornell University Press.

Falvey, Rodney E. 1981. "Commercial Policy and Intra-Industry Trade." *Journal of International Economics* 11: 495–511.

Franko, Larry G. 1976. *The European Multinationals: A Renewed Challenge to American and British Big Business.* Stamford, Conn.: Greylock.

Glickman, Norman J., and Douglas P. Woodward. 1989. *The New Competitors: How Foreign Investors Are Changing the U.S. Economy.* New York: Basic Books.

Graham, Edward M. 1996. *Global Corporations and National Governments.* Washington, D.C.: Institute for International Economics.

Graham, Edward M., and Paul R. Krugman. 1995. *Foreign Direct Investment in the United States.* 3rd ed. Washington, D.C.: Institute for International Economics.

Hackmann, Rolf. 1997. *U.S. Trade, Foreign Direct Investments, and Global Competitiveness.* Binghamton, N.Y.: Haworth Press.

Hatch, Walter, and KozoYamamura. 1996. *Asia in Japan's Embrace: Building a Regional Production Alliance.* Melbourne: Cambridge University Press.

Helpman, E. 1984. "A Simple Theory of International Trade with Multinational Corporations." *Journal of Political Economy* 92.

Hoekman, Bernard M., and Michael M. Kostecki. 1995. *The Political Economy of the World Trading System: From GATT to WTO.* Oxford: Oxford University Press.

Hufbauer, Clyde Gary, and Jeffrey J. Schott. 1993. *NAFTA: An Assessment.* Washington, D.C.: Institute for International Economics.

Hymer, Stephen. 1976. *The International Operations of International Firms: A Study in Direct Investment.* Cambridge, Mass.: MIT Press.

Institute of International Finance, Inc. 1998. *Capital Flows to Emerging Market Economies.* Washington, D.C.: Institute of International Finance.

Irwin, Douglas. 1996. "The United States in a New World Economy? A Century's Perspective." *American Economic Review* 86, no. 2: 41–51.

Julius, DeAnne. 1990. *Global Companies and Public Policy*. London: Royal Institute of International Affairs.

Kindleberger, Charles P. 1969. *American Business Abroad*. New Haven, Conn.: Yale University Press.

Korten, David C. 1995. *When Corporations Rule the World*. West Hartford, Conn.: Kumarian Press.

Krueger, Anne O. 1995. *Trade Policies and Developing Nations*. Washington, D.C.: Brookings Institution.

Krugman, Paul J. "Does Third World Growth Hurt First World Prosperity?" *Harvard Business Review* 72: 113–21.

_____. 1995. "Growing World Trade: Causes and Consequences." *Brookings Papers on Economic Activity* 1: 327–62.

Lawrence, Robert Z. 1993. "Japan's Low Levels of Inward Acquisitions: The Role of Inhibitions in Acquisitions." In Kenneth A. Froot, ed., *Foreign Direct Investment*. Chicago: University of Chicago Press, 85–107.

Levitt, Theodore. 1983. "The Globalization of Markets." *Harvard Business Review*, May-June: 92–102.

Lincoln, Edward J. 1990. *Japan's Unequal Trade*. Washington, D.C.: Brookings Institution.

Lipsey, Robert E., Magnus Blomstrom, and Eric Ramstetter. 1995. "Internationalized Production in World Output." NBER working paper no. 5385.

Luttwak, Edward. 1999. *Turbo Capitalism*. New York: HarperCollins.

Markusen, James R., and Anthony J. Venables. 1996. "The Theory of Endowment: Intra-Industry and Multinational Trade." NBER paper no. 5529.

Mataloni, Raymond. 1995. "A Guide to BEA Statistics on U.S. Multinationals." *Survey of Current Business.*

McRae, Hamish. 1994. *The World in 2020: Power, Culture, and Prosperity.* Boston: Harvard Business School Press.

Naisbitt, John. 1996. *Megatrends Asia.* New York: Simon & Schuster.

Ohmae, Kenichi. 1990. *The Borderless World: Power and Strategy in the International Economy.* New York: HarperCollins Press.

_____. 1985. *Triad Power: The Coming Shape of Global Competition.* New York: Free Press.

Organization for Economic Cooperation and Development. 1999. *The Future of the Global Economy: Towards a Long Boom?* Paris: OECD Publications.

_____. 1996. *Globalization of Industry: Overview and Sector Reports.* Paris: OECD Publications.

_____. 1999. *Measuring Globalization: The Role of Multinationals in OECD Economies.* Paris: OECD Publications.

Porter, Michael E. 1990. *The Competitive Advantage of Nations.* New York: Free Press.

Ramstetter, Eric D., ed. 1991. *Direct Foreign Investment in Asia's Developing Economies and Structural Change in the Asia Pacific.* Boulder, Colo.: Westview Press.

Reich, Robert B. 1990. "Who Is Us?" *Harvard Business Review*, January-February: 53–64.

_____. 1991. "Who Is Them?" *Harvard Business Review*, March-April: 77–88.

_____. 1991. *The Work of Nations: Preparing Ourselves for 21st Century Capitalism*. New York: Alfred A. Knopf.

Rodrik, Dani. 1997. *Has Globalization Gone Too Far?* Washington, D.C.: Institute for International Economics.

Rugman, Alan M., ed. 1994. *Foreign Investment and NAFTA*. Columbia, S.C.: University of South Carolina Press.

Servan-Schreiber, Jean-Jacques. 1968. *The American Challenge*. New York: Atheneum House.

Sigmund, Paul E. 1980. *Multinationals in Latin America*. University of Wisconsin Press.

Slaughter, Matthew J. 1998. *Global Investments, American Results. Mainstay III: A Report on the Domestic Contributions of American Companies with Global Operations*. Washington, D.C.: Emergency Committee for American Trade.

Stopford, John M., and Louis T. Wells. 1972. *Managing the Multinational Enterprise*. New York: Basic Books.

Global Strategies: Insights from the World's Leading Thinkers. 1994. Boston: Harvard Business Review Press.

Swenson, Deborah. 1993. "Foreign Mergers and Acquisitions in the United States." In Kenneth A. Froot, ed., *Foreign Direct Investment*. Chicago: University of Chicago Press, 255–84.

Tokunaga, Shojiro, ed. 1992. *Japan's Foreign Investment and Asian Economic Interdependence*. Tokyo: University of Tokyo.

Tyson, Laura D'Andrea. 1991. "They Are Not Us: Why American Ownership Still Matters." *American Prospect*, winter: 37–49.

United Nations Conference on Trade and Development (UNCTAD). 1991. *World Investment Report: The Triad in Foreign Direct Investment*. New York/Geneva: United Nations Publications.

_____. 1993. *World Investment Report: Transnational Corporations and Integrated International Production*. New York/Geneva: United Nations Publications.

_____. 1994. *World Investment Report: Transnational Corporations, Employment, and the Workplace*. New York/Geneva: United Nations Publications.

_____. 1995. *World Investment Report: Transnational Corporations and Competitiveness*. New York/Geneva: United Nations Publications.

_____. 1996. *World Investment Report: Investment, Trade, and International Policy Arrangements*. New York/Geneva: United Nations Publications.

_____. 1997. *World Investment Report: Transnational Corporations, Market Structure, and Competition Policy*. New York/Geneva: United Nations Publications.

_____. 1998. *World Investment Report: Trends and Determinants*. New York/Geneva: United Nations Publications.

_____. 1999. *World Investment Report: Foreign Direct Investment and the Challenge of Development*. New York/Geneva: United Nations Publications.

Vernon, Raymond. 1966. "International Investment and International Trade in the Product Cycle." *Quarterly Journal of Economics* 80: 190–207.

_____. 1971. *Sovereignty at Bay: The Multinational Spread of U.S. Enterprise*. New York: Basic Books.

Weidenbaum, Murray, and Samuel Hughes. 1996. *The Bamboo Network: How Expatriate Chinese Entrepreneurs Are Creating a New Economic Superpower in Asia*. New York: Free Press.

Weinstein, David. 1997. "Foreign Direct Investment and Keiretsu: Rethinking U.S. and Japanese Policy." In Robert C. Feenstra, ed., *The Effects of U.S. Trade Protection and Promotion Policies*. Chicago: University of Chicago Press, 81–116.

Wells, Louis T. 1972. *The Product Life Cycle and International Trade*. Boston: Harvard Business School Press.

Wells, Louis T. Jr. 1983. *Third World Multinationals*. Cambridge, Mass.: MIT Press.

Wilkens, Mira. 1970. *The Emergence of Multinational Enterprise: American Business Abroad from the Colonial Era to 1914*. Cambridge, Mass.: Harvard University Press.

_____. 1974. *The Maturing of Multinational Enterprise: American Business Abroad from 1914-1970*. Cambridge, Mass.: Harvard University Press.

_____. 1990. "Japanese Multinationals in the United States: Continuity and Change, 1879–1990." *Business History Review*, December 22.

Woodward, Douglas P., and Douglas Nigh, eds. 1998. *Foreign Ownership and the Consequences of Direct Investment in the United States, Beyond Us and Them*. Westport, Conn.: Quorum Books.

World Bank. 1993. *The East Asian Miracle*. New York: Oxford University Press.

Yamashita, Shoichi, ed. 1991. *Transfer of Japanese Technology and Management to the ASEAN Countries*. Tokyo: University of Toyko Press.

Index

About the Author

Joseph P. Quinlan is a senior global economist at Morgan Stanley Dean Witter in New York. His professional career has been evenly split between Wall Street and industry. It was during his seven-year tenure as chief economist at Sea-Land Transportation, a leading global transportation firm, that Quinlan began to research global trade and investment flows and the strategies of multinationals. Since returning to Wall Street in the early 1990s, his research efforts have been concentrated on global trade and capital flows, multinational strategies, and the emerging markets.

Quinlan has published numerous articles on global economics and trade and has authored or coauthored two books—*101 Trends Every Investor Should Know About the Global Economy* (Contemporary Books, 1998) and *Vietnam: Business Opportunities and Risks* (Pacific View Press, 1994). He also lectures on global business and finance at New York University, where he has been on the faculty for the past nine years. He has given guest lectures around the world. Quinlan was nominated as a Eisenhower Fellow in 1998, and under the auspice of the Taiwanese Eisenhower Association, has spent time in Taiwan studying cross-straits relations between Taiwan and China. He resides in Buckingham, Pennsylvania.